Acknowledge

My wife Ellen

Without you none of this would have been possible. You've given me the time and inspiration to write time and again. Supported my every decision and more importantly made me believe that not only can I do this for everyone else. I can also do it for me and an endless supply of coffee and encouragement always helped. Thank you!

Wendy B

It's no secret I'd not be here if it wasn't for you. You put everything into perspective for me and I'll be forever grateful. Thanks for being the light.

Nigel M

My therapist and my friend. I love and miss you dearly. You were an inspiration.

Melorna

When I got over confident you knocked me back into place. When I didn't have the strength to stand you dragged me back up whether I wanted you to or not. Thank you! Much love.

David L

I may still be stuck in a very bad situation if it wasn't for your contributions David. Of course a suede pair of shoes and a cigarette always helps! Thank you.

Shirley

You trusted me when I didn't even trust myself. Forever grateful.

George & Shirley C

The only couple I'd ever have let take the place of my parents.

Thank you.

Mark S
The only social worker I ever trusted.

Julia M
You're a tribute to your faith. Thank you, not only did you teach me maths. You taught me self respect.

Rose D
One session, one meeting, one of the most inspirational people I have ever met. I am honoured to know you. You changed my life completely.

Miss Whalen
Writing those twenty eight pages that day made me realise I could create anything and so I created this.
Thank you for your guidance.

Mum
Until we meet again.

www.samm.org.uk

Tracie's Story

Chapter 1

My mother was stood next to an old table drinking a glass of water and looking out over the pond outside in the back garden, I can remember the water was more green than clear from previous trips out there amongst the trees. I must have been no older than six and I knew nobody was out there, she looked relaxed. Her thin tall frame silhouetted against the cool autumn morning showing through from the glass doorway. My earliest memory. Brown hair flowed down her opal shaped face bouncing the sun's rays into an arch through the kitchen and warming the dark wooden table which was brown, like her eyes.

Wenzel was my fathers name, he bought me a tractor toy; it was red and had buttons on the back which were black there was four which made the vehicle go forwards, backwards and lifted up or down the dipper. He'd also bought a robot that turned into a monster. I was terrified of it and he loved to chase me with it. I recall this vividly. He'd place me on the sofa and the robot beneath the cushions and then soothe me by talking softly and leaning forwards. He would stroke my neck until I was calm and then he'd slide his hand down the sofa and press the button to make the monster appear from within the robot. I'd freak out again and again. He loved this game so much it got to the point if he placed his hand out of sight I was scared of what might appear. He lived to taunt people, he tried often to get my mother Bernie on side. She wasn't amused but this simply gave him another avenue to exert his authority. "Shut up woman. I'm only playing. Have a little fun in your life for god sake" he'd snap throwing her a filthy look which lingered several seconds longer than it should have. Although the appearance was of snapping, he was in control. He was always in control.

My sister and I were in the garden, it was summer, by now I must have been seven. I had a toy handgun Wenzel had brought back from the shop he was working in. A man walked past our front fence and I shot him "Bang!" He pretended to die. The day was hot and he'd made me laugh. I looked around behind me to see if mum had seen through the window. I knew she'd be watching. I'd be in trouble for playing with strangers and she'd be in trouble for letting me if Wenzel found out. Nobody saw so I shot him again as he walked away. I wish he'd come back and play. Caroline was running around somewhere beside the house, she was three years younger than me.

Wenzel was English his mother was Austrian. He was the only one of his family to get an Austrian name. His brothers and sisters had English names. He was upstairs whilst my mum was downstairs with me one time and we were sat in a rocking chair together beneath mum and Wenzels bedroom. My mother's hair was down around her shoulders and I was leaning on it whilst my nan "Pat" my mum's mother was stood by the window talking to mum. I wasn't listening I just remember the smell of cigarette smoke and her swishing hand movements as she spoke. Between the combination of nan's voice, the hypnotic hand movements and leaning into mums hair I was becoming quite comfortable when we heard a huge bang from upstairs. Nan ran into the hall "Wenzel!? You alright?" she shouted in her half Mancunian half Macclesfield accent. "No, blew my foot off." He replied I could hear movement upstairs. Mum and I were at the bottom looking upwards. "What!?" Pat asked looking at mum half in nerves half in shock. Nan went up stairs and we heard her shout down in disbelief "He bloody has you know. Call an ambulance."

The story went that he'd been cleaning his shotgun and forgot it was loaded. That he accidental blew off three toes, of course It was purely co incidental that he'd done this exactly above where my mother and I were sat. Years later he'd change his story and say he was attempting suicide but couldn't go through with it.

Wenzel appeared huge despite only being five foot six, a trick of the light as he blocked my view into the back garden and the sun. We weren't allowed to talk to the neighbours who didn't work because they buried cars in the garden and believed that items had spirits. I was told they were sheiks. I'd never heard of them but believed my father. Why wouldn't I? They did have a car half buried in the drive.

We needed a bigger place because mum had me and Caroline and was now pregnant with my brother – Jonathon. To add to the home we also had an Alsatian called Lance. It wasn't long before Wenzel said mum couldn't cope with two children. His attitude got worse and he told the social services that he couldn't cope with his wife's illness. Mum had depression but I saw no signs of it back then. I remember clearly playing in the garden on a sheet mum had put out for me and Jonathon. I was playing with the leaves that had fallen from the tree, counting the little red dots that were on its dark green surface. I was amazed at such a huge world on such a tiny leaf. The veins like roads that could take me anywhere and the red dots like villages of people. It was beautiful. I can still smell the freshly laid tarmac from outside the home. Mum was stood out in the sunshine with me and Jonathon. My sister had been taken away to live with our aunt and uncle Lesley and Lisa. Pat's sister and brother in law. The leaves were mine and I pretended I could see Caroline in them. It was strange without my sister. I don't remember her leaving but I remember her being gone.

We had moved at least three times already, I don't remember the actual moves just recall the different properties and their related stories I was so young. We moved once to have our own place as a family and then again to move nearer to nanna Pat. We then did another exchange to Moorhill road Macclesfield. All our properties were in Macclesfield and all of them on the Moss Rose estate.

Nanna Pat lived next door but one to Wenzel who had told the housing office it would be easier on him if he had a carer for Mum.

So now Nan was to be mum's carer. Where mum was quiet, shy and never raised her voice, Nan was a complete opposite. She was strong, loud and took no shit. She was known on the estate as "the battleaxe" because if you needed something taken care of. You spoke to Pat. Where mums eyes were calm and brown. Pat had a steels glaze which seemed to protect with the same ferocity as it warned. Where Wenzel was rude and belittling my Granddad Alan was Kind, fun and caring. Pat soon decided she wanted me permanently, and as she was mum's carer I was to move in with her to help mum get better.

I loved my grandparents and It wasn't long before I was calling Pat and Alan my mum and dad. I couldn't do this when Wenzel visited because nanna said it would make him angry but it was very rare he visited at all. Mum was diagnosed as agoraphobic, the furthest she'd travel was her garden despite only living next door but one to us and so my grandparents became my immediate family.

I have a lot of happy memories around Pat's house. Nan was looked up to on the estate not always for good reasons. Her son Clive had been inside a lot and if anything happened or a friend had a problem, it was usually Nan who provided the favour. It was always Clive who was sent around to have a chat or give someone a slap. It was a rough estate right next to the football ground with a pub at either end.

Granddad Alan was a gardener, cash in hand on account of his epilepsy. Strong as an ox. Short and balding but very well built. He was Irish and had a wonderful southern accent. He used to draw men doing martial arts for me and then explain the moves. He would add swords or bats to the pictures, we'd watch wrestling videos together and both loved Hulk Hogan and the Ultimate Warrior. Every time the Bushwhackers came on he would do their theme dance all around the house and body slam me onto the sofa! It was harmless fun, and giggles filled the house.

It was summer and he was tiring from digging up a tree from the back garden. We decided to go to the shops a short walk around the corner. He bought apple pie and lucozade and we walked home. He was sat in the wheel barrow outside, the heat blistering down on his broad bare shoulders. I was sat on a green milk crate whilst we supped out of bottles and ate pie. He lay back with a roll up on the go and fell asleep. When he woke up Pat told him off for falling asleep in the sun. He laughed grabbed a plastic crab which had adorned the shed and chased her around the garden with it making clicking noises! We all laughed. "Put it away you stupid, stupid man!" Nan chided slapping him away gently.

I spent that night sat on his bed peeling the burnt skin off his back in huge white sheets. Most nights we would watch through the bedroom window as the drunks went past. One night a group was outside and had turned violent. Which wasn't unusual but this night Alan shouted out of the window "that's enough lads! Leave him!" They didn't listen. He shouted again this time towards the house but with the window still open "Pat bring the shotgun!" they vanished. We didn't even own a shotgun. We did own a blank firing six shooter pistol though. I don't know why. Alan told me to wait in the kitchen down stairs and close the door. I waited until people stopped walking past the gap I'd made between the door and door frame and then I peeked out. There was a man on our sofa, Pat was blocking my view, Alan told her to lock all the doors and check the windows. When she moved I could see he'd been stabbed. There was a fair amount of blood and the knife was still in him. I knew I should feel something about this but I didn't. I just felt "oh, there's a guy on our sofa who's been stabbed. I hope the front door's closed" I wasn't worried because nanna Pat and Alan were there and whilst they were there I knew I was safe.

Chapter 2

Most memories of Nan involve her cooking or knitting, she was short but far from a small woman. Depending who you asked her nicknames ranged from Sergeant major to the Battleaxe. She also made bugs. They were little wool balls with feet, plastic eyes and a ribbon that was placed along the dash board of cars or mantel pieces, You don't see them much nowadays but back then they were a great source of advertising. She used to buy them loose from the company and make them all up. Then she'd sell them back for double the amount. She was very strict with money because we didn't have much of it. Each week a small amount would go towards Christmas and no matter what we weren't allowed to touch it. She loved Christmas we'd decorate everything from the ceiling downwards, we always had a star on the tree and there was loads of food and presents. One of the ways we raised money was going door to door and asking if people had anything for the jumble sale for Nan. Most people donated something even if it was just an old pair of trousers. Pat and Alan didn't drive so we used to take it in turns to carry the bags home. I knocked on one door as she watched from the roadside with a cigarette in her mouth, she was taking long puffs and seemed relaxed but expecting something. A round lady opened the door "anything for jumble..." I started as I held the black bag up. "What? Why would I give you anything?" She asked me looking downwards. I didn't know why she would either and was put completely on the spot. I turned back to face nan for an escape route. The round lady looked up and met Nan's eyes as she sucked hard on a cigarette and slung a paw onto her hip. "Oh Hi Pat, didn't know he was your lad. I'll go see what we've got" she said vanishing behind the door. She returned several seconds later with several pairs of trousers and some sweets. "You're doing such a good job helping your nan" she said sweetly handing me the sweets and putting the trousers in the bag for me. Nan didn't even speak she simply let out a snort and we went on to the next house.

My favourite film was The neverending story. I watched it back to back with nan whilst she did the knitting. I'd nicknamed the flying dog Gofax and wished I could just fly on his back like that young boy had done. We were out browsing the second hand shops one day when I came across a Gofax teddy! He had a zip up his belly and I wanted him immediately. "Look mum, Gofax!" I said running around the store flying with him "Can I have him? Can I? Please mum. Love you. Can we get him? Eh? Can we?" jumping up and down on the spot with excitement. "No, we don't have the money" she said. I put him down and slung my head down to make nan change her mind. Alan called me over and showed me a tiny black key ring that had a little blade inside it. "Nan's birthday soon lad, She'd like this for knitting" he said all love and affection in his voice. I rememebner being able to see the top of his green woollen hat as he'd bent down. I bought it for her with my Granddad and left. I hung my head down all around town that day. When I got home Pat said "bed time, you've been miserable all day." "What mum?" I asked shocked. Pat was never like this with me. "I said bed time. Don't argue" she replied I looked at Alan and he winked. I knew when Pat said don't argue she meant it. She'd not hesitate to slap me and she always wore big heavy gold rings which helped get her message across. I slumped up the stairs swinging my shoulders and opened my bedroom door. Sat right there in the middle of my bed was a brand new Gofax. I grabbed him and he was so soft! I ran downstairs full of excitement and hugged my mum and dad. That's the kind of people they were, with me at least.

I was flying down the back garden path granddad had made around a year before from paving slabs whilst on a skateboard when I hit the edge of a slab and was momentarily in the air. I remember clearly thinking "that's not good" before landing heavily on my wrist. A white pain went through me like nothing I'd experienced and I knew I was in trouble. Nan put me in a buggy whilst Alan tried to get me to move my wrist. I was having none of it. "Don't touch it! Don't touch it!" I yelled. Nan ran me in the buggy the mile plus to the hospital. She was so worried about me that she threw up when she got there, a nurse ran out thinking that nan was the patient! I'd had a green stick fracture in my wrist.

It wasn't long before I was back on my feet and helping Alan make my first mountain bike from old parts he'd gathered up the tip track. We just needed a front wheel and we were good to go I remember tinkering with the Alan keys in the sunshine as he explained the difference in sizes to me. It having no front wheel didn't stop me trying to ride it around the back garden though. The white front forks dropped deep into the grass every time I lifted them to peddle. It was fun for the few seconds I was able to remain moving before sinking in the mud again.

I was in pain, my throat hurt and it felt like I'd been on the sofa for weeks. I was aware Alan was reading his western book in his jeans and cotton shirt with his green woollen had pulled down. He was lying on the floor leaning against the sofa that I was lay on, his black hair peeking out slightly. When he noticed I was awake he folded his book and made wrestling gestures along with the television to try and cheer me up. I smiled but had no energy to join in. My mind was willing but my body just couldn't make the effort. It was Hulk Hogan vs The Ultimate Warrior my favourite match. He rewound the tape each time so we could watch it over and over. I had tonsillitis pretty bad. Nan had been spoon feeding me but I couldn't take any more. I'd gone from crying when she tried to flat out refusing. I was on a waiting list and could hear her getting upset when I didn't eat. Nan had called my father around as I'd been on liquids for two days she told him as I lay on the sofa "I don't know what to do. He won't eat and the hospital won't see him yet" she said stood in the living room next to Wenzel. My father looked down at me in his suede jacket, blue jeans and shiny chrome looking spectacles and said "Fuck him, tell him if he won't eat his throat will close up" and walked out. I started shaking with fear involuntarily. I didn't know what was happening to me. I knew I couldn't eat and believed if I didn't my throat would actually close up. I had no reason to doubt him. I lay shaking whilst nan tried to sooth me. I could feel her anger towards Wenzel as she brushed my hair back "Ignore him. He talks a load of rubbish that man. I don't know what Bernie sees in him I really don't" I'd like to say I relaxed under her touch. However the truth is I was arching my back and gasping for breath to check I could still breathe. The more I flapped about worrying about my breathing the worse I got.

Finally it was operation day, I'd had the anaesthetic and was asked to count to ten by a polite man dressed in white. I did and Pat and the male nurse exchanged a look. I was placed on a heart monitor and asked to count to ten again. I got to three before I was out like a light. I woke up with Pat right beside me. I was so excited to see her I flipped up off the bed shouting "mum!" I'd stood straight up before the effects of the anaesthetic hit me and I fell straight down. I had no energy to lift my arms and ploughed face first into the white tiled floor. It hurt but not as much as I'd imagined. The worst part was having Nan and a nurse get me to the toilet so I could pee whilst they held me up, one either side.

My throat was sore "talk to me darling, you've done so well. I'm proud of you" nan said. I lifted my head as though willing the words out "Ice, cream" I managed. Nan had promised me ice cream every day since we'd found out when my operation was. I was looking forwards to it more than a holiday at Blackpool. I wanted to see the giant lights surrounding my ice cream and feel the cool sensation on my throat like a waterside all the way down. I knew I could eat anything after the operation and knew I'd get ice cream because nan had told me and if she said it, it was true. I got toast and ate it grudgingly. There were several other children at the table when Nan promised me Ice cream when I got home. I noted that the other children didn't have parents present. I was lucky to have someone I called mum there. I felt sorry for them.

Alan had finished tightening the front wheel and placed my big heavy green bike next to the kerb. I had to jump to get on it whilst he held the seat for me. He taught me how to ride down our road by pushing me away from the kerb and holding the seat whilst I peddled. I was safe because he was always there, until he wasn't and I was peddling on my own. Then I panicked and fell off. There was plenty of scratched knee's and each one would get the same answer all calm and relaxed "get up, back on" and when I'd finally had enough falling, when my knee's hurt and hands were rough from pushing up off the pavement he'd pull me and the bike to the kerb where he'd bend down and look me gently in the eyes. "You're not quitting lad, back on". I learnt to ride and ride well. After a few weeks I'd think nothing of standing on the cross bar as I went down the street. We'd take trips to the tip track together or the allotments. One day it was beautiful we were in a field with a huge conker tree. Alan climbed up and I went into autopilot "Nan wouldn't like this. Your epilepsy granddad?" He laughed. "It's okay lad. Nan ain't here is she?" It was rhetorical but I looked around anyway. If she was I'd get a thick ear for letting him climb the tree. I laughed "but Nan wouldn't.." I started as he shook a branch and made monkey noises to drown out my questioning. I creased up laughing as conkers rained down on me. I can still remember the laughter tickling it's way through me today.

We filled an entire bin bag with conkers and I felt real proud. I was proud of him and I was proud that I was his son and everything felt just perfect. He put his giant paw on my head and ruffled my hair "I love you lad" he said. "I love you too dad" I replied honestly. When we got home we tipped them all out on the living room floor and put strings in hundreds of them. When nan came home she went nuts "look at this place you stupid man!" Alan just laughed her off. When she went into the kitchen he winked at me and said "guess she ain't playing conkers with us lad."

Chapter 3

I don't remember my brother and younger sister being born because they didn't live with us. Each time there was another birth I was just told that I had a new brother or sister and that I was to take care of them. I was told by Nan and Alan who'd take me around to see the baby for an hour or two as Wenzel, nan and Alan would play cards whilst Bernie played with the new born or did puzzle books. The baby was called Jonathon and mum said he was special because he was born with a hole in his heart and a squint in his eye. She said we were very lucky to have him and he needed special attention.

I saw Jonathon near Christmas but otherwise we rarely saw one another. Bernie didn't go out because of her agoraphobia and Wenzel was always working either on a farm or at the local shop, I was told he specialised in bedding plants and worked long shifts so didn't come to see Nan and Alan often.

On the odd occasion my brother Jonathon would be allowed around to play and we'd make swords and shields and play warriors in the garden. He loved our manual lawnmower, a big green metal thing with huge handles and would run around the garden with it for ages he mustn't have got out a lot because of mums agoraphobia and how protective she was of him. Those times being able to play like two normal boys were both rare and cherished.

Caroline had been sent to live with me at nan and Alan's house. I was told it was so that mum could get well enough to look after her again. I wasn't old enough to question this or really understand it. I was just happy Caroline was there. This meant more people to play with and I wanted to show her my toys and my room. Unfortunately we didn't get much playing done because nan didn't like girls like she liked boys.

Nan's attitude changed as soon as Caroline was in doors. Where she spoke to me like a little adult she cared about she spoke to Caroline like she had been very naughty and was disliked immensely. I liked playing with nans jewellery and would sit and put the rings and necklaces in size order then mix them up and re do it all over again. I liked to see the light shining off the different gems. I'd put a ring in my pocket to play with. Nan wouldn't mind as long as I returned it but I forgot about it and went off doing my thing when later I heard Nan shouting at Caroline in the bedroom. She sounded really angry. Caroline was crying and only had a nightshirt on as I went up the stairs.

"Where is it you thieving little bitch?" Nan snarled bent down leaning into Carolines face. I'd never seen her like this and she'd never swore at me.

"I don't know" Caroline replied stuttering and sobbing. I was scared, scared for Caroline and scared for me. Nan had never been like this before. The room seemed darker even though I knew it was daylight out and nan seemed to take up the whole room. The curtains were blowing slightly in the breeze which seemed to give nan an angrier look as the shadows crossed her face and wall.

"Err Mum?" I asked "Don't interrupt! She's taken it I know she has." Nan said turning back to me and swiftly back to Caroline and jamming a finger into her chest and then holding it an inch from her face. I am ashamed to say I stood rooted to the spot and said nothing. I didn't care about the curtains any more, that prod alone must have hurt.

The more Nan went on the more Caroline insisted it wasn't her and the more she cried. It probably lasted about five minutes and yet felt like forever. Nan eventually grabbed her hair and dragged her over the bed where she hit her repeatedly, slapping her body and head. Caroline must have been terrified because a brown patch appeared down her nightshirt. Nan grabbed her hair and dragged her to the bathroom. She ripped off her nightshirt and slapped Caroline around the head and body with it. "You dirty little Bitch!"

She pushed the soiled shirt into Caroline's face. I ran behind her "Mum!" I was pushed away easily "Don't!" She stepped forwards and lifted her arm. I legged it into the bedroom and sat with my knees to my chest on the double bed listening to Caroline crying as nan hit her. Caroline was pulled into the bedroom about ten minutes later and made to stand still, she was naked. Caroline almost fell over with fear as nan followed behind her and slapped her down and then as soon as Caroline had hit the floor, she dragged her upright by her hair. Caroline covered her face out of reflex every time nan moved in anticipation of being hit, she was petrified. Nan told her "Put your fucking hands down or I'll chop them off!" Caroline was repeating "sorry nan, sorry, Sorry nan" over and over. I'd never seen someone so afraid. She was made to stand there for an hour. I was told to sit and watch her to make sure she didn't move off her spot. If she moved off her spot I was to get nan immediately.

I was eight, Caroline would have been five or six. I did as I was told. I watched her knowing the ring was in my pocked the entire time and that I'd said nothing because I was scared. I didn't want the beating Caroline had received and yet knew somehow I wouldn't have. Maybe Caroline deserved it? This couldn't have been about a ring. Nan had never been like that with me. I justified it away that Nan was always right and so Caroline must have done something really bad that I didn't know about.

Caroline had done nothing wrong. I knew it and yet I played nan's game and I watched Caroline. This was the first time of many I'd have to watch her stand straight. About ten minutes went by and I pulled the ring out from my pocket and looked at it. Why had this ring caused so much trouble? I just wanted to play with Caroline. Caroline saw the ring in my hand as I sat cross legged on the bed and her eyes went upwards. She looked at the ceiling and held her gaze there, her long brown hair matted where nan had dragged her around. She couldn't even look at me and I realized. I'd caused this.

She was hurt because of me. I watched tears roll down the outside of her face as she tried to hold them back and then shook them off and returned her gaze to the ceiling. I couldn't have felt smaller. I went downstairs "You okay mum?" I asked as she did the knitting. "Yes darlin, I'm not angry with you." She said sweetly as though she'd not almost knocked out my sister. I entered the room a little more "can Caroline come and play then?" I asked her "No Caroline has been very naughty she's been stealing she has to stay there for a bit" she replied not looking up, her hands still making that "Tick tick tick" sound as she knitted.

"I found the ring. It had fallen behind the curtain" I said putting my hand out. Nan put her knitting down gently and the ticking stopped. "Did you take this?" she asked gently but in a tone I felt could mean I was in trouble. "Yes mum, I just wanted to play with it for a bit" I mumbled. She laughed "Why didn't you just ask? You know you can play with my jewellery whenever you like. Just ask me first" she replied all smiles. "Sorry mum, won't happen again" I said waiting for a thick ear.

"Come here" she said playfully. I was still expecting a slap but stepped forwards. Nan hugged me and took my hand in hers then tapped it gently "That's for not asking don't do it again!" She said. "Okay Sorry mum" I replied walking back up the stairs towards Caroline. Nan close behind. I saw Caroline flinch as nan came into the room. "You're starting to annoy me girl" Pat said. Caroline said nothing. Why was Caroline annoying nan? She'd just been told it was me who'd taken the ring. I looked at nan "why didn't you tell me he'd taken it?" She asked staring at Caroline from three feet in front of her.

Caroline looked at me. Nan bend forwards eye to eye with Caroline closing the space between them to a few inches "he won't help you. Nobody will, you live with me now and you'll do as you're told, understand?" Nan said harshly. Caroline nodded. "What?" Nan asked shouting stepping forwards and almost touching her. "Y,y,yes. I understand" Caroline stuttered. "Your hour starts now" nan said and left the room.with her yellow leather flip flops slapping against her flat feet as she went down the hall. I followed nan.

I couldn't watch Caroline standing there, naked.

Chapter 4

Not only did we have mum, dad, Jonathon and Jodie living on the same road as my nan, granddad Alan, Caroline and me but we also had two uncles and two aunts as well. Uncle Lesley and auntie Lisa. Uncle Lesley was a quiet round fella with light hair and a deep voice and Lisa was a total opposite, a thin chatty alcoholic who was borderline screechy. Lesley liked a drink as well and although he was a regular presence and quiet enough, he always had an odd vibe about him that I couldn't quite place. As though he was always acting relaxed but was really awkward around people. They'd come over to see Pat and Alan.

I was playing Buckaroo on the floor which I'd got into when I had tonsillitis Caroline wasn't allowed to play with me. She was told to be on her best behaviour for when they'd turned up and she was sat quietly in the corner in her night gown. Alan was watching T.V he didn't seem to agree with how nan treated Caroline but he never spoke up to stop it either. Lisa asked Pat why Caroline was still in her night clothes as it was after lunch time and Pat replied that she'd told her to get dressed but wouldn't so she was being punished by not being allowed to play. Later on Caroline asked if she could play with the dolls and was told "no" flatly by nan. Lisa seemed to like Caroline and wanted her to be able to play games with us all. The cards had come out and we were all playing crash. "Can I play with the dolls now please Nan?" Caroline asked gently. "Yes with pleasure" nan replied. Caroline sat still for five minutes a little bit closer to our group playing cards and then gingerly said "where is it Nan?" As she clutched the one doll she'd been allowed to play with. "Where's what?" Nan asked sighing like she'd been stopped mid way to picking up fifty pounds. "The pleasure?" Caroline replied innocently unaware of what it was she was saying.

This story was retold by Nan many times when someone asked about Caroline to point out how unwell mentally she was and why she was under whichever punishment nan had designated for her at the time. Caroline had no mental problems. She had a stutter because she had been scared so much as a child. Unfortunately the story sums up how nan was with girls perfectly. There was no pleasure.

I am ashamed of my own actions even though I was around eight years old. I am ashamed I said nothing to prevent these occurrences presuming them normal but not half as ashamed as I am about the night time events.

I had started to have bad nightmares, I didn't know why at the time however I had a naturally vivid imagination in the daytime and the negative things going on around me can't have helped. They were usually involving monsters or the woman from prisoner cell block H who used the press, a programme Nan loved and would let me watch before bed. The nightmares were so bad I refused to sleep in my own room because I felt like I was being watched or could see faces in my curtains. I remember clearly waking up one night convinced my pillow was a head next to me. I lay there for ages screaming until my nan came in and turned the light on. Even then the pillow had the same look about it, like it could change at any minute. So I slept on the floor in nan and Alan's room. I never questioned why Caroline was stood up beside the old black and white T.V or why a plastic potty was underneath her. I knew Caroline had told Lisa she didn't like it at Nan's and was to be punished for it. "Knickers down" Nan said calmly watching T.V, "Sit" she said, Caroline did as instructed "Stand, knickers up" Caroline did as she was asked. I looked at Nan thinking that was the end of it. "Carry on" she said. Caroline did repeating the process. Alan had his head in a western book beside nan in bed. I was on the floor in front of Caroline lay down with my legs stretched out. "Keep going" Nan said before falling asleep.

Nan and Alan would watch Married with Children, Hale and Pace and Prisoner cell block H and Caroline well, some nights she collapsed. Some nights she fell asleep on the floor and if nan woke up and Caroline wasn't doing what Nan had come to call potty practice she'd kick her until she continued, other nights I was told "if she stops. You wake me up" The first time nan was asleep Caroline looked at me pleadingly. I shrugged my shoulders. What was I to do? I was given orders. I sat watching her. The T.V had gone to the night screen thing. We'd watched Married with children, Hale and Pace and prisoner cell block H, All the while Caroline had done Potty practice. She must have been so tired and yet she continued because I was awake and I was told to watch her. I remember the really bad nights where I tried throwing myself into the television because I couldn't look at Caroline without feeling guilty. The nights where she begged to stop, Said she was sorry. Said "please," over and over as she slapped herself in the face in anger and was told "You finished your paddy?" By nan. Caroline would stand up and arch her back because she ached and look at nan for respite, "carry on" nan would say and she did.

Whenever family came over again nan was totally different with Caroline. I enjoyed these times. Caroline was told to go and put her dress on. It was black and red and looked great. Alan would put Buddy Holly, Elvis or the Beatles on the CD player and we'd be asked to dance together. We danced rock and roll style to all the songs and had a great time. It was the only time I got to dance with Caroline and it felt nice. It felt for a short while like we were both on the same level playing field. Like both her and I were free and really brother and sister, not like either of us were treated differently. I loved to dance, there was something special about being the centre of attention and showing off exactly how we could move. It was hypnotic and I thoroughly enjoyed coming up with new routines together.

When it was just me, Alan and nan again though things were back to normal. Caroline had started pulling her hair when she thought nobody could see her. Nan told people it was because she was retarded, that the doctor had said to leave her to it she'll stop in time. She wasn't retarded nor had she seen a doctor. She was frustrated and stressed and who wouldn't be? She wanted to escape her life the same way I'd of wanted to in her situation. However a big part of me believed that nan was right, I had no reason not to and nan had taken care of me through everything without complaining once and so I truly believed Caroline must have done something to deserve the treatment, however I won't justify my lack of action by saying I knew no better. However I will say I was a child who was lead by adults who should have known better and am not fully responsible for that reason. I'd been programmed to allow harm and sometimes to cause it. "Pull your hair again my girl and I'll pull your head off" Nan warned pointing her knitting needle towards Caroline like a rapier ready to strike. "Want a brew mum?" I asked trying to ease the tension. "Please darling" she said lowing her needle and placing it back under her arm "don't upset her" I whispered through the side of my mouth as I walked past Caroline . When I came back in Caroline had a chunk of hair twirled around her finger and was trying to eat it, I don't think Caroline even realised she was doing it. She must have been bored silly just sat there. I guess she was hungry I don't remember when she ate. Nan was walking towards her fast "Mum!" I shouted too late. She'd punched Caroline to the floor and grabbed her hair yanking her up straight up and then slapped her all in one fluid movement. Caroline was in tears immediately. Her eye's dazed from the impact. Nan grabbed her hair and dragged her to the sofa's arm and flung her over it holding her hair. "Mum!" I shouted again. "What!?" She said sharply. I stepped back holding two brews. I must have looked shocked. "Sorry darling, Put them over there yeah?" She said all sing song chirpy pointing to the coffee table. Caroline was trying to push her face out of the cushion whilst most of nan's weight held her down. Nan stood her up by her hair slowly as though moving a chair out of the way and seemingly forgetting about the beating she had just lay down on Caroline "Potty practice" she said flatly and pushed her through the hall door towards the stairs.

Nan, my mum was always great with me. I was fed well and when I was ill she always made sure I was taken care of. I was spoilt rotten to be honest. Everything I wanted I got. It was October and I'd already started filling in my Christmas list. Nan was in bed eating an onion sandwich and I was on the floor with an open catalogue. I wanted a master system 2 console like my friend had. I wanted the version with Alex the kid on the inside and it was expensive. Nan told me the same thing she said every year. "Wait and see what happens darling. You never know what Santa will bring". I got my Master system 2 around a week later, well before Christmas.

nan had spoken to Bernie and told her Caroline was not fixable and she couldn't handle her and me at the same time. Caroline would have to go! She was sent to live with Lesley and Lisa who I was told really wanted children and she'd have more fun there than she ever did with us.

Fora while I wondered what Caroline was up to, if she was still chewing her hair or if she had lots of toys. I was told not to worry about her, that she wanted to live with Lesley and Lisa and so wasn't here any more and so life was back to normal for a short while. Nan took driving lessons with Clive her son who'd been driving for years, I remember him owning a beetle that he'd painted a big smiley face on with his friend. soon nan started having headaches quite badly. She was in bed for a couple of days and wasn't making the bugs any more because of the pain. Alan was working most days and Nan's ear had begun to bleed but she wouldn't see a doctor. "Look after her lad" Alan ruffled my hair before he left "love you Dad" I said as the door closed. I watched T.V all day and kept checking on Nan who was asleep way past lunch.

Nan came downstairs. "You okay mum?" I asked. She waved me off

"I'm fine. Nothing a couple of paracetamol won't fix" she wasn't fine. I could tell. She was walking differently for a start and was leaning on the sideboards to get around the kitchen. She downed two paracetamol and I followed her into the living room where she lay down on our big red rug in front of the coal fire. I remember the rug, it was the same one I used to sink my hands deep into after a bath. She was face down and seemed to relax. Her whole body just kind of sank, I just sat watching her breath. The T.V was off and the light shone through the window in front of her face. If she fell asleep I'd cover her up and put the fire guard in place of the coal fire, around forty seconds passed before she started shaking and being sick. The smell of onions was instant, she wasn't trying to move away from the sick. She just lay there throwing up, lay in it. I ran next door but one to Wenzel's house and hammered on the door. He opened it and gave me a roasting for waking him up and clipped me around the head. "Nan, s,s,s,ssick" I stammered and he sent me upstairs to sit with mum.

I'd find out later that my uncle Clive was on his way home from the pub when he saw me run next door but one. I'd accidentlaly closed the door behind me so he'd kicked the door in to check on his mum. The doors were old council and had thin plywood in a square across the bottom so was easy enough to kick in and then climb through. Clive explained it all to us afterwards although we knew Clive had done this way before having to check on his mum. Clive was over six foot and had to have shoes especially made for him. He wasn't particularly built but he was tall and had huge hands and feet and so taking a door out wasn't a big problem. Wenzel went around to see what was happening and Nan was taken via ambulance to the hospital.

I waited with Bernie my blood mum whilst my brother Jonathon and sisters Jodie and Caroline were in bed. Mum told me how Caroline had said she didn't like living with Lesley and Lisa and that she'd come back home. I knew mum had always wanted the family together and she said it was better this way. "Maybe one day I'd choose to come back too?" She asked me softly. I'd always lived with Nan and Alan, they were like my mum and dad, I doubted it. I didn't like Wenzel and didn't know why. I loved my real mum but I hardly saw her. "Maybe" I smiled at my real mum. She always had a sad face even when she smiled, she was pretending. Mum made me a fried egg with chips. I didn't like it or want it. I played with the lego technic and made a huge train which mum helped me with. She sat close by me the entire time with her side touching my left arm. I'd missed her and hadn't realised it until that moment but even then my mind was elsewhere. My vision went hazy, it was as though someone had just removed everything I could see and replaced it with another scene, I saw someone pushing down on a female's chest. I looked down to find my fingers were interlocking and I was pushing down hard on the cushion on my lap. I stopped after five or six compressions and was aware of where I was and that there was a feeling like electricity in the room. Mum was looking right at me "You know" she said softly with her voice and eyes. I didn't have time to respond. The front door opened and Wenzel walked in with a bunch of flowers. He was wearing blue jeans and a white shirt with his white trainers on, most noticeably He had a little bit of spittle falling from his lip. I screamed "aaaargh!" As I brought my arms down several times on top of the train set in front of me. It took Wenzel and Bernie to hold me down. I was in tears. "She's gone, She's gone" Wenzel said breathlessly.

Chapter 5

I knew I'd be affected. I'd said to Nan many times before she slept "don't die mum" and she'd replied "just resting my eyes don't be so silly I'm going nowhere" I don't know how I knew or if it was just my over active imagination connecting invisible dots. I don't know why I did the compressions on the cushion. I'd never seen it before on T.V and didn't know what I was doing. I only knew it meant the person I'd called mum for nearly nine years wasn't coming home. Nan was in the living room, bedroom and everywhere I went. I just couldn't see her. I'd look up to see her but she wouldn't be there. I was numb. Just numb with no room at all for anything else.

I fell asleep crying on her white bathrobe in the bedroom at Alan's because it smelt like her and then I punched myself in the face because I'd put tears on it and that might take the smell of her away. I sat on the floor and leaned the back of my head on it with the tears welling up as I stared at the ceiling.

Alan took me to the chapel of rest where she lay in a coffin, The lid stood up against the wall with a gold crucifix on it. I say she lay there but the truth is that was just an empty shell of some woman. Alan touched her hair. I stood beside him convinced Nan was stood beside me, Her energy was huge in the room. She wasn't dead and she'd be back soon, but I knew she wouldn't.

We'd left and were approaching home, neither of us had spoken until Alan said "did you" I knew what he was going to say "yes" I said before he'd finished. "Me too, She was there" I knew what he meant and we didn't speak of it again.

Before the funeral I was getting my suit on and looked really smart. Alan was really pleased until I went to walk down the stairs and caught my sleeve on the banister. It ripped my shirt. Alan had to cut off the entire arm and stitch the cuff into my suit to make it look like a full shirt from outside. I was not pleased but looked okay. He turned to me downstairs and handed me a few pounds "This is last of what's left of Nan's money, She'd want you to have it" I didn't know what to say, as I took the money a coin rolled out and under the sofa. I watched the last piece of my mum roll away and leaned down to lift the sofa. I screamed and the sofa rolled backwards and hit the wall. It must have been adrenaline because apart from the odd spout of anger I was dead inside. I took my coin and turned to Alan who didn't comment. He took my hand and we went to the funeral.

It passed in blurry moments and Alan cried. They played The old rugged cross and White Christmas. I wasn't looking forwards to Christmas any more. I remembered the winter walks we used to take looking at the frosty cobwebs on the hedgerows and singing together whilst walking to and from the town centre. We'd always stop by the cobblers to see the robot man in the window hammering shoes. I came home and it was empty, more empty than I ever thought a building could be and yet nan was still there. I could feel her watching me and she was often near Alan too although he never said anything. Alan used to make a brew and biccies every morning and we'd sit on the double bed scoffing them from a huge biscuit tin that came up to my elbow. We didn't watch T.V in a morning. That was our time to talk and nan was always brought up. "If she could see us now eh lad? She's looking down you know" I'd nod a reply with a mouth full of Bourbon biscuits. He gave up work totally to look after me and soon he'd started to drink, which didn't help his epilepsy medication at all. "You're a good lad trying to take care of me. I'm awight you know lad? I'm okay I miss her loads but we spoke about this day and I promised her, I said I'd take care of you no matter what happened." I didn't know what to say. He was sat on the big comfy chair in the corner of the living room. The curtains were closed it was early evening and he'd been playing old Irish songs for hours. I didn't mind. I liked them but I was worried he'd go into a fit at any minute. "It's okay dad, We'll be alright you know. I love you" I replied sat cross legged on the floor in front of him in the same spot Pat lay down and died. I kept touching the deep red rug with my fingers, Sinking them into it. It felt nice. "Don't call me that lad" he said a tear appearing in his eye. I wasn't sure whether it was because T-Rex's Woman of gold had come on the CD player or whether it was because I'd called him dad. I just looked at him waiting for him to explain. "What I have to tell you now lad, well... I promised Pat I'd not say anything until you were old enough. You're old enough now lad. If I don't tell you now you may never know." I had no idea what he meant "Granddad, what's wrong?" I asked calling him by his true title even though he was in fact only my step granddad. My blood granddad had been stabbed outside a pub in Manchester before I was born by two men. One had ended up dead the other had been blinded. "Well lad, You can't tell anyone understand? If you do there will be a blood bath okay? Give me your word"

I knew a lot about giving my word. Granddad Alan spoke about that a lot. If I made a promise it was alright if I broke it as long as I broke it for the right reasons. So if I said "I'll never lie to you I promise" but then the person asked me how they look and I lied and said they look amazing then that is okay because I'm lying to be nice and so I don't upset them. However If I gave my word then I'd have to tell the truth no matter what. If I gave my word to keep quiet I'd have to. I'd have no choice. "What's wrong?" I asked "I'm sorry lad, I really am. Your word." I nodded "I give you my word I'll not tell anyone whatever it is you'll tell me" I said. "Good.. okay. Before you were born my brother and your mum were friends. One day my brother saw your mum Bernie across the road getting changed at the bedroom window. Your mum always liked my brother you know what I'm saying lad?" He asked. I shook my head "Liam and mum are friends? I know. He saw her get changed...so?" I shrugged and occupied my mind by sinking my fingers into the deep red rug and thinking of nan. "listen lad, Liam and your mum loved each other. Loved one another for real. Love like Pat and I.." His breath caught "a lot of love lad. They slept together only once because your dad was on the scene but they did sleep together lad and then you were born" I remembered every word Alan had said but I didn't understand and it was upsetting him telling the story. "Okay Dad." I replied as Woman of Gold played on repeat in the background. "Your dad might not be your dad lad" I looked at Alan and knew then what he had meant and knew as long as he was around it didn't matter in the slightest. "You're my Dad Granddad. Even if you don't want me to call it you that's okay. You've taken care of me. I love you. You're my dad we'll be okay" he leaned forwards and ruffled my hair. I stood up and gave him a hug. He leaned into my stomach and I could feel his tears falling onto my hand. "Dad" I said patting his bald spot. He lifted his head and I leaned over and pressed "off" on the stereo. "Time for tea".

Alan was always trying to teach me something about self defence or how to use my mind. It didn't matter if we were drawing or cycling he'd be telling me stories of southern Ireland and telling me the importance of being able to defend myself if I had to. We'd been up the tip track cycling as soon as he'd got home he pulled the three seater wooden sofa into the middle of the room. "Remember before Nan's funeral?" He asked. I nodded we'd been talking about adrenaline earlier and I didn't understand what it was other than a kind of power. He'd explained it like when the Ultimate Warrior shakes the ropes or when people hit themselves before a fight. He went on to tell me all that showmanship wasn't required to use adrenaline accurately. It's like a strength Chi, Mana he tried to explain. "Turn it over" he said pointing to the sofa. "No," I said stepping back. "It's okay lad you won't break it and it doesn't matter if you do. I'm trying to show you something about adrenaline. Turn it over" I bent down and tried to turn over the sofa. My hands could barely fit under the long wooden beam running along the bottom let alone lift it. I stretched and grabbed hard and arched my back. Nothing happened. I pulled with my arms and tried to stand using my whole body weight it moved about an inch and I dropped it. "No – too heavy" I said stepping back yet knowing it was the same sofa

I'd flipped with ease previously. "Right – now I want you to focus. Think of something that makes you mad, Upsets you but don't get upset. See it as a circle..." he went on to explain in detail and with big examples that basically I should control my anger and then release it in one go. I should learn this and learn to switch it on and off until it's automatic. The shutting off being the most important part. I didn't get it and nobody would until they'd tried it but after standing there for five minutes then pacing then seeing Nan throw up again in front of me and watching myself run to Wenzel's house I saw him return with that little bit of spittle on his lip. I started vibrating and then full on shaking physically. I watched myself smash up the train as I brought my hands down I stepped forwards and screamed "arrrgh!" The sofa flipped completely over and I knelt down on the floor crying. Alan came round and hugged me "It's okay lad. You needed to do that. You need to let go" he held me tight as I cried. "She's dead, dead funny, dead, dead funny" the only connection I could make with the word dead that didn't hurt as much as my mum not being present. "I'm sorry. I should have done something. I shouldn't have left her. She was being sick it smelt I didn't know what to do... " I sobbed as he assured me I did everything right and Nan would have been proud of me.

When my chest had finally stopped jumping he said "make a brew lad" as he pulled the sofa back beneath the window. I caught something different in his tone. "Dad?" I asked. "Make a brew lad. Now" I didn't argue. He was never angry not ever and I knew enough of violent people to know that if someone never gets angry and tells you to leave you get the hell out of the way – fast. I'd been in the kitchen maybe several seconds when I heard a scream and a crunch then a torrent of swearing in Gaelic I popped my head around the doorway to see Alan stuck within the door he had punched a hole through. It was the old hollow council doors which weren't that solid but it was still some feat to get himself stuck beyond the elbow inside one. As he stood cursing he started laughing when he spotted me. "Well, that was fucking stupid wasn't it?" He said laughing. "No – you needed that" I replied and finished making the brew. When I returned he'd managed to free himself. We sat together on the sofa and I felt myself go from being a little boy of eight or nine to a grown man.

"It'll never be the same, will it?" I asked him looking at the fire and not at him.

"No lad" He said. Several seconds went past "Be awight" he added patting my back. I'm certain he was reassuring both of us.

I knew even though his words said the right things the spaces between them told me totally the opposite. No, nothing was going to be alright. No things were never going to be the same and if we were going to get through this with any degree of acceptance we'd need to help each other. I'd need to grow up a lot and make sure he was okay with his medication and epilepsy and he'd have to do all the house stuff for me like buying food. I knew logically we were capable of all these things between us. However I had that bad feeling again. The same feeling I got when I saw Nan walk downstairs and go for the paracetamol. The same feeling I got when I was pushing that cushion waiting for news from the hospital.

Chapter 6

Wenzel had started insisting I spent three days a week with him. He seemed about as happy about it as I was. It happened so fast one minute I was with Alan and visiting Wenzel's every so often and then I was living at Wenzels house and Alan was leaving. I was staying with Wenzel because hey what he says goes. I'd hugged Alan and said my goodbye's and he'd said as though so down hearted "See you soon lad" I was sat cross legged on the floor watching the empty doorway he had left through. Wenzel stood in the doorway to the living room white T-shirt and blue Jeans. His glasses dulled by the living room light with no shade."You can't run around here like you did with him you know. He can't look after you now it's not fair to him now there's only him there" he said. I noticed he had a paper-clip holding his glasses together. He wasn't saying it in the form of explanation he was saying it as an order.

"He can, he wants me there and I want to be with him. Where's the problem?" I replied innocently.

"Did you just answer me back?" He asked with a tone that said I'd see trouble. He had a way of extending his words way beyond the sound they'd finished making. It wasn't like when a parent tells off a child. Sometimes you still hear the echo of when they've said "stop!" as it resounds. It wasn't like that, with this guy it was something more and intentional.

I wasn't used to the rules yet. Caroline had made a sharp exit and Jonathon was following suit behind her they held their heads down and went up the stairs. "No, I'm just saying. He wants me, ask him. He said I could live with him as long as I want" I stood up I was about four feet in front of him. He leaned forwards. "Well he's not your fucking dad is he? What I say goes. Understand!" He took a few steps forwards and tapped my head with his finger hard a few times on "understand". I shook him off. "Don't look at me like that boy I'll knock you senseless" He said doing a half laugh. I was starting to realise why Nan and Alan didn't like him.

I soon learnt mum was only happy when she had a drink beside her. She loved the kids and played with them a lot. Especially Jonathon who mum let know was her favourite. Jodie was in the play pen dancing around in a little yellow dress thing whilst Caroline was playing with her dolly and toy crib. Mum loved puzzle books and did them as she played with Jonathon. I remember her clearly with her feet curled beneath her on the sofa. She was allowed that luxury and although Wenzel complained when she doodled on the cover she did it anyway. I remember having none of my toys at Bernie and Wenzel's house who I'd started calling mum and dad because I'd had to. In my head it was still mum and Wenzel's. The longer I was there the more I thought about what Alan had said about Liam. I never told anyone of course but I knew I wasn't like Wenzel and felt very strongly that I didn't belong with this family. I loved Jonathon, Jodie and Caroline very much although I was often mean to Caroline because that's how I'd been brought up at Nan and Alan's and so we generally avoided each other.

Dinner times were totally different. As soon as Wenzel came home from work the 80's music which was current then would be switched off and the T.V would go on. We weren't allowed to watch the snooker or boxing that he'd watch and nobody wanted to watch Emerdale apart from him. We'd have to sit cross legged in a line in height order from smallest to tallest facing the sofa and wait for our food in silence. When he was home it was his time not ours. We'd had all day to play so couldn't do that when he was home. Food would be placed in front of us and we'd have to wait until Wenzel had received his. Then he would ask if we wanted salt. It didn't matter what was said. There was never any salt passed around. He would take a handful and sprinkle it on his plate and then rub his fingers together over our food pretending to put some on. Mum wasn't a great cook like Nan had been and most food was under cooked if I'm honest. We didn't mind but it gave Wenzel another excuse to pick on her. "What's this? That's not bacon it's a fucking crack in the plate. Can't even cook properly can you? Ah well least you're good for one thing eh?" He'd always phrase things so as she would have to reply. She'd often try to ignore him to which he'd make her respond. "Oi woman I'm talking to you. I said at least you're good for something aren't you?" she'd look at the kids embarrassed "yeah" she'd say and return with her food. When he picked up his knife and fork we were allowed to start eating. If we started before he'd stop us. "Think you're the man of the house do you? Now you can wait until everyone else has eaten" sometimes we'd get to eat after they had. Sometimes he'd just say "didn't want it did you not? Fine then" and take it away. This happened to me a few times because I would throw my mind to Alan's when Wenzel was home as I wasn't concentrating he'd take the food. "No, I was waiting for you guys to finish. I'll eat it" I said. I only asked once "should have thought of that before shouldn't you?" He walked off with my plate and I heard it slide into the bin.

I had to be really careful at meal times. Well we all did when he was home. If we ate all of the food we got insulted. "You're a gannet you know that? Like a big bin. Food costs money you know. You think I work for my health?" If we left any and I did a fair few times because I didn't like peas or onions then he'd go off on his favourite tangent. "There are kids in Africa dying who could have had that. You're nothing but a waster you care about nobody apart from yourself. Don't even care about your old dad do you?" I'd never reply. If I replied I'd have to tell the truth. Yes I care about my dad but my dad is next door but one.

I looked forwards to going to Alan's and when I was there we spoke a lot about going back to live with him which is what he wanted and told me all the time. "We just have to do what Wenzel says for now that's all lad. When you're a little older you'll be able to decide for yourself where you want to live" of course I complained constantly but there was nothing Alan could do. He wasn't family in Wenzel's eyes.

I may have been at my parents but my heart was with Alan. I daydreamed about living with him a lot although sometimes I'd get snapped back to reality by mother dancing with us, which was nice and I really enjoyed, until she came too close and the alcohol from her breath caught in my throat. I didn't like that at all but I loved the dancing. I'd not felt more connected nor more free than when dancing with Mum, Jonathon and Caroline. It was okay for me to call her mum now and not just okay because I had to, but okay because I wanted to. I'd grown to understand her, She kept that straight face on because it was her protection against Wenzel she could control whether to smile or not. What to eat or if not to eat. Wenzel controlled everything and everyone. She needed a little space that was hers and as she didn't have it outwardly in her life she found a way to get it mentally. That was okay. I understood. We all wanted that and it would manifest itself in different ways for all of us. Caroline had a stutter and mum had agoraphobia and obsessive compulsive disorder. I don't really think it was obsessive compulsive disorder though. She would hide the sugar and separate the coffee into two pots so as one was for Wenzel and the other for herself. If you ask me she just wanted something for herself that wasn't contaminated by her husband.

It was food time again mum had brought the last plate of food in for herself and sat at the end of the sofa in the corner of the room Wenzel beside her, "smile" he said looking at her. "Miserable cow, smile" he added when she didn't smile. Mum ignored him. Usually she'd give him a half second smile. She hadn't and everyone noticed. This wasn't good. I'd learnt to be very aware of body language and this was not good at all. Wenzel's shoulders were up. He relaxed them and prodded mum with a fork in her arm. "Ow!" she said pulling away and shooting him a look. He did it again. "Don't that hurts" she said. "That doesn't hurt" he said laughing and prodded her again this time in the fore arm. She pulled away and put her knife and fork down. "Oh don't be silly I'm only playing" he said grabbing her hair and pulling her down towards him. He held her as though in a headlock but without putting any pressure on and then let her go. Mum was holding her plate steady as Wenzel played the idiot. Mum sat up "you find it funny don't you?" he asked the kids. Of course if we didn't reply we knew we'd be hit. If we said no we'd be hit so we said yes or worse if we acted scared in any way. That was Wenzel's thing, fear, he thrived from it. "You're not scared of me are you?" he said in such a way he'd made it sound like "you weren't before but you soon will be". He continued to prod mum with the fork until she threw the meal on the floor and stormed into the kitchen. He followed calmly rising from his chair and giving us a very brief "I know what I'm doing" smile before he went into the kitchen. I didn't see what happened but there was screaming coming from the Kitchen and it wasn't Wenzel.

Chapter 7

I wanted to be back with Alan so much. I wasn't allowed out of bed apart from to pee at Wenzels where as at home I'd of had the run of the house. If I set foot on that landing floor and wasn't heading to the bathroom I was slapped around I don't remember the first time it happened. I do remember how the skirting board looked close up though. I'd seen it enough times before I learnt to close my eyes quickly with my head between my arms and my legs tucked up. I'd learnt to curl up pretty quickly. I knew the sounds of Jonathon turning over in his sleep, Caroline having another nightmare and the difference between Wenzel's trainer and Wenzel's bare feet on the floor. I had to. I didn't want him behind me without me knowing he was there. That said I didn't relish the thought of being in bed either. I couldn't get out of bed, literally. If my foot hit the floor and he heard me the door would swing open and he'd come in guns blazing.

I'd always had a very vivid imagination so much so that when Nan and Alan watched horror films I could actually see Freddy Krueger stood behind Nan's chair watching me and sometimes over lapping her face. Pat had to take me to the toilet as I wouldn't go up the stairs on my own.

Wenzel seemed in a good mood. He'd been hunting that day shooting rabbits and told us all the details when he got home. He got a rise out of telling us about the ferrets, that if you place a ferret and a rabbit in a hutch together the ferret will kill the rabbit and then eat its way through the rabbit from the inside outwards. He was pacing in front of us as he told the story and doing the hand movements as though actually holding up a rabbit. I didn't know if it was true but I knew he was in a good mood. When he'd finished his show he sat down and told mum he was going to watch a film. "Bed time guys" mum said. "Can I watch it too?" I asked. He looked down at me sat cross legged on the floor as though I shouldn't exist and was somehow disturbing his reality. How dare I talk? "You want to watch a film?" He asked doing that thing again where he extends each word and the silence echos. "She's told you to go to bed and you want to watch the fucking film? Who do you think you are?" He added. Jonathon was already half way up the stairs having given mum a kiss and Caroline was following suit. She shot me a look "don't annoy him" it said. "Yeah, I thought we could watch it together?" I asked ignoring the who do I think I am. I didn't know who I was and I was happy not knowing all I knew was my parents were gone and they'd have let me watch it. "Put the kids to bed" he told Bernie. She didn't argue I got up to go to bed "not you" he said. I stayed motionless half stood waiting for the impact, none came. "You want to watch the film, you'll watch the fucking film" he said walking into the kitchen.

He came back with a wooden Kitchen chair and pointed at it. I thought this was going to be fun, I was wrong. "Sit" he ordered and I did nervously waiting for whatever he was going to do next. "Don't leave that chair and don't take your eyes off that T.V. I'll be checking on you if you move you won't know what's hit you" He was calm but meant every word. He turned the light off and pulled the door mostly closed. The adverts were just finishing. I sat and watched children of the corn all the way through on my own. I don't recall what happens but I've never watched it since. I was eight.

It was a few days after and definitely not the work of my over active imagination. Wenzel was at work. I was upstairs on my bed playing Alex the kid on the master system Nan had got me for Christmas I'd got it early because I'd been good. It was still early December and Nan had died in the November. I wasn't thinking about anything much just lay there going over levels I'd completed a hundred times before when I felt the bed move down beside me like someone had sat down. I could see just fine from my position and presumed it was the cat as we always had animals at Nan's and then I realised Mum and Wenzel didn't have a cat. I looked at the spot and the bed •

was dipped as though someone was sat there. I felt Nan watching me and knew she was there. I couldn't see her just the spot where she sat. I didn't know what to do and carried on playing my game, around two minutes passed by which is a long time when you're concentrating on something you don't understand. I felt both peaceful and comfortable. I knew I was experiencing something magical. Suddenly the bed adjusted itself and Nan was gone. The room was empty again. I ran downstairs to mum and she asked what's wrong. I waved her to the stairs where we always spoke in private and told her "I've just seen something" I said.

"Ah" she replied not at all fazed "what did you see?" She asked. I shook my head and my mum smiled a real smile quite possibly the first real smile I'd ever seen her have. She had a brown checked shirt on and light coloured jeans. "It's okay, she won't hurt you" she said turning her head slightly. I let it out defensively "It's Nan of course she won't" then I caught myself "You've seen her?" I asked my mum a woman I only partly knew. I was looking into her eyes for the truth "Yes. They won't hurt you. They can't" she said and her eyes agreed. I smiled "now go and play, let's not tell your dad yeah?" She tapped my arm and I shot off to play.

I still hadn't drawn the conclusion Wenzel was abusive in part because it was all normal to me, in part because I'd seen Caroline abused by Nan and in part because my parents in my mind were Nan and Alan and they always said he was crazy and not to upset him, I presumed it was okay that he's crazy it and it was equally okay that I couldn't stand him. I'd seen his ways and didn't want to be there. I was going to run away with the full knowledge that if he caught me he'd kill me. I had no doubts about that in my mind, he would kill me, but if I got to Alan's before Wenzel then Alan would protect me. I'd had the thought in my head for a few days. I can't remember why but it had something to do with Wenzel calling me a bastard. I was eight years old but I knew what a bastard was I'd replied "I'm not a bastard Alan is my dad" I don't remember what happened but I knew it hurt and I knew I was leaving.

I had it all planned out. I'd wait until Wenzel and mum were busy just before food time. They always argued or she cooked whilst he banged around getting gear to go fishing or hunting, either way it was the time I'd chosen because they were both occupied. He'd taken me fishing twice I caught sticklebacks on Macclesfield canal and I hated hurting animals. When I told him he'd told me I'm no son of his. "I know" I thought. I went for a walk down the canal by myself instead.

The second time he took me he wasn't happy about it but mum said I'd not been out in ages. We didn't go fishing we went to a ladies house where I sat watching her fish tank in the living room whilst he took her in the bedroom. I wasn't allowed hunting. He had a twelve gauge shotgun and two friendly ferrets called Jack and kill, Lovely creatures but working pets so I couldn't handle them often. I never asked I knew it was bad. Asking for anything was bad so whilst he banged around in the gun cupboard I was stood shaking in the bedroom preparing to run away.

I could see myself stood shaking. I could see me from up above and knew I should be packing my bag, hiding it. Putting the clothes in the wardrobe and on the bed to make it look like nothing's missing. I knew the rest of my plan. It was ingrained in my veins from the amount of time I'd spent going over it. Each step, each movement. I'd have food with my parent's and act normal. Then I had to ask him about his day because mum never did and he always has a go at her for it. Sometimes he'd walk in and start having a go at her because he saw a cobweb, a glass on the side or simply the T.V wasn't on his favourite channel. She'd ignore him but look at him listening. "What? Not even going to ask about my day?" He'd ask. "You've been sat here all day doing fuck all, all day, who do you think pays the bills?" Then he'd go into another onslaught of verbal abuse. We didn't ask about his day. We didn't care about his day but nobody dared say it, but if I asked him about his day maybe just maybe he'd be happy and that would be enough of a distraction for me to be able to get out. It wasn't logical. I was eight but it made sense in my head. If he was happy he was less switched on to his surroundings. I didn't, I just stood shaking staring at the wardrobe imagining my bag filling itself, me climbing out the bedroom window and shimmying down the drain pipe onto the conservatory roof and into next doors Garden, then over two fences and I'd be into Alan's garden. From there I could just knock on the window and he'd let me in. It would all be fine.

I heard movement on the landing and immediately snapped out of my daydream. I'd stopped shaking too. It was mum "tea" she called and I went downstairs immediately sitting cross legged on the floor in front of the sofa with my back to the T.V. My usual place.

I was beside Caroline and she was beside Jonathon. I'd glanced at the T.V on the way in and received a look from Wenzel as I'd sat down. I knew the look, by now I could tell with the slightest of gestures what I'd done wrong. This one was safe and meant "sit down you're here to eat not watch fucking T.V" despite his words echoing in my head his pupils hadn't changed and so I knew I wasn't getting a beating.

Mum brought food in one by one. I wasn't hungry but then I was never hungry. He told me "sit down" as soon as the kid's plates were out. "Just getting yours and mine" she replied it was never "ours" it was always "yours and mine" She handed him a plate he snatched it and grabbed her wrist pulling her down "about fucking time! Sit down I'm trying to watch this" she rubbed her wrist and he laughed "that didn't hurt" he added.

"Yeah" mum said lowering her head.

"That did not hurt, look" he started tapping her face with the back of his hand repeatedly. She pulled away "stop it" she said glancing at him and then putting her head down.

"That didn't hurt" he said grabbing her wrist with both hands and pulling her towards him in the middle of the sofa. "No, please!" she said high pitched. He Chinese burnt her hard. She winced and tried pulling away but he wouldn't let her and gave her a "you know what you'll get in a minute" look. "The kids, please" she said he looked at us "well? Should I do it?" I couldn't let others answer I knew whatever they said this was bad. This was trouble waiting to happen. If anyone said yes mum got told "see even the fucking kids hate you, you're useless" and he'd burn her. I know I'd seen it before. If we said no then we'd be stood in the middle of the room and slapped until we cried and then told to stop crying, or mum would be hurt in front of us to prove he could do what he wanted no matter what. I looked him dead in the eye and said the only thing I could think of "Good day?" He laughed "good day? Eat your food you smart ass little shit your mums gone to a lot of trouble over this sorry state of a meal haven't you babe?" He said twiddling her hair as she tried not to pull away.

I was scared. I knew I couldn't let him see I was scared if I did he'd enjoy it all the more. Fear was his drug. If I was scared he could do anything. Total control. It could have ended in me being dragged upstairs his fingers biting into my arm. Even though I'd walk and never let myself be dragged sometimes it just happened. I couldn't run ahead to help my momentum catch up, If I ran ahead he'd just yank me down the stairs by my shirt and that was worse. Anything that involved falling or lack of balance was bad, very bad. I'd just walk and accept whatever was coming. Usually it was slaps, head, arms, legs, back anything he could hit. Sometimes he used the slipper and yanked my trousers down. I'd be dragged across his lap. It hurt bit nothing like slaps. I've taken a few punches. Had my head rock when I took a punch which felt like marbles rattling in a box even after my head had stopped moving. Like the pains echo lingers just to taunt for a while longer.

Some nights I would have made one mistake or another to be told to sit back. That meant I'd have to move myself backwards away from my plate at least three feet and watch the others eat. I remember automatically looking at mum to save me and know that she'd feel guilty and she'd not eat. He'd have a go at her again then which would naturally be my fault. When everyone else had finished I'd watch my plate get taken away. "What? You want it now? Should have thought of that before shouldn't you?" Myy food would vanish into the bin. I'd still have to reply "yes sir". If I said sir and he thought I was being sarcastic it was slaps time. If I didn't say sir then I was told "yes what?" to which I'd have to reply "yes sir". I wouldn't look at Caroline or Jonathon. I knew he'd start on me again usually with a "they won't help you – corner."

Corner was another one of his games. I knew the rules. One step away from the corner of our yellow living room wall was my place. I had to have my hands by my sides relaxed and facing straight ahead with my feet together. I'm surprised I recall the colour of those walls I spent so much time staring through them rather than at them. It's strange to explain those feelings where I'd be stationary for so long staring at a wall and yet aware of everything going on around me. More often than not the slightest sound and I could place what it was and who had made it. If you are walking around busy you don't really notice your legs that much because you're moving in different ways, however stood in one spot for hours eventually you notice it., a lot. So it's good to move your feet and legs around a little.

The key was not being seen. At first I'd just chance moving my legs apart a little "stand straight!" he'd yell if he saw me move at all. I did but figured he's just yelling as long as I can move now and again even if he yells I'll be fine. My freedom didn't last long. Wenzel had found a new game. I was stubborn and wouldn't let my legs give way. I knew if I did I'd take a beating and couldn't curl up. Worse than that though If I did collapse I'd be playing right into his game and he'd win.

Boxing was on television. I'd been sent to the corner after having the slipper because I'd said "don't" he'd slapped mum in the face whilst they were both in the middle of the living room. she'd replied with some off hand comment or other and as he raised his fist and moved forwards I'd said "don't". I wasn't thinking. It wasn't heroic. It was reflex. He immediately turned from her and looked straight at me. I eyed him it lasted maybe five seconds I didn't care by this point. Better I take the beating than her. I was in my usual place on the floor Caroline and Jonathon had gone for the corner and I don't know where Jodie was. "Get up" he said as though he wanted a man to man chat. I did and he knocked me straight back down half slap half push. I stayed down and he turned back to Bernie. I was on my feet before he was anywhere near her. I kept my eyes on his "What? Got something to say?" I ignored him and didn't take my eyes off his. I was knocked down again this time he put my arm up my back and pulled me over to him whilst he sat on the sofa. He said he was going to teach me some manners. My face was near his groin he had blue jeans on and a white T-Shirt, The zipper was brass. His left arm held my right wrist. He pinned my left arm under his leg. Mother was curled up at the other end of the sofa. She said something but I didn't catch it. He shot her a look. My shoulder hurt but I could breath and partially turn my head so I was okay. He slapped my face against his leg with his right hand. It stung but was nothing compared to the ache now in my shoulder. He pulled my arm upwards and pain tore through my shoulder. He must have hit me thirty times all slaps then he applied pressure to my shoulder again "say mercy" he said calmly like a question.

I was shocked and scared. When in doubt stay silent. I didn't know what mercy was or what would happen if I said it. I was saying nothing. My face went from mild stinging to numb in no time. My shoulder hurt. He began turning my wrist upwards behind me "say Mercy" he ordered. I grunted with the effort of trying to put my mind somewhere else and leaned forwards to try and ease the pain in my shoulder to no avail. Mother said something again and

Wenzel brought his knee up and his hand down at the same time simultaneously kneeing me in the stomach and slapping in between my shoulder blades. I could hear him yelling but couldn't make out what he was saying. I was winded and my back stung like hell. By now he'd twisted my arm so much I could feel the tension like a stick about to snap. I had tears down my face from the pain and my nose was pushed so hard against him I could hardly breathe.

He pushed me away and I hit the floor with a roll and lay there with my arm was limp. I held it straight down beside me and let out a number of whimpers. Then I realised the mistake I'd made. Not only had I let him know he'd hurt me but my roll had left me with my back to him. I spun around on the floor in time to see him standing above me smiling. I'll never forget that smile, I knew I'd fucked up and was so angry with myself. Mother was used to this. She was sat in the corner staring into the distance again trying to pretend this world didn't exist. I'd had enough "no!, No! Please!" escaped before I could stop myself "get up" he smiled. I'd taken too much I didn't think I could take any more and it felt like I'd never use my arm again. I lay there, helpless. "Get up or you'll regret it" I got to one knee with my arm dangling besides me before he'd grabbed it, pulled it straight and had my arm out behind me. This left me leaning forwards and screaming in pain. "When I say get up. You get up do you understand me?" "Yes" I replied in between rapidly begging for him not to hurt me. He turned my wrist upwards and grabbed my elbow. So now he had complete control. He pushed me towards the stairs and I had no choice but to go with. "What did you say?" he hissed into my ear. I thought it through in a split second "what did he want to hear? I'd said yes then I realised I'd missed the sir off"

"Yes sir!" I said. "What?" He shouted pretending he couldn't hear me and turning my arm back into the position he'd first had so now he's stood behind me and I'm against a wall in the corner of Caroline's bedroom.

"Yes sir" I answered

"Yes sir what?" He asked

"Yes sir I'll get up when you say?" I replied. I was on tip toes trying
to remove some pain from my arm. I couldn't feel my shoulder any
more than to say it felt like a burst balloon. I'd gone through
discomfort, ache, pain and fire to just plain deflated. The outside
was tender the inside was missing I can't explain that kind of pain.
He let me go and I turned around out of instinct. The light was off
he made motions as though he was going to slap me but didn't. He
liked that game. Making me wait for a slap. I stepped back and he
laughed. I couldn't protect myself anyway. My arm was shot and lay
like a weight down my side. I was trapped but even if I ran he'd kill
me when he caught me and where would I run to? He sat on the
bed facing me. "Take my shoes off" he said. I didn't hesitate I was
on the floor before he'd finished the sentence and untying his laces,
I noticed one arm moved a lot slower than the other. He had white
socks on with a blue trim my fingers wouldn't work properly but I
blanked it out because I was more concerned that he was going to
spank me with those trainers. The soles were really thick.

He shouted Caroline and immediately she was by the door head
down and arms down. "Bring my slippers" he said "yes sir" she
replied and our eyes met briefly as she left the room. "I'm glad it's
not me" they said "what did you do this time?" They asked. She was
wearing just a night shirt. She was gone and back in seconds. I was
just relieved. The slipper I could handle.

"Don't go anywhere" he said as Caroline tried to leave. "I didn't..." I
presume she was going to say move but he snapped "shut up!" He
looked back to me I was facing him as he sat on the bed slippers
beside him. Caroline was stood in the doorway looking inwards.
"Trousers off" he said which scared me. Usually he'd hit me through
them or just drag them off. I guess I hesitated because he shouted
"Five!" I knew if he got to one I'd be slapped down. I was stood

there naked by the time he got to three.

He motioned me forwards and leant me over his legs then took a slipper by the heel and slapped my arse with it. I remember him counting and remember he hit me more times than he counted. I was very embarrassed and kind of angry. Angry at me for fucking up and being useless and angry at Caroline for watching and not being punished. Angry at mum for it not being her which made no sense but was totally how I felt. I made no sound until he hit the tops of my legs. That hurt and I screamed and caught it as soon as it came out. Then gritted my teeth whilst he did it again and again. When it was over I was sent downstairs to the floor to T.V time with family before bed. It wasn't long before Caroline was back down too but time changes when you're in pain. Wenzel came in last "you, up" I darted up straight and he stood in front of me for what seemed like ages just looking at me. Then he took my arm "say mercy" I didn't hesitate "mercy" he let me go without applying any pressure to my arm. I'm not sure what stunned me more. Him letting go without hurting me or that I was allowed to watch T.V. He sat down next to mum so I sat down on the floor next to Caroline and Jonathon. "Not you – corner" he said.

Ah...a new game.

 So Caroline and Jonathon are watching T.V with the family and I'm in the corner staring through the wall thinking about my dad Alan and I know if I tell Alan about tonight then he will kill Wenzel. Their was not an if or but or maybe in my mind. I knew without a doubt if I opened my mouth Wenzel would be dead and I'd lose Alan. So I can't because then I'd have to live with mum all the time and Alan would be in prison. Oh and yeah, I'm leaving. I really am.

Chapter 8

I was staring out of my bedroom window and certain I was leaving. I 'd try not to get caught. I'd plan. I knew his routines and his actions. I knew his thoughts they were like my own. I had to if I wanted to know what he'd do next. I'd use that window. I'd decided to go when they were asleep. Our clothes were always in bin bags next to the bed so I'd fill the bag with toys and place clothes on top then put my full bag in the wardrobe. I'd place my books beneath my sheets so it looked like I was sleeping. My packed bag would go in the wardrobe until it was time to leave. I was visualising what I'd do as I walked around my room pointing at areas and then I packed and planned all morning re arranging my room and looking at it from Wenzel's perspective. All clear. My mother came up the stairs as psychic as ever and sat beside me on the bed. "What's wrong?" She asked and seemed to look more pale than usual. More as though all her clothes just shone lighter. Perhaps it was the dull light from the window I was looking to escape through. I said "nothing. "You can tell me anything you know?" She added.

"I'm running away." I told her "Wenzel is wrong. Alan wants me. I know it." I added to her silence without looking at her.

"Please don't. We need you here. You know what he'll do with us if you do go?" I hadn't thought about that. I'd thought only of me. I knew if I left he'd take it out on mum. I couldn't win. "I won't tell him you're planning to go but please stay. It's up to you but please don't go" she asked and walked out.

I'd been allowed to visit Alan and kept asking to stay the night. Alan wanted me to but said Wenzel wouldn't allow it. He said we had to do what Wenzel wanted because he is my dad although Alan would love to have me with him. I was really unhappy and had to stay at parents.

I stopped talking first. I remember mum asking me questions and I just sat there in the living room ignoring her. If you're not going to talk get upstairs so I did. I expected a beating when Wenzel came home but none came. At food he remarked "you not talking?" I ignored him. I could feel him looking down at me with my head down over my food. "Oi! Shithead I'm talking to you!" I clenched my teeth.

"Don't you fucking ignore me!" His plate went flying he got up and punched me in the head. I'd expected a slap and although I'd been sat cross legged when it hit I hadn't braced myself for the fall so my head clunked into my shoulder as I hit the deck. Surprising even myself I simply sat back up.

Looking back most people would have been upset, ran off or shouted. There would have been some kind of reaction. This was normal it really was like missing that piece of fluff with the Hoover or misplacing that book you love. It wasn't nice and it fucking hurt but it was normal. Just another bad part of the day and not only was it normal it was okay too. I deserved it. I'm useless so who cares? Fuck me I'm a nobody. I deserve it. It had got to the point I didn't even care about me. Pat my mum was dead. Alan wasn't allowed to have me because of Wenzel and that was worse than any beating and most of his mind games. He loved power. I didn't care. He could have it. Kill me. I welcomed it. I wasn't even angry I was just dead inside.

"You answer me when I'm talking to you I'm your fucking dad, Do you hear me?" By now he had me by the scruff of the neck face down on the floor ready to hit me again. I ignored him concentrating on making pictures in my head. I was playing wrestling with Alan and he kept throwing me body slam style on the sofa and I was laughing. He even sang Hulk Hogan's theme tune in an Irish accent. I was yanked up and my jumper which choked into me. Then I was slapped down and dragged up again. "I'm your dad and you will listen to me" he pulled me towards the stairs "no" I said calmly. He stopped. "No? Did you just say fucking no!?" He roared louder than I'd ever heard whilst spitting in my face. I was finding it hard to breath because of fear and adrenaline. Fear because this was all new it could get worse then I'd ever seen and adrenaline because I knew I was going to answer back anyway. "No, No! Alan's my dad!" He let me go then took my shoulders instantly calm and turned to face me square on. He knelt down "what did you say??" He asked. I replied "you're not my dad. Alan is my dad" I don't remember the trip upstairs but I remember being thrown against the wall. I remember seeing him reach for his belt and running towards him to try and get past. My brain had decided I was off and my body followed suit. I seriously had not thought it through other than to get out the front door and fucking run. I made it as far as the bedroom door before I was stopped by the thud of knuckles hitting cheek bone. My brain was outside running like hell, my body unfortunately was curled up on the bedroom floor holding its head in both hands.

"I'll teach you some respect" he'd taken his belt off and I crawled onto the bed and curled his knees beneath him. I must have blacked out. Maybe it was a punch. Maybe it's because my brain has blanked out a lot of shit from this time but I don't remember a thing after him walking towards me with his belt and then kneeling beside me.

It must have been a few days later because I was told Alan had been but I hadn't seen him. I had been at home all the time and was told I was in bed. I don't know if I was ill or what I can't recall but I remember thinking "Oh no, poor Alan. He needs me now more than ever as Pat has gone"

Strange how as an adult the abuse affected me yet as a child I just got on with it. I guess I had no choice and it feels as though realistically the things that occurred not only should never have done so to anyone let alone a child but that I shouldn't have been physically capable of withstanding all that I did. However I did.

We were sat on the floor again. Tea time. Usual drill. He'd done the salt thing and allowed us to eat. When he started "Alan called and said he's heard what you said to me and never wants to see you again" he said trying not to look smug. The shock must have registered on my face because he smiled "I'm your dad. You eat because of me. You're here because of me and if I say you do something you do it. Understand?" He added. I nodded.

I started crying how could Alan hate me? It's not true. It can't be true. Alan? My dad? I was heartbroken. He loves me. The food in front of me looked like a giant ball of mess through my tears. I didn't want it and didn't deserve it. I was useless. Mum didn't love me. Alan hates me and Pat is dead. "Eat your food you ungrateful shit" Wenzel said. I could feel Caroline's eyes drilling into my skull. She'd never seen me cry. I was the oldest and it was my job to be strongest. "Just eat it" she whispered" her voice carrying a million warnings. I pushed the plate away two inches and kept my head down. I couldn't eat. He slammed his fork down and sighed "ungrateful shit. I work hard so you can eat and you don't want it? There's kids in Africa that would kill to eat that." I said nothing. I was busy pretending my world didn't exist and me along with it. He looked at Bernie like it was her fault. She shrugged. "OK get upstairs if you won't eat but don't ask for anything later and don't leave your room" I headed to bed. I heard the others get told to eat which was nice because it meant they had stopped. They were concerned about me. Fuck them. I don't care.

Food became a disaster area for me for some time. After the third or fourth occurrence of not eating it became habit. I was hungry but wouldn't eat. I had breakfast because Wenzel was out but wouldn't eat at all if he was home. On this occasion I'd pushed the food away and stood up to go upstairs when he asked "where you going?" I pointed upstairs. "Answer me" he demanded. I ignored him.

"Answer me or you're going nowhere" he said. "Upstairs" I

answered and made a big show of sighing.

"Sit down you can watch the others eat" I looked at mum."Please don't" her eyes told me. I sat down. I could smell the food and hear people eating every now and then Wenzel would comment "isn't this nice Caroline?" Caroline would reply "yes sir, it's nice" he never addressed us by name. Caroline had no choice but to reply, It was like I just didn't belong which is exactly what he wanted. Every now and then Caroline would glance at me. Sometimes she'd throw me a secret smile that said "it'll be OK" Then one day during one of these meals there was a knock at the door and it was Alan.

Chapter 9

I don't know what he said but he was immediately invited in. It's the first time I noticed he had a weird walk. He kind of shuffled his legs. I only noticed because his stone washed blue jeans dragged slightly on one side. I could see he was looking relaxed but taking in everything. My heart leapt I'd been wondering how he was doing since I'd been told he didn't want to see me. He sat down and said "OK kidda?" I smiled. Wenzel piped up "come on then eat your dinner" everyone else had nearly finished it was obvious I hadn't touched mine. I ate the lot. Alan said "what no hug?" I looked at Wenzel and he nodded faintly the light not reaching his eyes. I didn't care about the warning. I ran to Alan and threw my arms around his neck. "I thought you didn't want to see me?" I said.

"Nonsense lad what made you think that?" He asked.

I said nothing but I learnt the lesson to trust nothing Wenzel says.

I was sent upstairs again by mum this time. I just looked at Alan he said "Go on you heard your mum" I sat upstairs wondering what type of punishment I'd get for my actions this time when Alan appeared in the doorway. "I heard you've been asking to stay with me? He said fake hiding a big smile.

"Oh no" I thought. I really didn't want Alan to tell me off. "I don't like it here" I told him honestly.

"Best grab your bag then" he said with a huge smile. I looked up at him "Really?" I asked.

"Come on before he changes his mind" he said.

I don't know what was said downstairs but I was packed and out the bedroom door like a rocket. Alan was chatting to my mum and Wenzel waited by the front door hopping foot to foot as I ran past them and upto the gate in the front garden. "Here lad" Alan called to me. I came in hoping I was still allowed to go. "Say goodbye and thank for being allowed over" with no hesitation I fired off "thanks mum bye dad" I wasn't intending to be rude or sarcastic it's just what I knew. I knew mum would have wanted me happy and knew Wenzel couldn't care less. As I was walking the short journey next door but one to Alan's he told me "you shouldn't be rude to your parent's you'll make it worse for both of us" I told him I didn't mean to be but I'd missed him. When I asked him why I couldn't stay with him before he told me "you could but you weren't well" I told him about father saying he didn't want to see me. "You'll always be welcome here son...hey...I missed you too kid" he patted me on the head. "Now stick a brew on and grab the tin."

I never told Alan about Wenzel's violence. I secretly thought everyone knew and yet also thought Alan can't because he'd of defended me if he did. That's what Macclesfield was like. Things got settled. My uncle's dad who I never knew was stabbed by two men outside a pub in Manchester and died. One of the guys died the other was blinded. My uncle had upset some people one year and they came down to Moorhill road looking for him. Alan went out to protect Clive and half the street came out. Petrol bombs, axes, hammers pretty much anything that could be used as a weapon was used as a weapon. I was too young to remember but I heard all about it from Alan and Clive. This was commonly referred to as "the Moss way" So I couldn't tell Alan because if I did then I was a "grass" and you don't grass. It didn't matter anyway. I was back with Alan and everything was perfect. Alan told me I had to be good at Wenzel's otherwise I wouldn't be allowed to visit. That was the deal. Three nights at Alan's place a week as long as I behave at Wenzel's. I agreed.

It was party time which was weird without Nan. I don't remember one event that didn't include a punch up or a row and this one was unfortunately no different. Alan, Clive, Lesley and Lisa who used to look after Caroline and Maggie Clive's wife were all downstairs drinking whilst Caroline and I played on the scalextric Nan had got me before Christmas. We heard a bit of shouting and Alan appeared in the doorway. "Clive is not in a good mood okay?" I nodded. Alan had saved Clive's ass numerous times when the police were looking for him or random people turned up on Alan's doorstep after being told Clive lived there. I knew Nan had liked the power it gave her in having Clive do whatever she said but Clive could turn at any minute. Nobody gave her shit because Clive was her son but with his mum dead Clive was dangerous. I looked at Caroline and we exchanged "here we go again" glances then carried on playing. It was maybe twenty minutes later Maggie ran up the stairs crying and hid in the bathroom slamming the door closed behind her. Clive soon followed banging on the door. "Come out you stupid bitch I didn't mean anything by it" Maggie just sobbed. Caroline looked at me and put her finger to her lips "shhh" I'd got the message. If he didn't know we were here we weren't a target.

The bedroom door swung open and Clive's six foot plus frame stood over us swaying and blocking the door way. "You!" He pointed at me. "What?" I replied quietly. "What? Come here!" He tried to grab me but had to bend to reach me and step forwards. I was lucky he was so tall and so drunk. "Get Alan!" I told Caroline and darted through his legs hitting his knee on the way through with my shoulder. He grabbed my jumper and I shrugged him off and pelted for the stairs and ran into the living room. "Where's Alan?" I asked the smoky room looking around confused. "Here lad" he said raising a giant hand. He was short but twice as wide. I spat out "Clive wants me upstairs! He wants a word with me". Alan slammed his cup down "fuck, okay come on then" I knew he wasn't upset with me and knew I was safe but still didn't like the idea of Clive and Alan going head to head.

We met Clive going down the stairs as we were heading up. I presumed Caroline was hiding as I was taken into Pat's bedroom. Clive said to Alan "You don't say nuthin, no answering for him" Clive bent down as I was sat on the edge of the bed his beer stained teeth in front of my face so close I could taste it. "Don't lie to me! " he took a breath then added "Because I'll know!" He pointed in my face. "I won't" I stammered looking confused. I dared a "help me" glance to Alan he nodded a "listen to him" expression. Clive said "right, did you trap my Harry's finger in a door?" It took me a minute to realise Harry was his son and I hardly saw him. I knew nothing of a trapped finger. "No, no ,no" I stammered. "N,N,N,N,no!" he repeated taking a step back "don't lie to me!" He shouted. "I'm not! I don't know anything!" I screamed as he grabbed my jumper and turned his hand so the jumper dug into my neck. He lifted me clean off the bed and towards the wall at speed. I couldn't breathe. Clive's fist came back and as it did Alan cannon balled into Clive from the side. I hit the wall then the floor. Choking I got my jumper off and realised why I couldn't breathe. I'd had a whistle on a chain Nan bought me on beneath my jumper as he'd twisted his hand it had dug into my neck. As soon as I released it I was OK but panting.

I hit the floor hard clutching my throat then I looked up and saw Clive punching Alan in the back and head. Alan was bent over and saw me he grabbed Clive's arm "Run!" he said. I jumped across the bed out of reach and turned to see Alan lift his arms above Clive's neck leaving Alan's face free to get hit. He took a few hard punches but managed to grab Clive's head and pull it downwards where Alan went to work with his knees. Clive's face took several knees before Clive pushed forwards knocking Alan onto the floor and Clive falling on top of him. The force had sent Clive sprawling so now Alan's face was by Clive's feet. Clive stood up and kicked at Alan. Alan was fast though, he Hooked both arms around his leg and sank his teeth into Clive's Ankle. Clive grabbed his leg in pain.

I arrived at Wenzel's in seconds and banged on the door. He answered gingerly "What the fuck do you want?" I told him "Clive and Alan are fighting!"

"Upstairs" he said and closed the door on the cool night air.

Later I would find out Clive got up and tried to kick Alan again when he was down. Alan had grabbed him and thrown him into the bedroom window. After a few punches Alan told him "I promised your mum years ago I'd take care of you but if you ever touch that boy again I'll kill you" The next day Alan picked me up and told me everything. Alan didn't drink because of his epilepsy however later when Clive popped in with eight cans Alan accepted and they were fine again. Macc rules, it was the Moss way.

Chapter 10

I'd remembered what Alan said about my real dad and how he might not be my real dad. However at eight years old my Nan had just died who was like a mum to me I didn't quite get it. Kids are pretty durable there was no "could it get any worse?" feelings back then and no "why me?" feelings at all I just took it on the chin. It was like being told I couldn't play outside because there were drunks out there. I'd understand I couldn't go out but not the full ramifications that if I did I could be harmed.

I recalled the stories I was told about Alan's epilepsy, the time he moved house and had a fit a few days later. That night he woke up and walked downstairs. He opened the front door and peed in the street thinking it was the toilet. Nan wouldn't wake him in case it set a fit off, It did cause a bit of a scene for the people having a garden party across the road though.

In another story he'd flip up out of bed repeatedly into the wood chip wall paper, smacking his face into the wall in the process. He'd spent a week in hospital and Nan and I visited him. We brought apple pie which was his favourite. I don't remember it but Alan told me all about it. When we'd left he asked the nurse who we were "that's your wife and son" she'd replied. "Holy shit, I'm married?" He'd responded.

I knew exactly what to do if he had a fit. I'd learnt not to let him grab me if he went into a fit and all about the recovery position. He'd usually come around within an hour and take another half hour to get his bearings.

It was Christmas Eve and the place was bare. "She'd not approve of this lad" Alan had said earlier in the day. I pretended not to hear him. It didn't matter. We had each other. "I'm tired dad" I said later heading to bed. He was right the place was bare she wouldn't approve she'd always made a huge show of Christmas but hey she was dead. That was the bottom line. She was dead and we were here and we had to be ourselves and just survive so sod it. I hated Christmas and I hated people.

I got up in the morning and Alan smiled "brew?" I jumped on the bed beside him and tucked into some biccies. Come on then let's go and see what today holds for us. He said jumping out of bed pushing me backwards playfully. I wasn't excited I had no reason to be. Alan nodded for me to go in front of him as we went down the stairs. I opened the living room door and it was magical. There were lights everywhere! Along the top of the curtains, over the sofa, around the fire place even the T'V had a set of lights around it. Stood in front of the window was our huge tree and on the top was an electric Angel that had a halo and a book that lit up in gold. The wings sparkled. Every year Nan had a star and this year she had her heart set on that angel. Alan had done it all by himself on his own on Christmas eve. Beneath the tree were loads of presents.

I knelt down in front of the tree, Alan joined me. We weren't praying. Neither of us were religious as far as I knew. We just took those five minutes for Nan and sat in silence. Neither of us spoke we didn't need to and then it happened. We cried at exactly the same time we both just burst into tears and the heavens opened and ran down our faces. We held each other and cried until we could cry no more. I remember his big green jumper being soaked from my tears; He took his green woollen hat off and wiped his tears away too. He passed me a parcel and I pushed it away. "We'd got you these" I went and got the parcel from upstairs and Alan opened his new western books Nan and I had brought him. "Thanks lad" he said rubbing my head. My granddad and my best friend. That night the black and white portable T.V clicked off "night lad" he said. "Night Granddad" I replied and there was an emptiness where we both thought "Night Pat"

The huge water butt was full and had iced over outside because of the snow. I'd chucked my wellies on as I could see Alan pushing down on it hard and it looked fun as the huge ice circle wobbled around. I could see it bouncing softly over the lip of the huge blue bucket and it was really thick. "Here lad" he waved me over as I plodded through the snow towards him. He lifted the whole circle out and placed it standing up on the floor in front of me. "Go on then!" He said with a huge grin. "What?" I said.

"Give it a whack lad" I laughed it was very thick and cold. It looked amazing but I wasn't going to hit it.

"Give it a kick then" He said and I did a few times and it didn't break.

"Your turn Granddad" I said raising my arms to hold the top of this thing. We rolled it against the fence post. Alan asked if I wanted another go before he broke it? "No, you won't break it!" I said knowing he was capable of such things with ease.

He stepped back and I heard him take a short breath in rapidly and then let it out twice as fast as he stepped forwards. "Hai!" the Ice ring went clean in half and fell to the ground and I bowed to him Aikido style.

I was sleeping on the floor in Nan's room as I had when she was alive. It was still Nan's room although she'd been dead more than two months. We could still sense her there and were in the same routines as though she was still alive. We even watched the same programs. I knew he'd not settle straight away. He hadn't since Pat passed. I waited for his breathing to change before I let myself sleep.

I woke up it was dark and I could hear movement. The moon left enough light for me to make out a figure on Alan's side of the bed. He'd got up to go to the toilet. I had an idea! He wouldn't even see it coming and he'd find it funny! I heard him curse as he walked into the corner of the bed and I knew one of two things would happen, either he'd walk past, I'd trip him he'd fall and we'd play fight on the floor or he'd see me trying to trip him and he'd kick me away and jump on me and then we'd play fight on the floor! Neither of these things happened.

Chapter 11

Granddad took a step in front of my feet and I reacted. I spun to the side straightened my leg and ankle keeping them tense and turned my foot knocking into him perfectly just how he'd taught me. Got him! He tripped and the second he started to fall I knew something was badly wrong. He fell forwards and immediately went into a fit. He toppled and fell hitting the radiator by the wall. I heard it rattle in the dark but didn't see the impact and then he was upright again and falling backwards, straight down like a falling wall. His head hit the floor hard. He'd landed on Nan's bathrobe which I'd used to cover myself up with because it still smelt of her, it did nothing to hide the vibrations through the floorboard of his head hitting them. I remember the sound of pipes rattling to this day.

I grabbed his face and tried to remember everything I'd been told. "Don't move him, Get help! Don't put anything in his mouth. Don't let him grab you. When he stops shaking put him in the recovery position" all the information hit me within milliseconds. He wasn't shaking, he wasn't moving and as far as I could tell he wasn't breathing. I knew if he wasn't breathing he needed immediate help. He must have slept in his jeans because his keys were on a chain attached to them and currently in his pocket. I could see the chain and the bulge. I crawled over him and dug my hand down deep struggling to remove the keys on a metal clasp. I ran downstairs and into the front door, literally. I fumbled with the keys and ran outside. My memory blanks here I don't know who I told first. I don't know where I went or what happened. I do recall the verdict. Brain haemorrhage just like nan. I also remember it was two days until his Dobermann lay down and died oddly the only memory I have of our old dog, I couldn't tell anyone. I was destroyed. I'd lost my parents as far as I was concerned.

I was moved back to "mum and dad's" and everything changed. Mum looked after the kids and did the cooking. She wasn't very good. Her depression got worse and she drank heavily after losing her mum. On the very rare occasion she tried to go out she'd get to the lamppost and freak out. She'd only go because Aunty Betty or Maggie would promise her a bottle of sherry if she made it. I'd watch from the bottom of moorhill road usually stood beside Wenzel who'd repeat "she won't make it. Silly cow never does fucking waste of space". As soon as she'd get home whoever had taken her and Wenzel would say how well she'd done and how proud they are of her for trying. Then our visitor would leave and he'd start up "waste of time that wasn't it? Don't know why you bother"

"if it wasn't for me you'd have nothing. Fucking useless you are. What are you?" He'd ask.

She'd look down and he'd repeat. "Well? I'm talking to you" he'd pull her chin up to meet his gaze "what are you?" He'd sneer.

"Useless" she'd mutter.

"That's right. Don't fucking forget it" he demanded walking off.

We all knew if she didn't reply he'd slap her around and if that didn't get a reply he'd start on the kids, usually me. I'd take a few whacks and he'd insult Bernie and Caroline until mum said "I'm useless" then he'd stop but not until he'd dished her an order "make food" or "get upstairs."

Even he knew his limits, he never hit Jonathon. I remember that day well. Jonathon was playing with the plastic washing basket and Wenzel gave Bernie the "sort him out" look. She replied "he's just playing". Wenzel stared at her and she moved the basket from Jonathon who promptly went back over to play with it. Wenzel slammed his plate down and stood up heading towards Jonathon. Bernie threw herself at him. I'd never seen her move so fast. Like a cat she'd gone from feet curled beneath her on the sofa to on top of

Wenzel instantly. "I'll kill you! You bastard! Touch him? I'll kill you!" he spun and she went flying. Jonathon and I ran to opposite corners of the room. She clawed his face. He hit her and grabbed her wrists forcing her downwards. She was in obvious pain but looked straight at him "you can do what you want to me but you do not touch him" her eyes were like steel. That's the only time I saw her stand up for herself and I knew beyond doubt that if he touched Jonathon she would kill him.

He wasn't violent for a while after that incident maybe even a week. The thing to remember is that as a kid these things were not unusual. The insults and violence was a normal part of everyday living and we totally accepted it because we'd known no different. We knew something wasn't right. Like I knew from day one Wenzel didn't want or like me and that was OK because Nan and Alan had. In a warped way when he didn't tell us off or hurt us it was worse because then it was like he didn't care at all. Then at least when he hit us he wanted us for something. We protected him too. He never did it in front of people. If I was out to the shop and someone asked me a question I'd look at him for the OK to reply. If I didn't get the nod I didn't speak. He controlled my voice, my actions, and my life. He held all the keys to all the doors. I was his to do as he pleased. I hated it however that was my life and it was normal. I had an advantage the others didn't though. I'd known another life. I'd known love or at least a form of it.

I was starting to be programmed. I didn't realise nor did I understand a lot of my actions would be wrong. Some even cruel. I started to copy what I'd seen daily. Clive screaming at his wife. Nan abusing Caroline. Wenzel attacking Bernie. I learnt to believe a few inaccuracies and by believe I mean I knew them to be true, they were fact.

My words were a powerful tool. I could lie easily to escape punishment even if I deserved it.

I could predict people's actions because of their body language and tone of voice. If I knew how they felt I could use this to my advantage.

I knew to feel good all I had to do was control another and that was okay to do because every male I'd known apart from Alan was doing it.

I'd started to understand Wenzel got a physical and sexual kick when he controlled people. If he told Bernie she was useless she became below him and he became useful. If he made her cry he felt strong. He physically felt superhuman if she was depressed because of him. At the same time it was a circle. If she didn't look happy when he wanted her to then he felt useless as a husband, which he was. He'd fix this by making her do what he wanted "smile" was his favourite quick fix. Mum would for a half second. She knew his games as well as we did and we all knew little ways to rebel against them. The split second smile was one of her ways. By her fake smiling he felt in control and happier by her not holding a full smile she felt more in control of his ways and therefore not as controlled.

I'd started seeing it everywhere and not only was it normal but that was right and exactly how I should be.

I remember Caroline being told off because she felt sick and so wasn't eating her food as fast as Wenzel would like. I looked at her with disgust. I knew how she felt and I'd been where she was more times than I liked to. I'd made the choice to join Wenzel's ways. I hated myself all the more. Caroline looked at me like I'd slapped her. "What's your fucking problem?" Wenzel shouted at her. "Feel sick" Caroline replied. "Eat your food" I said loud enough for all to hear but without shouting. I didn't look at her and tucked into my own as I waited for Wenzel to hit me. He didn't, he laughed "you heard your brother, eat your food" a few days of me siding with daddy and I was rewarded with two things. Firstly I was allowed out on my own which had never happened before and only happened this time because when I asked mum had said no and Wenzel would disagree with anything she said. My second reward was that he would take my word over Caroline's and sometimes Bernie's too.

I knew I'd made my life easier but also knew this gave me leverage. I could prevent him hurting them by making him laugh. They would hate me because I'd put them down but they wouldn't be hit either. I got special treatment. I could watch T.V and eat at the same time. I knew how his brain worked and used it to my cause.

On one occasion Caroline was talking to Jonathon. I can't recall what was said it was trivial normal Kid's stuff. Wenzel piped up "what was that?" We weren't allowed to talk unless spoken to. Never to each other at dinner or in his presence. My mum was OK with it but he wasn't. I repeated what was said which was something like "want to play Lego later Jonathon?" Wenzel blew up. "Lego!? Fucking Lego! You're supposed to be eating you little shit not talking!" He was red in the face and looking to hit people, it was seconds away.

"Upstairs twenty slaps with slipper. Knickers down!" I said and carried on eating not looking at either of them. I could feel Caroline's eyes on me. She hated me but didn't know what I'd just done. Either he'd beat me rotten for taking his role or he'd calm down because I suggested it and as it was his normal suggestion he'd feel it was the right thing to do but didn't need to be done because everyone now knew it had been suggested. No control in knowing what's going to happen. Control comes from shock and fear. I chomped my egg down smiling waiting for the outcome. He laughed "maybe later, eat your food" he said nodding at me calmly.

I nodded and mouthed a "sorry dad" I knew my place. Below him and above them and I was starting to get the same kicks of control he'd got.

Chapter 12

My rewards had grown and being able to see Conran whenever I wanted was one of them. He wanted to swap my Maccano for his Lego and I'd agreed so he took the Maccano home. Conran was okay, about a year older than me and very pale. I'd play on his master system console with him whilst his mum was with clients in her bedroom. The story goes that she was a masseuse but everyone knew the truth. Alan told me she was on the game years ago. It took me a long time to realise that didn't mean she played Sonic the hedgehog.

Conran put the control pad down and went around the corner of his high sleeper bed. He told me to wait there so I did for a few minutes until he shouted me. I went to him and he had his trousers around his ankles. Touching himself. "Touch it" he said pointing it at me. I stood there looking at it and then at his face. "Want to touch it?" He said. I turned around and walked out, him pulling his trousers up behind me and shuffling along "Please don't tell anyone!" He begged. I nodded by the front door "lego still okay?" I asked. He nodded and I left.

A few days later Conran was at our house which was unheard of. We rarely got to play together as brother and sisters let alone have friends over. We totally didn't know what to do but I knew there was no way I was playing Sonic the hedgehog with Conran again. So we watched T.V instead sat on my bed. When Wenzel got home he asked what we had been up to all day. I told him "just watching T.V" pointing at the portable. "Good lads. Come on. I'll take Conran home" He replied. We sat down for the evening meal and Wenzel told me "You can't find anything else to do but watch T.V? That's last time Conran comes over". I didn't argue and we all had an early night.

I went to get a drink from the bathroom sink and before I knew it Wenzel was behind me. My mistake for thinking I was untouchable.

"What you doing out of bed?" He asked.
"I heard something I was checking what it was she was doing but she's asleep" I lied referring to Caroline He grunted and pointed to my room. My lies came easier each time.

The cycle went on for a long time. One minute I was the useless punch bag that belongs by the wall where he'd throw things at me if I moved. He started with socks, slippers things that don't do much damage and then one day when I slipped and fell because I was stood on the side of my foot to take the pain away from my calf, his bunch of keys hit the wall next to my head. I jumped. "Pick them up" he said. I bent and fell because it hurt. He laughed. I got his keys and gave them to him and stood there like a lemon waiting for instructions. "What? Back on the wall" he said and I returned to the corner waiting, always waiting. More than once those keys hit me square between the shoulder blades and want to or not I hit the floor in pain and stood bolt upright again.

The next minute I'd be the chess buddy and tell tale butter wouldn't melt. It all depended on his mood and how I played it.

I'd been out with Conran, no sooner had I closed the door behind me and I heard the screams. Caroline was upstairs with Wenzel. I ran up knowing they'd not hear me over the noise. He'd never punched Caroline before it was always a hit with an open hand. "Off!" he said as I reached the top of the stairs. He was sat on the edge of the single bed as he was when he spanked me. Caroline pulled her knickers down as I walked in. She had nothing else on. He pulled her over his knee and I went to back away. "Where you going?" He said. I stood there stock still. He must have slapped her over a hundred times. When she pushed her arms back he'd grab her wrist and slap her arms instead.

After Caroline had taken that beating I tried to keep him calm though it was dangerous. He never gave a slap because it was deserved. It was always because he enjoyed it. I knew Alan hadn't been like that and after seeing what I'd put Caroline through I realised I wasn't like that either. I'd blamed myself because I was out when she took the beating.

It was late and a couple of months after Alan's funeral which I don't remember going to but remember wanting to. I know it was nearly bedtime but knew seconds before that we'd not be sleeping. I had a great antenna for danger and I as soon as the door went thud I knew bad things had arrived. Wenzel looked scared. I glanced at mum "upstairs all of you" she said and we legged it, me last I had to make it look like I was running. Caroline took Jonathon's hand and was taking steps two at a time and almost dragging him. I'd just reached the top when the door burst open and two men came in. Clive and my great uncle, Phil who was a renowned wimp. He was the guy who'd always shout his mouth off or put the boot in when someone is down but never do the heavy work himself. He was nothing but a shit stirrer as Alan used to say. He moved Bernie into the kitchen by pushing her in the back and closed the door "just a chat. Stay there" he said as Clive pushed Wenzel into the living room.

I'd made myself small by bending down and looking through the cracks in the banister railings. They were cracked white paint. The living room door was partially open. There was lots of shouting going on and Clive was pacing. Wenzel had curled up in the corner between the sofa and the gas fire. I'm sure he was hiding. Bernie came out of the kitchen, luckily she didn't see me. She entered the living room and the door was more closed but still left a gap. I heard the ironing board rattle and Wenzel scream. Clive was over six feet tall with enormous hands. He had to have boots specially made for him, He grabbed the ironing board from the floor again and I saw him hold it above his head by the sides as Bernie was dragged away by Phil. Clive let fly with the ironing board slamming it several times into a curled up Wenzel, He didn't fight back. He just lay there and took it until he couldn't curl up any more and had to straighten out face down which is when Phil started putting the boot in. I watched the ironing board slam into his back and then after a couple of minutes at the most the noise stopped and I went upstairs. Clive shouted something and the front door slammed shut.

Wenzel went to the hospital via Ambulance although Phil and Clive hadn't seen me on the stairs as they left Bernie had she sent me back up with a look.

Wenzel was out of hospital less than two days later on crutches. Apparently they had broken his back. At least that's what he tells everyone. Yes he looked in a lot of pain however he was able to walk and with him you just never know what's fact. What was definitely real though was his fear. He was absolutely petrified of Clive and anyone connected to him. Wenzel hadn't been home half a day before he told us "grab some clothes we're leaving".

A normal person would have called the police or got an injunction. A normal person may have called friends and family for somewhere safe to stay before moving his wife and children and a normal person may even have money to one side in case it's ever needed in an emergency. Wenzel was not a normal person nor was he mentally ill or crazy. He was simply a psychopath. A person who lives for control and thrives on it.

We were bundled into the car. Bernie in the front seat despite her plea's of agoraphobia, Jonathon, Jodie and Caroline side by side in the back and me well, I was wedged against the back sloping window.

Chapter 13

Wenzel had this idea that the social services would immediately house us because he had four children, a mentally ill wife and had recently been beaten up. He was sure that a few hours down at the social services base and he'd have a house well out of Macclesfield. He was wrong. We'd made ourselves intentionally homeless and nothing could be done. Wenzel decided if we couldn't get access to the property we weren't intentionally homeless so we drove back to the property and posted the keys through the letterbox. By the time we got back to social services it was closed. We slept in the blue Volvo estate.

I was curled up and couldn't move without kicking Jonathan so I didn't move. I gazed out of the window. I don't recall every trip we did in that car but I know Bernie tried to cheer us up by playing tapes. I heard like a prayer by Madonna and I wanna dance with somebody by Whitney Houston so many times. Wenzel at first would sing with us and play eye spy. We would have sandwiches in the car for dinner and on one occasion my carrier bag flew out from underneath my sandwich and wrapped itself in the rear view mirror. Wenzel turned red and pulled off the main road all the while shouting at Bernie for not keeping control of us. "Do something useful instead of just sitting there!" He stormed. "Like what?" She asked echoing all of our thoughts. What were we to do but sit here? We were homeless. "Well you can start by not listening to this shit" he growled flipped the cassette out and threw it at her. "Let's have some real music" he said smiling into the rear view mirror behind his clip on sunglasses. So that's how I learnt every song by the Police and the Eagles.

At night we would stop by the car park in Wilmslow and have chip shop chips shared between us. Mum rarely ate and often Wenzel would take ours just as a control kick. I'd always put some in my pocket for night time when I got real hungry. This pattern went on for weeks rather than days although I can't recall an exact amount of time. It's hard to describe what it's like in a tin can in the summer days packed up tight. I accidently touched the plastic beneath the window a number of times. It was so hot that it hurt. Other times I'd get down from the back window and sat with Caroline, Jonathon and Jodie as it was the only time I could be uncurled. I couldn't stretch out but I didn't have the one position numbness I had previously. My arm would be wedged against the door and the heat would soon be too much so I'd crawl back to my window out of the way. One evening we had chips and sausage. I was hungry but was more pleased to be out of the car. I could stand but not walk very well. Caroline played on the swings with another family in the park. Soon they were playing Frisbee together. Jonathan asked if he could play with them and they agreed. He ran to tell me but I couldn't. My legs wouldn't let me. I knew we couldn't carry on like this. I wasn't worried about me which isn't ego. It's simply how it was. We wouldn't survive with one bag of chips and a sausage between four people with this heat and no change of clothes. The lack of bathing had meant sweat had started to make everyone irritable. To give Bernie and Wenzel a little credit occasionally they did turn our driving to different homes into an adventure. "New home will be great it's not far now", "we'll get somewhere soon! What colour do you want your room?" After a couple of weeks we'd all grown sick of it.

Mum had gone from rarely talking to not talking at all. I'd followed suit unless he asked me a direct question. I didn't bother half the time even then until he looked like he'd get violent. I realized he wouldn't hit us if other people could see us. That's what first sparked my awareness that "he's not normal" I still believed every family got hurt in doors. I just knew outside was safe and that I'd started caring about me less and less. Caroline wolfed down some two day old stale chips I'd given her that had been squished in my pocket. We were next to a big building I'd never been to. I don't remember getting changed but I remember standing at the deep end of the swimming baths in my Y fronts and T-shirt. Wenzel was behind me talking but I don't know what he said. One minute I was looking at the water in front of me. It was calming and I was just going with whatever was meant to happen here. There were a couple of people at the shallow end of the pool but otherwise it was empty.

The next minute I was hit in the back. I don't remember hitting the water. I do remember going straight down, bubbles coming out of my mouth rising in front of me. My only thoughts were "blue", "warm" and "quiet" as I sank downwards. I sat cross-legged on the bottom and then I breathed in. Panic hit me as I inhaled water. I flailed my arms but couldn't get up and then I was lifting rapidly my neck getting tighter and tighter where I was hauled up out of the pool and slung onto the side of the baths. I coughed my guts up and shook uncontrollably. Wenzel was making a show of tapping me gently on the back and looking around to do the perfect parent bit. It didn't stop him whispering in my ear "why didn't you tell me you can't fucking swim?" He faked innocence so well. Nobody had ever taught me. Closest I'd ever been was walking in the sea with Alan at Blackpool. That was bath time over and we headed back to the car.

I was supposed to be first in the back but it was a hot day. The sunlight was shining through the water on my face and I was hot and clean. I felt good physically but sick at the same time. I looked at the car and froze. I saw "my window" and "my spot" staring back at me like huge empty holes I'd fall into forever and ever. Their was so much space in the car park to move when something turned inside me. "Not again" I felt it like a punch to the stomach. *Not again*

I sent my brain outside to play whilst my body reluctantly curled up against the glass. I warmed up fast and dried off slowly. My underwear burnt into the creases in my legs preventing me from keeping the "me" in my mind outside and periodically dragging me back into the vehicle. I loved the outside. I was on a skateboard that could jump anything, cars, walls, lamp posts. I'd ride the house walls as we went past scoring points like I did on the Paperboy game on my Nan's old Game Gear console. Nan....No! Back outside. It's nice outside. I'm free ten points! My face hit the window as he'd stopped suddenly and my leg jumped out and hit Caroline in the back as I was snapped back to reality. She leaned back accidently crushing me. I kicked out sending her into Johnathon and him into the door on his side. He started crying. "Fuck" I thought. "What's going on?"Mum said. We'd turned off another road behind some houses. "Out!" Wenzel yelled. Caroline and Jonathan got out. I sighed with relief and clambered towards the door he had held open for me, Where I was met with a punch in the face. "You want to fight?"He said. I crawled back into my corner. I'd taken the impact well and wasn't fazed. It hurt but not like a full punch. I wasn't sticking around for more though. He followed me but could hardly reach because of his bad back. My face still hurt and he scared me but not as bad as not being let out of the car. I made enough noise to let him know he'd hurt me when he was swinging even though he barely made contact. He backed off. I smiled inside. I'd won. I wasn't hurt. I fooled him. We got back into the car and Bernie at him. He pinned her to the seat by her wrists and leaned over her. "You got something to say?" He spat. He was about an inch from her face and raised his arm to slap her. "Well?" He said. She ignored him. He slapped her. She pulled away and he slapped her again. "No" she said at the same time Jonathon said "no". "Ungrateful little shits all of you" he said slamming the car in gear and staring at me through the rear view. I didn't take my eyes from his. "What?" He said. "Nothing" I replied. My tone level strong and slow I was hitting that point of taking too much. Seeing too much and my adrenaline was kicking in. I knew about that stuff. Alan taught me....*Alan....No! I'm outside I'm skating through the tree's...*

In that car when not trying to escape my thoughts of Nan and Alan I had time to think but my thoughts were muddled. I'd always believed I'd grow up like Alan and be a gardener. I'd probably work with Uncle Clive and we'd do the tip track runs together. I'd marry and have kids and live on Moorhill road like they did. Yet now Alan was dead and Clive was scary. I didn't want to be like Clive. He ruined our family and Alan was dead and I certainly didn't want to be dead so what do I do now? I had nothing but I could skate even though physically I'd never rode a board at all. I'd cycled like Alan taught me. He built me a big heavy mountain bike. I loved that bike. Mum was quiet and I understand why. Yeah I'll be like mum. I mean I'll never see my friends in Macclesfield again. His name was Lee I'd gone to his house for lunch his mum was really friendly. We sat at the table and had dinner. I ate the lot and then she came through with orange juice and said "why didn't you tell me I'd forgot the juice?" she was smiling. I thought it was a serious question. "Sorry. I really am I should have said. I just didn't know I was allowed to" I replied.

"Don't be silly. You can have a drink anytime you want one. Just ask" she told me.

I can still smell the fresh cut grass his mum had cut outside. Later I approached her "I'm sorry I was silly earlier about the drink.....can I ask you something?" I said.

"Of course you can ask me anything" she said straightening her hair and putting her hands on her hips with a cock eyed smile.

"Please don't tell my dad I was silly" I said and walked out. I hated Lee. I wanted to be just like him. Have his parents and his garden. His life and his happy mum and dad and his house. We'd gone to his room. He had a lead amongst the electrical toys in a box. I pulled it out and it was barely attached to a digital alarm clock. I pulled the lead off and plugged it in. "It's dangerous. It will spark" I told him. It didn't though. I took a can of coke from his bedside table and put it on the desk. I touched the lead to the can. Nothing happened. "Touch it" I said to him as much a question as an order. He did and flew across the room. I legged it and never went to Lee's house again. That night Wenzel asked me if I'd had a nice time at Lee's. I told him I had and that I'd seen Lee's sister. He asked "did you see her stamp collection?" I told him "no" and shook my head. Did she collect stamps? "Next time you see her tell her to show it to you" he laughed. I didn't get it. I missed lee.

The car stopped and I realized where we were.

Chapter 14

We had pulled in to Uncle Karl's house back in Macclesfield. Suddenly everything was normal again. Karl's mum lived with him, she was Austrian and we could barely understand a word she said but she was a good woman and loved the kids. She made us bacon sandwiches each morning and gave us "coins" each as she either refused or didn't know their real names. Usually we would receive odd amounts and she'd give us extra to make up the difference when we explained the amounts weren't the same. They had a huge garden that went all around the home and it was beautiful. Large white rock salts dotted the front garden and snaked our around the back giving the illusion of a starlit sky in daytime. Alan and Pat used to camp with me in their back garden and we'd watch for shooting stars. I remember visiting Karl and Joanne's house one time when she said "I'm throwing these away. You can have one each" Uncle Karl had to translate but we got the jist, she was refering to several brass items on the table. "Can I have something else?" I'd asked. "like what?" she said looking back and forwards to Caroline and Karl. "A garden star?" I asked her. "He means a rock" Karl said.

When Wenzel came to pick us up I carried that damn rock all the way home. I stopped once as it was so heavy and Wenzel said "If you stop again it stays there" it was a lot of effort but I made it. I put it in my bedroom where I was convinced it shone at night. It wasn't long before Wenzel moved it to the garden. I knew there was something special about natural rock.

Caroline and I were to stay with Karl and his mum whilst John and Jodie stayed with another aunt called Petal in a caravan. Wenzel often spoke badly of Petal on account of her being very religious. She was always his parent's favourite and he hated it and therefore her too.

Joanne's was a great big new adventure. I had loads to do in the garden and Karl was brilliant. He'd served twenty two years in the

Cheshire regiment and boxed for his country. I'd stand for hours looking at his caps and medals. Karl had routines and he always stuck to them. From getting up to going to bed he'd go for a bath with three inches of water in and take no longer than fifteen minutes. I only found out because I walked in on him once! Then he'd have breakfast and head to work. On the way home he'd grab four cans of Skol and have tea whilst doing paperwork. Then it was drinks and the news before a movie and bed.

An odd habit they both had was covering up the electrical items before they went to sleep. I wasn't sure if this was Karl's idea or Joanne's but I presumed an odd logic that perhaps if burglars can't see it through the window they won't break in.

It must have been summer because I was hot and allowed outside a lot more than I would be had I been at home. Wherever that was.

I'd made friends with a lad called Michael around my age. I didn't know where he lived but he knocked on for me sometimes. This day we'd been going into people's back gardens looking for treasure. We didn't want anything we just wanted to see what was there. Michael said he knew of a great one where we wouldn't be caught. Somehow the danger made it more fun. We had entered down the side of a house and met a small wall we could stand on. Below it however on the other side was a very high drop and a lawn. It was too high to play on but the garden was surrounded by huge hedges an ideal place to play.

We kicked the ball around for a while and soon got bored when Michael asked me "you seen anyone at the house?" I hadn't. We went to the back door and pulled the handle down. It was open. Someone must be home. We opened it anyway. The kitchen was empty. I can remember a mixture of fear and excitement jumping through me. I went in first. There were ornaments in the living room and a wallet on the fire surround. "Man upstairs" I pointed and whispered. Michael walked back in and took the wallet and took it me in the kitchen. "Now what?" I asked. We had no idea what we were looking for and knew not to take the money because if we got caught we'd be in serious trouble. I put the wallet back exactly as I found it. When I entered the kitchen Michael had his head in the freezer. He emerged with a box full of jubilee lollies and laughed silently. He handed me a few and laughed with nerves loudly. We both burst out laughing and ran for the door. It was difficult to stand though laughing so hard. We sat in the next door neighbour's garden and ate the lot.

Karl said Caroline and I could go out together as long as we stayed together. We rarely played together as she'd grown up with an Uncle and Aunt and I'd grown up with my grandparents. We didn't really see each other apart from at home with Wenzel and we weren't allowed to play there at all. So we had no idea what to do together. I decided I'd show her the secret garden and we'd play Frisbee in it. No fear this time just walked straight into the garden and Caroline loved it. Enormous hedges and large lawn. I threw the Frisbee hard towards Caroline and the wind took it high into the hedge. Caroline gave me a "what we gonna do now genius?" look. The little blue disk was too high to reach...unless. "I know!" I said. "You wait here. I'll jump off the wall into the hedge, grab the Frisbee and land down there on the grass". Caroline was halfway through saying something like "are you sure that's safe?" when I reached the top of the wall. I tested my balance before I made the big jump. I can still feel the brick beneath my thin trainers. "OK I jump. Grab Frisbee, spin into hedge and land on my feet about there." I said pointing to an empty patch of grass."

I shuffled towards the edge and glanced down. My world span and my foot slipped out from beneath me. I don't remember falling I fell so fast. I do remember the impact. I had landed on my elbows and both shoulders jumped out of their sockets, secondarily I'd whacked the base of my spine sending a shock wave all up my back. "I can't move" I said. "Caroline stood beside me thinking I was faking it.

"Don't touch me!" I screamed as the pain ripped through where my shoulders used to be. I could feel the skin tightening in my right shoulder. I must have blacked out because when I woke up I was on Caroline's back. She'd somehow got my arms around her neck and was dragging me along piggyback style. My world was blurry and pain ridden. To top it off I was babbling. I blacked out again. I was on Karl's sofa lay against Joanne who was running her fingers through my hair and ranting in German. The only parts I caught were "Karl home soon" and "soon Karl home" It wasn't long until he was stood in front of me. He was so calm and quiet. "Can you lift your arms?" I tried my left and it moved a few inches. My right just lay there. Karl took both of my wrists and said "relax". I leaned back on Joanne and exhaled as he yanked both of my arms straight out in front of me, both shoulders went pop and my face burnt with tears but my shoulders felt like they fit my body again. I was up and about in a couple of days but wasn't allowed out of the garden so they could see if I had any problems because of the fall. Caroline told me in the front garden that I'd really scared her and she thought I was dead. I told her the same thing Pat had told me. "Don't be silly. I'm not going anywhere".

"You coming out or what?" A voice shouted from across the road. I turned to see Michael waving his arm to me.

"No mate, not today" I shouted back thinking of my sister beside me.

"Whatever, pussy" he yelled" I turned away to talk to Caroline as something hit the ground near her.

"Go play with your sister then!" He shouted.

"Go in" I told Caroline and picked up a piece of slate from the drive as she vanished through the front door. Another thud as a stone hit the front wall close to me. "Karl will be out in a minute you best leave!" I shouted to Michael.

"I'm not scared of him!" Michael yelled back.

"He's my Uncle and he was in the army!" I yelled back getting angry suddenly prepared to fight in my Uncles defence.

"Pussy" Michael yelled and chucked another stone. It had just left his hand when I let fly with the slate. It curled up into the air and he started running. I remember trying to guide it with my mind, visualising it hitting him. I just wanted to scare him. It arched and curled downwards towards him. He looked back and it hit him right above the eye. He hit the floor and got up running holding his head. He was covered in blood. I turned around to see Caroline watching from the hallway then she disappeared Michael had vanished by the time I looked back.

"My Uncle's in the army?" I heard said calmly from beside me. Everything with Karl was calm. I both respected him greatly and feared him greatly. Although I'd never had reason to fear him. "Sorry" I said. "Go on in" he replied and I did.

That night Karl had to go out and said Caroline and I could watch a film together. He wasn't used to kids and didn't know what we could watch. He told us to use his room so we sat on his double bed as he put a video in. "This is the most child friendly one I've got. Sorry" he said and he meant it. He genuinely had no idea what was good for us to watch. So we sat and watched Nightmare on elm street part one.

Joanne was making her usual bacon sandwiches for us in the frying pan. A small kitchen. Caroline and I were sat opposite ends of the table and she kept turning around to tell us how happy she was to have children around again or something in German to the same affect. We were never quite sure but we both nodded and smiled a lot. There was bacon cooking and it smelt great. I could never get bored of this. As she turned back something fast happened and the frying pan was on fire. Joanne started flapping "nein, nein, nein," and waving a dish cloth around until that caught fire too. She threw the lot into the sink as the curtains went up in flames.

Chapter 15

I was on autopilot and I have no idea how I knew what to do. I stood up from the table and pushed Caroline out the back door. Then went back and grabbed Joanne. The curtains were falling down by this point and she was waving her arms around wildly. I chucked the pan of fire into the garden and returned to the Kitchen. I jumped onto the sideboard and pulled the curtains down by the pole just ripping them loose and chucking them outside. Then I turned the cooker off. Karl came home and had an argument with Joanne. It was all in German and then he thanked me in English for helping her. He said I was brave. I didn't feel it. I felt scared. Joanne nearly burned and I thought I'd be in trouble for helping so as soon as I'd turned the cooker off I was silent all day. Maybe the fire was why we couldn't stay any more

Wenzel and Bernie picked us up and it was back to life in the car. Only a few days this time though as Wenzel had found us a hotel to stay at. Something called emergency accommodation at the Erosa hotel in Wilmslow. We would have our own room and so did Wenzel and Bernie. I was sad to leave Nan's but I knew I'd be okay once we reached the hotel.

It was night time when we arrived and their was a huge car park which was unlit. A van with men inside and a few men sat around it. A black man alone with a hat on of a type I'd never seen before. It was also the first time I'd seen a black man. "Well we're here" Wenzel said trying to keep our spirits up. His tone told me otherwise. Something was wrong. Our eyes met via the rear view window briefly and they told me everything I needed to know. "Keep an eye on them, It's not safe". Great we're fucked I thought. Wenzel walked mum, Jonathon and Jodie to their room which was next to Caroline's and mine whilst we waited in a dark hallway. Mum's was right at the end next to a toilet. Her door at the bottom left had been kicked in and boarded up badly.

There were men in the hall huddled together and two small groups but I could have sworn I was being watched. Our door was intact it was thin wood with gold numbers on it. It was brown and stained with liquid. Wenzel came back "it's only a few days" he said opening our door. We went in and Caroline stood by the window. I remembered what Wenzel had meant when he looked at me earlier. I walked around the thin single mattress on the floor. No slats, no base, no furniture, no pillows, no T.V. Just a single stained mattress and some burnt out candles with no holders. They had been wedged in the gaps of the floorboards. "We'll be OK" I said looking deep into his eyes. "It will be OK" I repeated. He stood for maybe twenty seconds holding my gaze and then tapped my arm. His one and only show of genuine acknowledgement that I existed in a positive way and said "No, no we're not staying here," we were in and out of that hotel inside ten minutes flat and I was for the first time pleased to get back into the car.

It's around now I started to notice Caroline was different. At Karl's she was happy and well herself again but around Wenzel she had a stony, hollow expression and she had it now in the car. Staring straight ahead not paying attention to traffic or Jonathon or me. Just hollow staring through the back of the front seat. I lost track of the time we spent in the car. I don't remember food or washing around this time at all. I just know we travelled. A lot. Then out of nowhere we had a house to go to. Wenzel had used his old house to get an exchange with someone on an estate in Rochdale.

The house had a front and back garden and windows that slid up to open them. I liked it. It wasn't home, but I liked it. We soon got used to the new routine. Wenzel was relatively placid as he claimed benefits because of his back and rarely moved. Bernie was running around doing everything for him and us kids not doing a thing in case we upset him. "Can I go out?" I asked mum. She said yes. Wenzel said no. I stayed put. Wenzel looked at me "Your mother said yes" he said. It was a trick. I stayed put. "Off you go" he said. I was out the door like a rocket but not before I'd caught a glimpse from Jonathon and Caroline watching me leave.

OK I wanted friends. How do I get them? Stand around until someone talks to me I guess. That's how I met lee and Michael so that should do it. I saw a group of lads on skateboards down the road. This was an adventure. I knew nobody and there was no danger, right? Wrong.

I stood around for a few seconds until someone said "new guy!" I made small talk about the skateboard until one asked what I did in Macclesfield. I explained about the Aikido and what Alan had taught me. I'd been in the local paper with my club. Next minute this lad is asking me to show him some throws. I show him one and he says "I can get out of that." I replied "there is always a counter.""

"Show me" he said. I go to throw him and wallop I'm on the floor and taking punches four maybe five before he steps back and kicks at my legs. "Street smarts" he laughs tapping his temple. His mates join in the laughter. I stood up "I think he wants some more" one quips. "New boy thinks he's hard" another pipes up. I made it to my door and closed it behind me with four lads running fast. "You're back quick" Wenzel says. "It's cold out" I replied and ran upstairs to clean up.

It wasn't more than a couple of days after that and Bernie had gone all quiet again. She was starting to shake visibly. She's not had a drink in ages I thought. Wenzel was pacing "They found us! It's your fucking fault!" His crutches miraculously vanished and replaced with a solitary walking stick he never once leant on. "Pack up!" He shouted "not again?" Bernie said screeching the word "again". "They've just settled" she answered referring to us kids. "Don't fucking answer me back! Pack up!" He stormed pointing at her. Bernie was heading up the stairs with her head down before he'd finished the sentence.

We were on the road again. Second property we had given up. What was Wenzel running from? At the time we were told "Clive tried to kill your dad. He's still looking for him and has a hit out on him" we knew what that meant. Bye dad. What we didn't know was why. Years later there was speculation that I can't prove that said it was because Wenzel accused Lesley of abusing Caroline instead of telling Clive like Macc rules dictate should have happened. He'd gone to the police instead and nobody grasses. They go to Clive, Alan or Pat and as Alan and Pat were dead he should have gone to Clive. Later I'd also hear it was because Wenzel wouldn't lend him his car and because Wenzel had hit Bernie and was planning on moving away. Rumours were rife and facts were like ghosts.

I'd later hear it from the horse's mouth it was actually because Wenzel didn't take care of Alan when I moved in with him. Wenzel was supposed to make sure he took his pills and Clive saw that as the ultimate betrayal to his mum Pat. Clive had done nothing when Alan passed and nothing again when Wenzel accused Lesley. However when Clive found out Wenzel was having an affair. He lost his temper.

We had been in the car a few days after another visit to the homeless peoples unit. The same story just in a different area. "I'm in danger. My wife's seen Clive in the street we live. We need housing. I have four children" the answer was also the same. "You made yourself intentionally homeless we cannot help you." This basic circle would continue into huge constructs but essentially the exact same conversation whilst we sat stock still on plastic chairs in the waiting room. I desperately wanted to walk as I'd been all cramped up in the car all day but we weren't allowed. The weather had turned colder as well so now my previously roasting window was freezing to the touch. Jonathon had taken to kicking out in his sleep and my shoulder would touch the window so I'd wake up. Ever since that fall at Uncle Karls when it gets cold my shoulder lets me know.

That was something else too. I never slept in any sort of real sense. My sleep from as young as I can remember until I lived alone was so light that a letter could come through the letter box and I'd be at the door as it hit the floor. "Mrs Daily your children are terribly well behaved they can play with the toys your know?" Wenzel was immediately at Bernie's side wanting to know what was said but not asking. Bernie knowing the drill as well as we did. "Is it okay?" She said to Wenzel. He said yes and Jonathon was off playing with toys. Caroline and I didn't move. We knew better. Ignore Wenzel at home meant a beating but embarrass him in the street and we'd pay for it for days. Jonathon wouldn't get the beating for playing with the toys but someone would. Either mum or us. He held mums hand when we left the homeless persons unit. I recall it vividly. He never held her hand. I got closer and realised why. He was crushing her fingers.

He used to do that to me if someone asked me a question and I remained quiet too long "squeeze".

My knuckles often felt like they'd been bust even though they hadn't. He loved his power games "say mercy" he'd say at home pulling my fingers back and forcing me to the floor. "Well? Give in?" He'd ask. We had this routine quite often and it was always with me. I figured it happened when he hadn't hurt someone in a while. I'd exhausted every tactic. At first I'd go with it until it hurt and try and pull away but he'd not let go until I said mercy. Then he'd apply more pressure for a few seconds and then let go.

When I got wise to that as soon as he touched me I'd say "mercy" that was a bad idea though because then he'd say "what? I can't hear you?" Until I said it louder then he'd repeat "what? Still can't hear you?" Each time applying more pressure until he chose to let go. My screaming excited him and yet it didn't matter if I screamed or not. He'd do what he wanted.

My way I don't recommend. However it worked for me. Don't say a fucking thing. Don't whimper. Don't show pain. Don't cry. Don't run and don't flinch. A flinch excites these types of people. So he'd grab my fingers and pull me around and I'd remain calm and stone faced looking at the floor. I tried to make it look natural, unaffected. The truth however is that I was checking the ground for where I was going to fall. Where exactly he'd make me hit the floor which he did at least twice during a game. When I felt too much pain in my palm where the bone in the finger wants more room to bend but doesn't have it. I'd breathe slowly trying to minimize the pain. It was always very bad and I was forever telling myself "I'm OK, Doesn't hurt" over and over. Often I'd go into my own little world where I was with Alan but that would upset me and make me angry so I'd come back again. Thud the floor would hit me as he'd pull my fingers straight down fast. I'd used my free arm to take the fall and be up on my ankles straight away. I knew the game. If I wasn't my fingers would be wrenched upwards and turned so I'd have my back to him and my fingers being in agony. By being up fast I could move with it. When I thought He would actually let me go, and his face was a good indicator of how much he was enjoying my pain if he looked to be enjoying it I'd say mercy and he'd let me go. If he wasn't enjoying it then there was no point in me saying mercy. The trick was to act in pain but not too much. Say mercy at the right time.

I let myself down only once. We'd played his game earlier and got stopped for dinner. Yeah he actually thought it was a game and Bernie saw it as a game too despite her knowing the pain I knew. Weird? No, not really. If we consider had either I or Bernie questioned him his game would have been played with us. By saying it's a game we justified it as okay and therefore neither of us were guilty of letting a bad thing happen.

He'd said something to Bernie. I can't recall what it was but I'd answered him back. "Come here" he said. I did and he held his hand out. He wanted me to be scared of putting my flat hand into his and I was. I was fucking terrified but I wasn't letting him know that. As soon as his hand was open I placed my hand in his. "Say mercy" he said softly as he pulled me to the floor. "No" I replied with the same tone as his. He threw me around that room like a rag doll until he was screaming "say mercy" and I was screaming "No!" This went on for what seemed like forever. My jaw hit the floor at one point and I grabbed it with my left hand to hold it on. It was fine but hurt like hell. I curled up but he still had my arm "say mercy!" He shouted. "No!" I replied. The next second I was face down over his lap my arm up my back fire hit my shoulder. "Say mercy" he said "mercy" I replied. "say sir please let me go" he said. I repeated it and he threw me to the floor. I was in a lot of pain. More than that I was disgusted with myself. I'd let him win. I'd let him make me cry. I vowed that day that he would never know my pain again. "I am Alan's son and Alan doesn't quit" I told myself. So when I saw him take mums hand, crushing it as they walked. I knew two things. One, she was in for it tonight and two, keep my fucking head down.

Chapter 16

Thankfully I don't recall what happened that night. I do remember going back to Rochdale to get more things from the house though. Wenzel sat outside in the car and sent Bernie in. He wanted to be able to make a quick getaway if he saw Clive around and believed Clive wouldn't hurt Bernie as he's her brother. He looked over his shoulder every ten seconds. I asked why we were running "Do you want me dead? Clive will fucking kill me. You'd like that wouldn't you?" Another trick. I won by not replying. This is how I managed some degree of control for myself, by telling myself when I earned a win and when I made a loss. A loss meant I had to change something next time. There was always a next time. A win meant I'd not got hurt or I'd made him believe I was hurt, at best it meant I'd found a way not to play his game. I knew if I'd said "no" He'd have called me a liar and I'd be punished for lying. If I said yes it would throw him for a few seconds but I'd take a worse beating. I lowered my head as he turned around to look at me. "Yeah, cunt you'd fucking love it" he said looking at Jonathan as if to say "Go on, tell your mum. I dare you".

Bernie came out with bin bag after bin bag full as we sat there whilst she piled it into the car with us which meant much less room. We were car bound for around a week before we were placed in Lacey Green in Wilmslow. A bed and breakfast ran by a gentleman called Barry and his daughter. The garden was huge as was the house but the garden was where the magic really lay.

The first quarter had a patio large enough to easily fit three trucks on it and then a pond to the right surrounded by flat well maintained grass and flowers. The pond consistently held frogs. Directly behind that was some gnarly old trees and twisting paths. I'd spend as much time as I could up there. I'd sit pretending I owned it and that one day I'd build my own hut in that garden.

My room was also Caroline's room. The white doors were clean. The single beds in our room were well kept and it even had a television in the room. Carpeted throughout and had large windows to the left of my bed looking out over the magnificent garden. I was in heaven or as close as I could be without Nan and Alan who always seemed to be in my mind.

Mum's room was directly opposite and smaller but still a good size with a double bed and dressing table that mum had a photograph on in a picture frame. We had full run of the hotel and garden until 6pm when we had to be in our rooms but it was great. I can't remember what mums photo was of but I do remember going to her room and she showed me the picture and took the back from it. Behind the picture was a newspaper clipping. She wanted me to know what was on it and told me to keep it a secret. "He doesn't know I have this. It means a lot to me. You should know it's here." She said. I was just happy mum wanted to share a secret with me. I knew Wenzel wouldn't be aware. Everyone needed secrets, especially from him.

It may sound simplistic but being a bed and breakfast two things were guaranteed to us. A nice clean warm bed and a wonderful warm breakfast. The two things that before I didn't much care for. However after living in a car on and off for God knows how long. These were luxuries and I took full advantage of them. It was always a full English breakfast and Wenzel would always tell the same joke every morning without fail "Is this bacon or a crack in the plate Barry?" Wenzel was one of those people with no sense of humour who thought they were extremely funny and to be fair to him if you hadn't lived with him you'd think he was a diamond. However we heard all his lines many, many times and it just becomes routine. We laughed because we had to. Laughed is probably too strong a term. Mum would ignore him until he said "that's funny" or "no sense of humour some people" and then she'd flash him a half second smile or a "sorry" with no enthusiasm behind it. The kids would just tut a short laugh. We had to humour him. His family, his rules.

Barry was brilliant with the kids he insisted we went outside whenever we wanted. Wenzel had started buying sweets when he went out and didn't hurt us once here. He would give us packets of skittles or opal fruits and Caroline, Jonathon and me would share them out. I was quite mean as a child and remember giving them colours that they didn't like because then they would trade me two of theirs for one of mine that they did like. I remember feeling especially bad one day after one of these sweet sharing moments when Jonathan approached me in the garden. His fair hair and squint both pointing in the same direction. He always looked cute and not odd. Some people their squint makes them more handsome. He was one of them. I remember the sun shining off his little red coat and blue rimmed glasses. He handed me his sweets "For you. I know you collect them" he said dropping them into my hand. I told him I'd trade them two for one and handed them back "no, you have them. It's okay I'm not hungry" he replied and placed them on the little wall and ran off to play. I was turning into Wenzel. I hated myself and felt guilty. Suddenly the sun didn't matter any more The garden was unimportant. Caroline and Jonathan were playing in the garden and instead of being a part of it and just enjoying the game like they were I was constantly looking for my next leverage. Constantly looking over my shoulder for trouble. Waiting to run, hide, respond. More than this I didn't like me.

Later Wenzel got the bags out of the car and Jonathon and I played with the action figures and old star wars ships. For once we had fun and nobody controlled anyone. Just me and Jonathon brother to brother, as equals.

Sandy was the cleaner's name. She was a nice lady who lived in Wilmslow. She'd always talk to us and have a clean bed ready. Things that if I'm honest Wenzel nor mum did much of. They didn't take time to talk a lot and mum only did when we went to her with a problem. Don't get me wrong I love my mum. She would play with us when we were in Macclesfield but elsewhere she either didn't or wasn't allowed to. So it was nice when Sandy would smile and ask how we were.

Jonathon and I had been playing so long Wenzel came into the bedroom and said "right time for bed" Jonathon looked at me and I looked at him. "Fuck it. What's worst that can happen" I thought. "Five more minutes?" I asked. Wenzel looked back at who I presume was Bernie standing in the hall "Okay. Five minutes only" he said closing the door. He must have forgot about us because we played well into the darkness.

I'd stay awake at night and watch prisoner cell block H and married with children like I had with Nan. I had to be careful though as soon as I heard a door creak or someone step on the landing I'd shut the T.V off and pretend to be asleep. He never caught me but it came close one night when I hadn't heard his bedroom door open but did hear my door handle slide down. I click the T.V off and closed my eyes. I knew not to be sat up If I was he'd know I'd watched T.V so to minimize any movement I lay my head on the pillow and watched T.V at an angle. He walked in and closed the door "I know you're awake" he said turning the T.V from standby to off so I couldn't use the remote control. Then I heard him walk to the door and it open and close. I hadn't heard his footsteps on the other side. I counted to two hundred slowly in my head to be certain, About halfway through my second hundred the door opened and then I heard him leave, cross the landing and go into his room. I made a big show of sighing and turning over in my sleep just in case he was still in the room. I scanned it eyes open just a slit as I moved over. Shit – that was close.

Caroline and I had been playing in the garden that day climbing trees. Neither of us were tired. We'd gone to the park and had chips and sausage with Wenzel and been sent to bed as usual. I'd waited to hear Caroline's breathing change and flicked the T.V on. I waited for prisoner cell lock H to start. I wasn't thinking about anything in particular I was just watching Prisoner cell block H and listening for Wenzel's footsteps or the door to go. I heard neither. My bedroom door opened and on this night I was sat up in bed. Unusual for me but I remember it clearly because I'd usually want to hide and pretend to be asleep. This night I didn't. The door opened and I had an amazing feeling of ease. Total peace. My Nan, Pat stood there plain as day, very solid but not as solid as a physical person. I could just about see through her but all of her features were visible from head to toe. She wore the same sandals she had done in life. She smiled, Waved her arm to me and in that second I knew I was going to be okay. I felt great. Then she vanished, She was just gone, Perhaps a second later the door closed. I looked at the door for maybe five seconds and then logic hit me. If Caroline had seen her then I had proof. I looked at her fast asleep. I looked to the T.V and prisoner cell block H was still on. She'd turned up during her favourite programme I thought. I smiled. I knew I had to tell mum in the morning and she'd be so excited! Pat is alive. Not here but alive somewhere. I fell asleep about an hour later more content than I'd felt in over a year.

I did tell mum. I remember clearly sitting on the bed beside her and her telling me how she'd heard Pat on the landing in Macclesfield and seen her outside the bedroom window a few nights after she'd passed. Mum went on a big talk about ghosts being people but I don't remember all of it. I was only interested in two things. "Why can't I see her all the time?" And "when can I see her again?" I was thinking If I can see her I can live with her but mum said it doesn't work like that.

I looked for Pat all day in the garden and I found another garden and thought maybe she'd got lost looking for me and had gone in there. So I spent the day up a tree where I could clearly see both gardens. That night I waited until Bernie or Wenzel had closed out bedroom curtains and then sat with the T.V off looking at the door. Caroline was already asleep. "They've gone now. You can come in" I said in my head. Nothing happened. I tried a few times then realised she couldn't hear me because I was talking in my head. I repeated "They've gone now. You can come in" this time loud enough for anyone in the room to hear me. Nothing happened. I lay on the bed willing that door to open. It didn't. I lay on the bed in a huff and then it hit me. Maybe she can only turn up during prisoner cell block H? So I turned that on but didn't watch it. My eyes were on the door. I repeated this every night and every night Nan didn't turn up.

Chapter 17

Wenzel had got quite chatty with Sandy, A good looking woman with a very bubbly personality. I noticed he wasn't at the breakfast table a few mornings and then when he was he didn't make the bacon joke and mum looked more agitated than usual. Even more so when Wenzel spoke about Sandy. On one occasion mum slammed her fork down hard and said "not in front of the kids" I can't hear their discussion from memory however I remember the tension vividly and I can see the tense body language between both of them. Bernie wanted to leave at worst and have a peaceful life at best and Wenzel wanted to reach across the table and slap her but couldn't because of Barry.

The next morning I was awoken and had to get ready for school. My first school since Ash grove primary and from the little I'd gone I'd hated it. I went because I had to. Lacey green had a big long open playground which was beautifully cut at the back. I was introduced to a lady teacher in the hall who's name I forget. She was pleasant as I looked around at something moving in a large box beside me. "Guinea pigs" she said "Do you like them?" She added. I'd never seen one before. I was amazed. "Pig?" I asked then jumped up next to Wenzel. I'd forgot to wait for the nod to speak in my excitement. I waited to be hit. "It's like a big gerbil" Wenzel said "not a pig" he added laughing. We were a normal family for the teacher's benefit. "Gerbil"....What happened to Arnie? I wondered I guess he was in Macclesfield alone for all this time. I was introduced to my class and they all seemed more quiet and calm than the kids in Ash Grove primary school. I could like it here I thought.

They had sums and words on big posters on the walls. I knew all the words but none of the sums. Nan had taught me to read from an early age and I'd spent countless hours reading make a choice books under my bed Bernie's. I was standing in the playground one lunch time alone watching the other pupils. I was wearing a coat with a fluffy hood and an orange interior. It was ripped in many places. I wore it because Wenzel told me to take it even though it was roasting outside. The other pupils didn't play like other children they mostly stood around talking. The people I did overhear talking appeared distant and spoke strangely.

I was in a classroom we had been given some basic words like with and then to put into a word search that we had to create ourselves. I was bored stupid and totally didn't think the teacher would notice so I did the word search and included a few choice words of my own including dickhead and bastard which were longer than any words we had been given to use. I was called up but not because I was in trouble. I'd later find out Wenzel had been questioned as to why none of us were in a school so he got us into the closest one. A school for disabled children.

I came home to Wenzel and Barry having a chat in the kitchen. Wenzel wasn't happy but looked like he'd been defeated. I went through my head to see what I'd done wrong. Perhaps it was playing snap with Brians daughter? Or when Brian's daughter slept in Caroline's bed and I talked about what was down our trousers. If it was that I was in trouble. Wenzel walked past me like I didn't exist. I went to my room and he was chatting with Sandy, his demeanour had totally transformed. Downstairs he was downtrodden like he'd lost money, Sad but not angry. Upstairs he was all interactive body language and smiles like he was fun. Upstairs I still didn't exist and I was more than cool with that. Not existing was a great thing when having Wenzel's attention was the alternative. I got a smile from Sandy as I passed through. Wenzel headed to the door and stopped himself. He turned back to Sandy with a smile "Thanks!" It'll be great!" Sandy smiles folded the sheet and turned to me as he'd left, She threw me a beaming smile I couldn't help but match. "Want to know a secret!?" She said. She couldn't hold it in any more I'd not even replied "You're coming to stay with me!" She said her green eyes sparkling her long hair bouncing as she laughed.

"What, really!?" I asked.

"Yes but shhh it is a secret!" She said quietly. I hugged her. I don't
know why....perhaps because I didn't get affection. Maybe because
she was always happy and that made me happy or perhaps because
she was hot but it was probably the affection thing. "Thanks" I said
and ran off.

I'd be sorry to see Barry's Bed and breakfast go but Sandy's would
be great fun! Bernie looked very flat at breakfast that morning. She
didn't talk at all which wasn't unusual but it was somehow more
noticeable. For her things had got worse over night and I wasn't
sure how. Wenzel was all smiles and even managed to throw Barry
a "thank you for lettings us stay but I'm glad I won't have to eat the
plate cracks any more" Joke. I didn't understand. How can you eat
plate cracks? But Wenzel and Barry seemed to get it. It wasn't far to
Sandy's. We passed my old Lacey Green school on the way and I
thought about the Guinea pigs and Arnie again. I'd not see Arnie or
Nan or Alan again. I was starting to believe I caused problems
wherever I went and good people always left me. Maybe I really
was useless. I looked at mum stone cold staring into the distance. I
knew how she felt and yet I was angry with her. If she smiled more
and just did what Wenzel said he wouldn't be angry and keep
moving us around.

We were going to Sandy's estate and it was the nicest estate I've
ever seen. There was a row of houses all joined together with a flat
on the bottom which had a garden and a flat on the top which had a
balcony. These rows turned into square's each with a large field in
the middle and a couple of trees. There were numerous blocks of
these dotted throughout the estate. It was very pretty. The flat was
quite small inside and only had one bedroom. Sandy gave us some

juice and we all looked to mum to see if it was okay to take it. Mum gave us the nod and we thanked Sandy. Juice was mum's job not Wenzel's. We gulped it down.

The sofa was a small two seater I sat beside mum and Caroline whilst Jonathan and Jodie sat on the floor. Jonathan spotted a games console and kept looking at mum hopefully who half turned her head "no". Sandy spotted this and asked if he wanted to play? "No it's okay" Jonathan replied as mum had said no. I don't know where Wenzel was. "It's okay if Sandy says you can" Mum said and Jonathan was off playing golf on the game. We took it in turns to play and Sandy asked mum if she'd like to join us "No it's okay. I don't know how" she said sitting quietly. Sandy offered to show her and again mum declined. Us kids were having a great time and mum was being polite but something wasn't right with mum. I'd never seen her be so nice and polite. She was always flat. She'd still not had any alcohol and I couldn't pinpoint why mum wasn't happy but she'd got worse since Sandy vanished ten minutes ago. I came off the game "What's up?"

"Just watching the game" she said pointing to the T.V.

Jonathan and Caroline were playing together Jodie was over by the wall somewhere doing the baby thing. "I know" I said all smiles "but what's up..seriously?" I added carefully.

Mum nodded to indicate behind her but said nothing. I could hear faint talking I can't remember what I heard but I remember needing to distract mum from it. "How do I do this bit?" I asked grabbing the control pad. "Just hit the ball" Mum replied. I did. "I can't do it" I said. "Here"Jonathan piped up holding his hand out wanting me to give him his game back to play. "Not yet" I told him. "Here, show me" I gave mum the control pad. I know what was said and it's one of the only conversations I can remember in depth with mum. Sadly although I feel the words. I still cannot hear her voice. I have no idea what she sounded like. This happens a lot with people who lose someone. I have relatives who had difficulty seeing her in their head but could hear her just fine. With me it was the other way around. I can hear Jonathon's voice very clearly. He still has the same sing song tone just a little deeper now he's an adult.

Yet when I tune into mums I get nothing but a "knowing" of what was said. She played on the golf game for a long time. She had a way of totally absorbing herself in a game or a book. She was very good at spelling and knew a lot of general knowledge especially about T.V and the supernatural.

Sandy came out of the bedroom and asked if anyone wanted a drink? Wenzel came out a few seconds later looking like a cat that got the cream. Wenzel wasn't attractive by any standards. He was probably less than average looking. A slim build and pale features. He was slightly balding and his glasses were a permanent fixture held together with a safety pin but he had charm, banter and humour on his side. He was very persuasive and woman seemed to love him.

Sandy went over to Jodie. I can't remember what Jodie needed but Sandy picked her up. Mum was on her feet immediately "I'll do it" she said "It's okay" Sandy said and Wenzel shot Bernie a look, moved from the doorway to stand behind Jonathan and rubbed his neck. A warning that would appear as affection to Sandy. Jonathan carried on playing the game ignoring him. Mum and I knew what he meant "Sandy does it or else. Any trouble and I'll hurt Jonathon" His eyes bore into Bernie. She sat down. "Sandy can we play outside?" I asked.

I knew I risked a beating but things had gone bad again. Outside we were safe. In here there were no hiding places.

"Of course you can dear" she said flashing us a smile. I looked at Wenzel "Off you go" he said. "Caroline, Jonathon let's go" I called pulling Jonathon to the door "my game?" He protested innocently.

"Will be there when we get back" I said hauling him out onto the balcony. Sandy chucked us a thick bag I briefly wondered why she had a football but took it anyway. "stay on the front" Wenzel yelled and we were free.

Chapter 18

We were just walking the field talking together. Caroline wouldn't say much as she didn't want Jonathan overhearing but I knew she was thinking the same thing I was. What the hell was happening with mum? How bad was our situation? How could we all live in that poky little flat and naturally when will we be moving on again?

One of us kicked the ball and Jonathan ran off to get it. As he did two boys walked over to him. One was wearing white on his top half because it made him look like he was concealing something. I slowly walked over but by the time I'd got there Jonathan was crying and one of the boys held a bag open. "Jon?" I asked and he turned and walked towards Caroline with the ball he'd retrieved. He was still crying. "Want to see too?" the lad said meeting my eyes for a split second then making a show of opening the bag.

"What?" I asked getting closer.

"A hand we have a human hand it's all bloody and orrible! Have a look" one lad said laughing. The other was grinning ear to ear and had a rounder face. I wasn't playing this game. I walked back to Jonathan took the ball and put it in the thick bag. "He's really upset" Caroline said. I don't know exactly what changed in me but something did. "Back in a minute" I did a one eighty and ran straight at both boys holding the football in the bag out in front of me. "Here' lads! Look what I found!" I shouted eyes wide. The boys stopped walking away and turned towards me. They looked at each other. "What?" fat face said who was obviously confused the other a little cautious. I got closer as the same taller lad said "What?" a second time as I punched him square in the teeth he fell flat on his back. "I have your fucking head!" I screamed at the other as he stumbled backwards and legged it I kicked his foot out from beneath him and he hit the floor. I didn't know what I was going to do or why I was really doing it. I just knew the only person allowed to upset us was Wenzel, and family protected family. Alan protected me so I took care of Jonathan. That's how it works. I grabbed Mr. stumbly. "Want to see?" I repeated as scarily as I could. "Come near us again and I will take your fucking head off and put it with this one!" I screamed into his face. I was suddenly stone cold calm. The lad was terrified. Job done. I instinctively knew how to scare them. Wenzel had done so many times before to us. Boy one was scared of violence and noise boy two didn't fear noise he'd heard a lot of noise but he didn't fancy a slap either. He didn't know me or know if I really did have a head in the bag or if I'd actually take his off, internally he was questioning everything without logic. Like a hamster spinning out of control he was just accepting what was happening without understand it. The lad I'd punched ran off. I let go of his friend and walked back to Caroline. "What happened?" she asked.

"Told him I had a head in a bag" I replied.

"What?" she asked.

"Nothing, Let's go home" I replied.

I don't remember how long we were at Sandy's. I don't know where we slept or what we ate or pretty much anything but I recall her long red hair and that we left and got back in the car. There was no promises of a new house this time.

There would be no new home and things would change into a new kind of pain I'd never witnessed before and wished I'd never had to then. A pain which echo's inside to this day, easing over time and experience. I have dealt with it and moved on. Yet I can never envision (nor would I want to) me doing to my family the things Wenzel did to his. We'd been in the car a few days at least as I was very hot and sweaty and I remember my arms were darker than usual. It wasn't the sun. It was dirt. The itching had returned to my side and I'd gone back to sending my mind away. I'd progressed from skateboarding and I'd recalled everything I'd learnt at Aikido over and over again in my head. I'd memorised every song on the tapes we had. I had no patience but didn't outwardly snap. I was ten years old and we were on a fast road when Wenzel stopped suddenly and slammed his hands on the steering wheel repeatedly. He gripped it hard white knuckling. Despite the change I knew we were safe. He was angry but not with us. "I had a good job you did fuck all!" He bellowed at Bernie "ungrateful little fucks!" He yelled at us. Still safe he was proper fuming but had no logic. He only hurt us when he was thinking clearly. He got out and paced without his sticks and then kicked the car. "Fuck" now we were in trouble pacing was bad. Very bad.

Luckily I was wrong. He got back in the car and was instantly calm. "I'm OK" He said although nobody had asked. He swung the car around and we pulled into a social services base. We sat in the waiting room. "What's happening" Caroline asked me quietly as Jonathan played with the toys and Mum and Wenzel were in the other room talking to social workers. "I don't know. It's not good." I replied putting as much emphasis on "not good" as I possibly could. I had that stomach feeling again. The one I'd had with Nan and Alan. This wasn't just bad. This was very bad. Jonathan kept trying to play with a plastic bat and ball set in the corner of the room. We kept saying no because we didn't know if allowed. A social worker came out "why don't you play outside this may take a while" Jonathan sat down next to me and none of us moved. "It's a nice day out" the lady said. We remained seated "Dad?" I called "it's okay, go out" he called. We got up and the woman handed Jonathan the golf clubs set and his face lit up whilst Caroline's and mine fell. This was not good.

I paced around a garden area with a tree in it. I was in my own little world. Why here? What is this place? What do they do? I had no answers. Is mum going to hospital again? Perhaps it's about the agoraphobia even though she'd been recently? No can't be that. It's a bad boy's school because of the word search perhaps? No this isn't a school "you okay?" Caroline asked me touching my shoulder. "No, this" I said pointing at the rooms "Isn't good, we need to leave and go back to Macclesfield, find a house. Any house, even Rochdale. This...not good" Jonathan trundled over to me holding a gold club "Bat?" He asked looked at it enquiringly.

"No Jon it's a golf club, go play" I said.

"Bat?" He asked holding it higher and pushing it towards me to play.

"No John it's a golf club hit the ball with it" a little harsher than intended. He smiled and ran to find a ball.

I talked to Caroline for around twenty minutes whatever we were saying kept being interrupted by John trying to get me to play ball "Bat? Play bat?" He'd ask trying to push it into my hand.

"No John I don't want to play" I said.

"Why?" He looked sad but kept his "bat" by his side. He walked a complete circle then stood in front of me "Play bat!?" He asked cutely. "I don't want the fucking bat! Fuck off and play!" I snapped.

Caroline gave me the same look Bernie gives Wenzel when he's being an asshole. "What?" I said and paced in the opposite direction. We must have made up because we were all playing hit the ball with the bat when Mum, Wenzel and a female social worker came out of the building. "We off?" I asked wanting to be out of there as soon as possible they could give me whatever bad news they had when we had left. I stood by Wenzel's car. The social worker spoke. "You're going to stay in a nice house with another family whilst your mum and dad find somewhere to live for you. Then you can come back" she said. She had yellow hair. I'd never seen yellow hair before. She spoke with authority. This is happening it's not a question.

I ignored her and looked at Wenzel and Mum, he was cold,

unfeeling just waiting for it to be over. Bernie had been crying. She had tears in her eyes but was holding them back. "Come back?" I asked anyone who was listening but replying to the social worker.

"Yes when they find somewhere to live" The social worker said. It was sunny but I couldn't feel it.

We got in the back seat of the car. There was loads of room despite being a small car because it was only Caroline and me. It appeared huge. "Comfy?" The social worker asked. She pulled away and I flipped around to look through the back window. Bernie stood watching us leave. She didn't wave. Just stood there, Hollow. Wenzel held her hand in the same controlling grip. His face was red but I didn't know why.

The social workers name was Trish and she told us that Jonathan and Jodie will stay with another family until we all got a place to live together with Mum and Dad.

She baby talked me. I didn't like her tone. Caroline asked her twenty questions whilst I sat ignoring the woman in the front seat. She's not my Mum or Nan. She shouldn't be here. By the time we got there I'd been told a man and woman had a house and garden to play in which also looked after other children. Trish had sweet she offered us, I declined and Caroline accepted. For my refusal I was asked "you don't talk much do you?" with a complete fake smile. I gave it the answer it deserved and ignored her. She then told me her car had a nickname "Pansy the Polo" or something. Naming cars, What an idiot I thought. I wasn't happy. Trish got out to talk to the foster carers and I launched into Caroline "what the hell are you doing?" I stormed trying not to be seen by the carers. "What?" Caroline asked me.

"She's not one of us and you spoke to her all the way here!" I said.

"She's nice" Caroline said.

"She's your best friend now bitch?" I said to Caroline. "Dad would leather you for that and you know it!" I told her.

I was outside a farm on one site and a large three bedroom semi on the other. It was built into a corner and the garden went all the way around. We were in Cheshire and it was the nice part not where we were used to at all. I met the foster mother and was told the same story as before but this time by a middle aged woman in a long skirt and flowery top. I'd later find out her name was Brenda, She had a very stuck up sing song voice when she spoke. It wasn't nice even if she spoke with good intent. I didn't trust her. She was definitely not from anywhere near Macclesfield. Their property was in a gorgeous town called Winsford. I was told I'd meet the foster father Jim who I'd call big Jim on account of him having a son also called Jim later tomorrow as he was at work.

I immediately felt I was in a totally different world and to be fair, I was. Brenda and Jim had a very regimented routine.

Chapter 19

The first few days were really strange. "My name is Brenda but you can call me Brenda or Mum as I'm your foster mum but only if you want to and Jim is big Jim or Dad okay?" She had a sing song voice which I didn't like and wasn't used to. It sounded posh. I blanked her whilst Caroline nodded and smiled there's no way in hell I'd call anyone Mum apart from Pat and my mum. Big Jim wasn't so big he was around my height and I was to turn ten in a couple of months making it around July time. He was however rather rounded, not fat but round with grey wiry hair that popped out everywhere apart from the middle. He was the quiet one. Brenda was obviously the boss of the house and he just rolled with whatever she said which was totally alien to me and made me twice as concerned about her as I had been before. I'd seen what Pat could do to someone she didn't like.

Later when I became accustomed to the routine I'd get up and dressed straight away for breakfast at the breakfast bar and when I say bar I mean a half kitchen length entire bar complete with wooden bar stools and a variety of cereals all in plastic containers. We could have cereal and one toast or two pieces of toast. If I wanted more I could top up on as much fruit as I wanted. Then it was upstairs for a wash and teeth cleaned. Grab my bag and sit downstairs in the living room until it was school time. Usually we would be watching Saved by the bell or The big breakfast. After school it was straight home and upstairs for homework and changed then down for a full meal with dessert, elbows off tables and back straight with knife and fork in the proper hands. No sandwiches! Bread was a side piece I could cut up on my plate but not make a sandwich out of my food. Then homework would be scrutinised and adjusted accordingly and if everything had been spot on that day then I'd be allowed a few hours free before a shower and bed at 7pm, totally different to my world. My world was a little erratic.

Swearing was also a huge no, no. I'd grown up with it to the point that it was part of my natural language. I knew a fucker from a bastard a mile away. If he could be a fucker he was usually an okay guy, but if he was a bastard he was plain evil. I remember walking into my room for the first time, up the well kept clean staircase and turn left past pictures of all the other children Brenda had looked after. "They all come back you know. They always do" she'd tell me. I turned left and was met with a poster of Robbie Fowler on the door with LIVERPOOL in bold letters straight across the top. I was hopeless at football. I had never played at school and the lads on Moorhill road who played were always cutting peoples clothes lines down and stealing from gardens so I rarely played with them. This wasn't going to go well. A ginger haired lad a few years older than me appeared out of nowhere. I'd never seen hair so bright! His face full of freckles. "Who do you support?" I guess he was being friendly but at the time it felt like intrusion. How dare he presume I support anyone? Or that I even want to talk? "Erm Liverpool!" I replied not having a clue about football. "Who's your best player?" he asked I pointed to the poster "him" I said and walked into the room I had been told was mine. He walked in behind me and I expected trouble wasn't this my room? The room had two bunk beds and Little Jim who was twice my width and at least a foot taller jumped up onto a bunk on the right and leaned on his elbow watching me. "Our room, my room" he said lifting his oversized head up slightly to get a better view of the new guy. "Yours" he said pointing to the other bunk bed. "Great, just great" I thought staring at the small shiny gloss on the wood of the wardrobe with no idea what I should be doing or where to look. I wondered where Wenzel and mum were.

I turned to my left as I sat on the bottom bunk. Huge garden, conservatory the size of my old living room a long drive and a farm beyond the garden. "They probably own that as well" I mused "would be beautiful if they didn't actually live in it" I laughed at my thought unintentionally. "What's funny?" Little Jim said "nothing, where's the toilet?" I asked he pointed behind him in reply. "Share the joke" he demanded rather than asked. "I need a piss" I replied and for the first time I heard my name screeched like a foghorn on speed. "Traacieee!!!" That sing song voice shouted in a long drawn out drawl up the stairs. I didn't pee and went to go down the stairs where I was met at the top by Brenda who'd obviously been listening in. "Okay, you are new so I'll let you off this once okay?" She was baby talking me but there was a threat behind her voice. The question was rhetorical but I didn't get it. "OK?" I asked. "We don't swear in this house, ever, and could you take your shoes off? I'll buy you some slippers for around the house"

"What did I do?" I asked her innocently.

"What did you just say?" she asked me and I believe she genuinely didn't hear me.

"I asked what it was I did wrong?" I asked again.

"You swore" she said.

"Can I go now?" I replied shaking my head in disbelief.

"Yes and try to remember what I said" she remarked. I looked down at my feet. Shoes off? What sort of game was this? I didn't swear...did I? I replayed the conversation in my head twenty times. I was good at that. I'd had to do it a lot. Then I left it that she thinks piss is a swear word. Silly cow. I left my shoes on but not out of malice, simply because she'd asked me "could I take my shoes off?" and well I could but it wouldn't help me much if I needed to leg it when someone starts swinging so no, unless I'm told to they stay on. It's worth noting that during all this I'd not seen any hint of violence in anyone. No anger, zero, which creeped me out more than if they had said "If you don't take your shoes off I'll slap you" That stuff I was used to. I could handle that. I understood that. Not knowing the people the ways or the punishments really concerned me.

Caroline's room was next to Brenda's bedroom and shared with Brenda's daughter Rita who was gorgeous at least eighteen years old with long strawberry blonde hair. Girls never went in boy's rooms and vice versa and nobody ever went in Brenda's room, not even her own children. What was she hiding? "Why can't people come see you in your room?" I asked her. "Well you wouldn't want me snooping in your stuff so I don't let people snoop in mine" she replied. "Snoop?" I asked never having heard the word. "look through" she replied "ah OK" I said. "Yup definitely hiding something" I thought.

The first time Brenda told Caroline it was bed time I was gob smacked. She was to go to bed at 6:45pm and I at 7pm as we got older it would get later she told us. We were not used to bed times. If Wenzel said "bed!" at 4pm we went to bed if it was halfway through the night and he said "bed!" We went to bed the time was irrelevant it was the order that held importance. I remember asking him once "Can I go to bed?" He asked "you tired?" I was cross-legged on the floor with my back to the T.V "yeah" I replied. "Stand up then" he said. I got up to go to bed when he bellowed "No!" I stood stock still mid stride and suddenly was wide awake. He stared at me so I stood up straight "that's better, won't fall asleep now will you?" He said "stay there" he added. I was too tired to care I accidently broke another rule by looking straight at him. He smiled at me "Caroline, are you tired?" he asked her ", "no sir" she replied quickly. "Okay, Jonathon?" He said. "Yes Sir" Jonathon said "Go to bed then" Wenzel told him. I said nothing. Made no movement nor sign that I could see what he was doing. "Goodnight" Jonathon said kissing Mum and Wenzel before bed. Caroline went up about an hour later. "What?" He asked me although I'd said nothing. "Nothing sir" I replied not taking my eyes off his. I wasn't tired any more I was angry and fully prepared for a beating. At least I could go to bed afterwards. Ten minutes or so went by "If you keep staring at me I'm going to knock your head off" He said turning from the T.V to face me. I held his gaze for a split second then lowered my head "better" he said, and now here I was in someone else's house being told I was to go to bed at 7pm? She's not my mum. "I usually watch prisoner cell block H" I queried. "Bed time is at 7pm here" she repeated. I lay in bed for around twenty minutes after my shower that night before I was up on the landing talking to Caroline in her room. "This is bullshit" I said. "I know" she replied. "It's not for long" she said trying to comfort me. "It's still bullshit" I told her. Little Jim came up the stairs. I didn't move. I'd already tuned into his walk earlier in the day he was heavy and shuffled on one side ever so slightly. He was slow to reach the top and I figured he's one of us like in Macc you had the kids and the adults. That's how it was he won't care. "You should be in bed" he said looking down at me as he reached the top of the stairs. I was a little shocked I eyeballed him disgusted. "You should be in bed" he said again. "I heard you" I replied with the same even tone he gave me. Then he turned and did what no lad I knew of in Macc would have ever done "Mum!" Me shouted down the stairs. She came up and I looked at her. "Bed time" she said. "I'm not tired I'm talking to Caroline" I told her turning around to point to Caroline who'd vanished into her room. Smart girl.

"Talk in the morning" Brenda told me. "Bullshit" I muttered walking as slow as I could manage past Brenda and sidekick. Little Jim had to go to bed himself so the slower I moved the longer he had to wait. I could feel his eyes boring in my head. He jumped to the top bunk and lay with his back to me. I etched "Bullshit" into the top bunk with my thumb nail making a mental note to get something harder to do it with tomorrow night.

A few hours later the bedroom door opened and a tall lad with black curly hair walked in. He was thin but with big long arms. "Alright lad?" He asked jovially, his arms kind of jiggled as he spoke. I nodded and he stripped and jumped into the bottom bunk on his side of the room. I liked him straight away.

Chapter 20

There was a picture of a fighter plane in the living room above the sofa. Big Jim was ex parachute regiment and had done a number of marathons in his younger days. He wobbled when he walked, grey in places little Jim was ginger. Take little Jim's muscle and turn it to fat and change the ginger to grey and balding and they were otherwise identical. When I'd found out he was ex military I was impressed and hoped for someone like my uncle Karl. I was disappointed. When he asked if I like golf I was more disappointed. I hated golf. I remember him hitting a training ball from one end of his garden to the other for hours on end trying to perfect his swing. I was bored silly. I rarely spent time with Big Jim but he was to be fair an okay guy. I liked my own company. I enjoyed being silent. It gave me power. Something people couldn't take away from me. My choice to speak. Caroline had developed a stutter and although we played together we rarely spoke. I was like that with everyone. Caroline had become pals with Brenda which was another reason for me not to talk to Caroline. I guess we were already brought up to distrust one another and I was just looking for reasons to distrust her more. Her relationship with Brenda increased that distrust.

Mum and Wenzel turned up for a visit. Mum remained silent on the sofa she didn't play with us or talk to us as much as I can recall. Brenda did the airs and graces bit with little china cups, saucers and a tiny plate with biscuits on and then added "Tell your parents what a great time you've had" Caroline jumped on that immediately. I remained quiet long enough for Wenzel and mum to pick up a problem to the point that Brenda said "Tell them what you've been doing then."

"Yeah, wonderful" I replied. I don't remember them leaving but mum had sat totally motionless the entire time. She was in her own world and whatever she was seeing it wasn't pretty. I wasn't offended or upset. I knew mum was dealing with things the best way she knew how. Our inner worlds can be really helpful when it comes to seeing harsh shit and she was rolling with it to survive.

It was about a week later and I'd been given new clothes and my old ones had been taken away. I was pissed off. I wanted my old clothes back. I didn't belong to Brenda and Jim. People always came and went here. Brenda cared for a lad called Simon and another younger lad named Stephen, Which with her daughter Rita took the daily household people up to nine including Jim and Brenda and Jim worked all day until late.

I'd got familiar with the routine. I didn't like it but I'd learnt where the cake cupboard was so instead of my bedtime involve me awake staring at the top bunk for eight hours it now had me stuffing my face with cupcakes each night. Result!

I'd daydream I was back at Nan and Alan's watching American wrestling with them and we'd all chant "I am a real American!" To Hulk Hogan's theme song. When I'd be startled awake by a door being opened and a light slammed on by Brenda "Time to get up" not for me though. They had not got me into a school yet. Brenda would walk off and I'd sit up and crack my head on the top bunk but on this morning I punched it repeatedly in frustration. I was pissed and being startled awake I'd felt I was being attacked by Wenzel. Fuck I was having a good dream as well. Was I awake? Nan dead, Alan dead. Me in care? What was next? This bullshit stinks. I want Caroline, Jonathon, Jodie, Mum and Wenzel all together again under one roof. Where are they now? The familiar pains hit me one on top of the other like layers of bricks numbing me each time they fell and they fell hard. Yeah I was definitely awake.

I hated dinner time but figured hey it's only for a week or so then I'm sure our parents will pick us up to move out. I started saying "sorry" If I forgot the shoes thing, If I didn't have the knife and fork in the right hands, I wasn't sat up straight or left my elbows on the table. Tow the line. It's not for long. I told myself repeatedly. I didn't relax; My mind was always on speed. I was always analysing waiting for a hit a need to run or a reason to argue. I was always in defence mode. I sat beside Caroline with Brenda's eldest Bob opposite and little Jim to my diagonal left opposite Caroline. Brenda beside me to the right and Big Jim to my left at the end of the table. Caroline rarely ate at the table and the kids had usually left by then. Cheese and crackers was my favourite dessert. We weren't allowed more than five which was looking back a decent amount, however I'd quite happily eat four and count it as two. Little Jim's favourite game was telling Brenda I'd eaten more than I should have.

Meals held a number of problems for me. It was always a *family* event and they weren't my family. Also because everyone there knew English and Math's and I only knew English, My maths were God awful simply because nobody had shown me. Yet it was me who had to stand facing the wall looking at the times tables sheet whilst everyone else sat down waiting at the dinner table for me to come up with answers so they could eat. Brenda would randomly screech out sums "6 x 7?" I'd have to turn to face her to answer and my brain couldn't do it. It could pick up the titters and laughs from the other room though as I got the answers wrong time and time again. I'd go red having not learnt the self control for this situation yet. Violence and ridicule I was used to yet embarrassment was new to me. I threw out Idle numbers "21?, 32?, 18?" I'd have three and then be told I'd have to try again tomorrow and sent as a spectacle to the dining room beside us to eat.

I can honestly say years later I knew my times tables backwards. I hated it however and it showed whenever I had to do maths whether in the presence of Brenda and Jim or alone I'd turn embarrassed and second guess myself constantly.

It was visiting day again and we were going out with mum and Wenzel! Yes! I'll bet they found a home! After Wenzel and Brenda exchanging pleasantries we were bundled into the car. We went to the car park just down the road by the River Weaver. None of us hugged. We never did. I wanted to just we weren't like those other families. It wasn't done. Mum stood watching the ducks whilst Wenzel sat on a wall nearby. I threw a stone into the water. Caroline sat on a swing by a very small children's area. Wenzel wanted to know what we'd been doing. We didn't say. He said they didn't have a place yet but would soon. That was the last time I'd see my mother alive.

Her name was Trish Pharro she was a social worker. I was sat on the sofa at Brenda's, It was blue. She sat opposite me and Caroline sat beside me. Brenda was in the doorway. I could tell by her face something was wrong. She wasn't upset, She was concrete faced. "Hi Guys! You okay?" Trish said with fake happiness. Something was very wrong. I eyed Brenda who was checking out our physical responses. I hated being read. I switched her off in my head. "What I have to tell you isn't easy to say" Trish said. She was going to go on to say something else when I cut in "what?" I asked.

She sighed. "Your mum was found dead this morning" Caroline had taken an instant stony expression. I could feel it. "How?" I asked. Trish looked at Brenda who gave a short nod "She was killed" she started. "Clive" I said staring deep into Trish's eyes. I was certain. It had to be Clive. "No, no not Clive" She replied. I must have looked quizzical because it didn't make any sense to me. "Who?" I asked her. "Your dad, he handed himself in to the police earlier on today" I don't remember the rest. Some said I went upstairs and was in the bathroom an hour. All I remember is being on a pushbike my granddad made me and flying around the Winsford estate over and over repeating "father killed mother" over and over again in my head. I knew I had to remember it. I had to drill it in so it couldn't move or else I'd forget it and I couldn't forget it. I'm the oldest. I take care of mum when Wenzel's not around. "Mum's dead, Nan and Alan are dead, who am I?", "father killed mother, father killed mother" over and over. Each turn of the pedals, each half turn, each moment. "father killed mother, father killed mother."

Chapter 21

Mealtimes no longer mattered. What did matter? I had my own demons to contend with and I'd started by trying to find a reason for the killing. Mum wasn't perfect however she didn't deserve to be killed. Wenzel was more than capable but I couldn't accept it. He was after all my father and it was time I acted like the oldest of four. Alan and Nan were dead. Clive was on some kind of rampage and I was sure he'd killed mum. I wasn't sure why but I couldn't believe Wenzel had done it. I needed to believe I had a reason to continue. I wanted to take Caroline, Jonathan and Jodie and move back with Wenzel. I'd find the truth and we would all live together, Wenzel would tell me what happened and it would make sense somewhere. I just didn't know where and then we would be a family again. I was oldest. I should have taken care of them. I should have known this would happen. I should have done something, anything. Alan was dead because of me, Nan was dead because I'd just watched her being sick and done nothing and Bernie was dead because I had not listened to my gut. I'd get them back together because that was my job.

"Where are Jonathan and Jodie?" I asked Brenda who was making juice in the kitchen. "With Winnie and Phil in Alderley Edge" she replied.

"Where's that?" I asked knowing that Wenzel had told me him and Bernie were staying in a caravan in Alderley Edge. He'd mentioned something about a Wizard and caves. "They are fine" she told me turning around and giving me a smile. "Do they know about, about, about mum?" I asked stopping my voice from breaking and holding back tears. "Yes, yes they do" she replied putting the juice on the side in a big plastic jug. I will not cry! I told myself. I told myself mum is not dead! Jonathan, Jodie and I will live together we will be with Wenzel and.... a big empty hole hit me. I will not cry! I demanded of myself. "OK" I said and walked off. I grabbed some kitchen roll from the wooden holder on the way through and blew my nose hard which hurt a little. I did it again and noticed that in the split second of pain my mind stopped everything apart from physical pain. I went upstairs blowing my nose over and over and not crying.

I lay on the bottom bunk and punched the thick wooden slat above me slowly. Pressure, no pain. "Father killed mother" I told myself and punched it again this time feeling pain. "Father killed mother" punch, punch, punch, pain... yes, pain was good. Alan flashed in my mind punch, punch, punch with each punch the days fell away and mum was alive. They were all lying to keep us here. Punch, punch. I'm in the living room at Alan's house. I'm hitting the sofa cushion he's holding up for me "turn your hips lad!" he's saying. Punch, punch, "again lad. It's good. Again" I hear him clearly and see him more vividly as my knuckles turn red and sore. I'm snapped back to reality as the skin splits. I'm in pain on my back at Brenda's house on the bottom bunk. Little Jim has walked in and looks down at me "aaaaaaargh!" I scream unloading lefts and rights into the wood. For around five seconds his eyes are on mine before he legged it down the stairs. I'd worn myself out by the time Brenda came up. "You're on the top bunk from now on" I was told. I ignored her that night and a few nights after. Yes I believe this is where begins the start. The true start of my story.

It had to be said that Brenda and Jim did a great job from what I saw with the other children and either genuinely had their best interests at heart or at least gave their best to make it look like they had. I however hated foster care and them along with it. Big Jim was rarely home so Brenda caught the brunt of my attention. I was coming down the stairs walking beneath the decorative plates she hung on the highest wall when the front door opened. Brenda was stood in the doorway with her back to me when I heard her say "HI Louise!" and a girl responded "Hi Brenda! Is the new boy in?" I stopped in my tracks. "Oh no, oh fuck no," I thought. I really didn't need this. I didn't have friends. I didn't want friends. Who was she? What did she want? I bet she wants to know why I'm in care and all that shit. Great, just fucking great. "Louise called for you isn't that nice?" Brenda said flashing me a smile. I just looked at her trying my best to make her vanish. No such luck. "Hi!" Louise waved hopping from foot to foot. I looked back at Brenda trying to convey my feelings of *seriously?* In my face."Go and play then, don't go off the front" Brenda sing songed me out of the door.

I'll admit the foot hopping thing was pretty cute. She was shy and that was odd but it brought the carer out in me. I still had no reason to trust her. "Hi I'm Louise I live next door!" She said overly happy about it and pointing to another huge house with a big lawn and daffodils lined up all along it. "I know" I replied. "Oh you've seen me!" She asked so excited I thought her pretty green eyes would fall out. I had seen her. She was out most nights with another lad and a girl. They would sit on Brenda's wall whilst I was in bed. She had red hair with that much lacquer on it that it looked like her fringe was a shield in front of her face and if I looked beyond it I'd of sworn her eyes would have swallowed me hole. "No, I've not seen you. I know because you just told me" I said. Push her away, "leave me alone!" My mind growled. "Okay" she said slowly in a happy voice. "Don't like them much eh?" She asked tilting her head back to Brenda's. We'd reached the edge of the drive. I stopped. I wasn't usually allowed off the drive without asking and although she said "don't go off the road" I didn't need the bullshit. I was certain she'd find a reason to bollock me anyway. Wenzel always had. "Father killed mother" hit me like an allergic reaction. I put my hands in my pockets and tried not to let it show on my face. I grabbed the tissue and stopped myself. I'd look awkward. "Well, I'm out. What now?" I said with a *when is this shit going to be over* appearance. "I get to know you!" she said. "Favourite colour?" She fired jumping on the spot up and down. I didn't know or care. I looked straight at her not changing my expression. She pulled a sad face. "Don't want me to know you? Okay!" She said springing to life and her eyes sparkling

"You ask me then? Go on! Ask me!" I couldn't hold it in any more. Inside I was laughing. "No, What now?" I said with the hint of a smile. "Okay, okay Mr Grumpy!" She said tilting her head left and right and getting closer to my face. She was stood leaning on the post at the end of the Garden. I realised she was humming a tune. I didn't recognise it. She put her arms on the post and lay her head on it. Her hair fell along her face and she moved it subconsciously. "I know!" she sparkled standing straight. "First to laugh loses! You'll probably win!" She said laughing. *Bitch* I thought with no malice. She had character and I liked that. "I'll go first!" She said and exploded into a dance around the post. I'd only ever seen mum and Caroline dance. Both had danced with me. It took me back to mums alcohol breath an inch from my face and then a happier memory as Caroline and I danced to rock around the clock at Nan and Alan's. She wore a red dress with black on the skirt and we rocked all night. We both loved it even though it was demanded by Nan. I looked up and realised Louise was still dancing but with no pressure. She wasn't making me dance or forcing me to do anything. She wasn't hurting anyone. She didn't have to be there. She chose to be there. She leaned forwards and puffed her cheeks out doing the head tilt thing again. I noticed she had lip gloss on. "Mr grumpy" she said blowing me a raspberry and hopping left and right. I creased up laughing! "You fucking idiot" I said. She flinched, I'd not meant to hurt her. As soon as I'd seen it on her face it was gone. "Made you laugh though" she said just as her front door opened and her mum appeared. "Louise!" She called. "Gotta go!" she said singing "Mr Grumpy" all the way to her door. As I walked off I heard her call "Oh yeah, I knock for you later?" I stopped and shrugged "whatever?" in a half assed fashion. She kept her eyes on mine and didn't move. Half in the doorway half out it lasted maybe five seconds. "OK" I said and turned away "Yay!" she exploded closing the door behind her.

Louise would knock on for me hundreds of times after that. I'd learn she was a happy, bubbly, fun loving character who could both dance and draw very well. She wanted to be on stage and sang everywhere she went usually breaking into song during conversation. I'd also learn it was all a front. If I had a best friend growing up it was Louise. She used to dance and sing to break up mundane conversation and when she didn't want to think about things that were going on in her life. She was always seeking adventure in some form of distraction or other, usually involving alcohol and always involving a guy with a car. When it came down to the bottom line after endless nights her sat holding back tears and thanking me for listening she simply wanted two things. To be loved and to escape feeling unloved. She became important to me. More than once I'd find her surrounded by a couple of lads on a bench somewhere trying to cop a feel and have to take her home. Louise seemed to interpret their attention as affection and hoped for it to be love. Seeing her like that made me angry but not with her. I was worried she'd end up just like my mum, an alcoholic or worse, dead. We spoke about it a lot Louise's answer was always the same "why do you care?"

Chapter 22

My bedtime had been extended to 8:45pm on account of a couple of birthdays going past that I did my best to forget. Louise wanted to meet a lad called Toby she'd been dating even though we both knew she was in love with someone else she never stopped talking about I'll call J. I chose to walk with her through the park as it was dark at around 8pm she'd told me she wouldn't be long and I said I would wait for her. "I'll be fine, go home" she laughed waving and walking off down a path with hedges either side. If she came out drunk and got picked up in the park she was in trouble I'd never forgive myself. 10pm came and went I'd been sat in a hedgerow where I couldn't be seen by passing drunks until she came out at around 10.20pm "Oh, you're still here?" she said as I jumped out of the hedge in front of her. She'd not seen me at all which meant she wasn't switched on and wouldn't have seen someone else who meant her harm either. "Yeah, you said you wouldn't be long?" I replied flatly. "Huh, I got chatting" she said dismissively and linked my arm. "Why'd you wait?" she asked leaning her head on my shoulder. "Because I said I would" I replied. "You're weird" she said giving me a nudge. "No, I'm not weird. I'm just not out for a shag, money, booze or to treat you like a slut" I replied without thinking. "What?" She said pulling away from me. "Come on Louise, you know what Toby's like he's a nobhead and we both know you love J" this prompted a debate about J and Louise's choices at which point she said "I didn't ask you to wait!" Fair play. She hadn't but Toby was trouble and so was his brother stinge, another apt nickname. I hadn't crossed paths but people I knew had. I didn't want Louise around them. She was better than that.

I entered the house through the back door at Brenda's and took my shoes off. She was awake and doing the ironing in the Kitchen. I'd been grounded before because I was fifteen minutes late but nothing this late. I'd upset Louise and wasn't impressed with myself. "What time do you call this?" Brenda said less sing songy and more clipped as she moved the Iron a little harder on the board. I ignored her and just stood there. She stopped ironing and looked straight at me. *Fuck it what's the worst that can happen?* I looked at the clock above her head "Eleven fifteen" I said. "Don't get smart with me Tracie!" She fired back. I blanked her "where have you been?" She asked sharply. I blanked her. I didn't need this shit. I stared through her. "Sit down" she said "I'm tired" I replied. I wasn't but I'd learnt she couldn't do shit too me despite her bullshit threats. She got paid loads to look after all these kids and not only was I nobody's child bar my mums and she was dead but I wasn't best pleased about being her job either. "You'll sit there until Jim comes home" she said pointing at the breakfast bar. I sat on a stool leaning on my elbows s and stared into the wall. She went off on a tangent about manners. I ignored her only replying in my head.

"We have given you a place to live," she said. I nodded. *That's true.*

"We have simple rules, you've been through a lot." *You're simple alright.*

"We all show respect here. We can't have you behaving like this." I ignored her *I don't care you're not my mother.*

"We don't have to have you here you know." She said. A veiled threat. *fuck it, enough!*

"One, You asked me the time. I told you. You didn't like it. Two, I was out with Louise making sure she got home safe if that means I'm late then I'd rather be late than see her hurt. Three if you think threatening me with Jim is going to scare me you're wrong and do you really think I want to be here?, kick me out! Do it!" I told her without getting up from my stool and without looking at her. I'd shocked her as that was the most I'd spoke in one go to her ever and my points were valid. *That's right bitch not just a dumb kid* I thought.

"I've had it with you, blaming Louise" she tutted "I thought more of you" she said putting the ironing board away by now she was visibly shaking and the board wobbled "whatever" I replied as calmly as possible. My insides were starting to shake and I was hoping it stayed as fear of the unknown and not adrenaline.

I sat there maybe ten minutes going over all Wenzel had done to me. It had been months since I'd had to run or hide at home or just take it, but the rules had changed. Jim wasn't Wenzel so would try different tactics I'd not witnessed yet and I'd promised myself I'd never hide again. Big Jim wouldn't hit me. He didn't have it in him. He came in and said something to the tune of "what are you doing up?" I blanked him and concentrated on his footsteps. I was ready for anything. He stopped about a foot behind me "turn around" he said. I ignored him. "What you doing up?" He asked me again and again I ignored him. He walked to Brenda who I heard say "you deal with him. I've had enough. I can't take it any more". Big Jim came in again ten minutes later asking me if I thought various things were right? I kept my eyes on the wall and ignored him listening to the footsteps. Brenda had come in and was stood in her spot in the doorway. She was silent and had slippers on. Big Jim paced but not energetically. He was calm. He'd walk behind me and pace backwards again talking. I'd relaxed unintentionally, He wouldn't strike. He was full of shit and this was all just show to do what his wife wanted him to do. I felt sorry for him in the end he's just got home and was given bullshit orders to fulfil otherwise he'd have the same shit from her that I listened to all day. Poor bastard. I laughed to myself as my arm disappeared from holding my head up and my face came crashing down fast towards the wooden breakfast bar. I hadn't seen Jim move but he'd knocked my arm out from beneath me.

Without thinking I stopped my head hitting the table and was on my feet Aikido stance arms up heading straight at him. I had zero thoughts in this action what so ever. What scared me the most was how automatic all of this came. He moved away with his palms flat against the wall by his side. In my head I'd already hit him, grabbed his head and was twisting his face upwards towards mine. I wanted to rip his head clean off his shoulders. I was scared as I stood there in front of him and he stood with his back against the wall flat. Brenda had taken half a step back and then forwards to regain her balance. I was scared of what I was becoming as I looked into his eyes. In reality when he'd knocked my arm out I'd saved my face from hitting the board and stood up nose to nose with him as he pressed his back against the wall. I didn't hit him. He said nothing. I wasn't a cowering child but I was scared. Scared of what I would do to him and knowing that on some level he was right for giving me that tap. He'd not hit me. He'd got my attention by knocking my arm out from under me. "Tracie" Brenda said very slowly and very calmly. I was eye to eye with Jim and his eyes were searching mine trying to figure me out. I don't know how long I stood like that it must have been seconds but felt like hours. I calmed myself but kept my awareness pinpoint sharp. If Jim had so much as twitched a finger I'd of dropped him. Every eventuality played out in my head. They all resulted in the same thing. *Drop Jim.* "Tracie" Brenda said a second time this time I could hear her more clearly. I dropped my arms not taking my eyes from Jim Adrenaline had started to kick in and I could feel myself growling trying to not shake. "Tracie go to bed" Brenda said softly. Little Jim appeared on the landing and popped his head over the banister "what's going on?" he said. "Go to bed John!" Brenda yelled her voice cracking. Little Jim eyeballed me I stood next to Jim and smiled the biggest fucking grin I could muster. *Go on nobhead, have a go. I'm through, all I love is dead. If I'm going I'll take you with me.* I thought. He stormed off in a strop and slammed the bedroom door. I pushed it open hard making it hit his bedside cabinet and rocking Bob's deodorant and stuff that was on top of it. I stood looking at Little Jim who'd jumped on the top bunk for three seconds then spotted Bob watching me. I gave him a nod. I liked Bob and respected him. He would protect his brother and I liked that. I'd do the same. I stood at the window just to piss them off. I looked out to see if Louise had gone back home, the wall was empty, I hoped she had.

Chapter 23

I had returned home from God knows where on the little figure of eight estate and had to go to bed early as I had clothes to try on for school and so did Caroline. High street country primary school. I remember waking up and putting on an ironed, clean uniform. Something as much as I remember the ironing happening at home in Macclesfield I don't remember ever having clean clothes. This was both new and weird. I felt like it wasn't me and then I remembered the last time I had a suit trousers on was at my Nan's funeral.

The school was small and all the teachers were really nice. I kept to my "don't talk unless severely have to" rule though. Nice people are nice when they want to be. It's all a front. Trust nobody. It wasn't a mantra. It was ingrained and automatic. I lived and breathed it in everything I did.

I learnt very quickly I was good at English and horrendous at everything else. I enjoyed learning about the Egyptians and the Mayans however when a teacher asked me what famous buildings the Egyptians had built I couldn't tell them. My mind wasn't on the task. I was seen as an outsider for three reasons. Firstly I was new, everyone else had been there a while before I showed up. Secondly my head was always down even though my eyes were everywhere no matter where I went. My senses always on alert but trying to show I was totally invisible, which made me seem strange to the other kids and finally I wouldn't talk. A question like "want to play football?" And my brain raced *stupid game, pointless, can't play, how did they learn? What's the reason? You're an idiot if I'd wanted to play I'd of come and asked. Moron.* I had a constant leave me alone expression and total silence just seemed to irritate people. One being a lad called Mark who was known as the cock of the school and a good football player.

Another lad called Will had asked me to play football. He had close shaved brown hair unlike Marks which was blonde and long in a centre parting we affectionately nicknamed a fanny parting. Will was a good two inches taller than me and a bit wider too. Mark was stocky and pale where Will was darker skinned and hard faced. I walked to the pitch with no idea how to play. The ball rarely came to me so it didn't really matter but then it did just above head height, I ducked and let it fly past me to the growls and snickers of the other lads. "Head it!", "Stop the ball! Duh!" Play continued and I tried to zone out the comments. I saw the ball once more sail downwards towards two lads who were about to head it. I could see them in slow motion both going to jump for it. I wasn't going to do that. It looked like it hurt when I'd seen them do it. *Get it!* My inner voice screamed. I took two steps and jumped turning my hip as I'd been trained both by Alan and my Sensei. I caught the ball with my foot, hard and way before it was anywhere near the first lad. However it was also just as guy number twos head made contact with the ball. The ball flew towards the other end of the pitch and guy two hit the floor and rolled. Everyone stood motionless. *Fuck!* I didn't feel it but apparently I'd kicked this kid in the face and what I didn't know is you can't kick that high in football. "What the fuck are you doing!?" Mark said grabbing the ball and forcing his face into mine, nose to nose. "Well dickhead?" he continued. I looked at him. Small, compact, mean and angry, hard to knock down, easy to outrun. *Never running again* my inner voice chimed in. I'm not running I told myself. I put my head down and looked through him. Will had got up "are you stupid?" He asked approaching me and touching his jaw. "Fight!, Fight!, Fight!" The chanting started as a circle of kids developed.

I tuned them out, too many to take on. Mr Davidson came over who was my sister's teacher and we all went back inside. "Did you see that?, He took on Mark!" I heard one lad say "Mark will kill him" another reported. I'd done nothing, I'd just stood there. The words "Mark will kill him" rang out in endless echoes through my head for the next hour. I was back in Mrs Avingtons class my teacher and was watching Mark from the corner of my eye. He pointed to me and hit his fist with his hand. "You're dead" he mouthed. I turned back to my book and took out a sheet of paper and started drawing, The word dead playing over and over in my head like a record I couldn't turn off. The faster I heard that word repeat the faster I drew and then it got faster and deeper like a chant "Dead! Dead! Dead!" As soon as it had started it stopped. I looked down to find I'd drawn nans coffin and a big cross on it with a vague shape in. I was now angry and hurting. I stood up folded the paper and walked over to Mark in front of everyone. I bent down next to his face and slid him the paper. "You dropped this" I said giving him my best "go on, take me on" glare.

"Tracie, sit down" Mrs Avington said politely. I held his gaze for three seconds and sat down not taking my eyes from his. He opened the sheet and broke my look to do so. When he looked back I could see the fear in his light blue eyes. I'd written "You" in big letters underneath.

After school I was to be picked up by Brenda. I made a point of being first out of the door and walking so slow I was the last out of the playground. They all had to pass me to leave. They couldn't say I ran. Mark walked with Will at a great distance then went over to his parents all smiles. I looked at Brenda stood where my mum should have been. "Good day?" She said all fake smiles. I flashed her a smile and got in the Mazda.

High Street was actually a really good school. Mrs Avington taught me a lot and I actually learnt to respect her. I noticed as I grew older I was learning more that women were equal and to be cared for, but before this the most important thing Brenda had done for me was to make me realise that some of my actions were plain wrong. I can't remember what Caroline had said but I'd lashed out and hit her. "That didn't hurt" I said mimicking Wenzel. "Did he hit you?" Brenda piped up from behind me. "It's okay" Caroline said nervously. "Say you're sorry!" Brenda squealed. "No" I replied "Say you're sorry now" she said this time less harshly. "No" I huffed. I wasn't expected it and Brenda grabbed me pinning my arms to my sides. "What the fuck are you doing you stupid bitch? Let go!" I yelled. "Hit him back" Brenda said to Caroline calmly. Caroline looked gobsmacked "Go on, hit him back" Brenda said. I threw all number of obscenities at Caroline and a fair few at Brenda. I don't remember if Caroline did hit me or not and I remember storming off. Most importantly what I do remember is when I was held I knew I could get out. I knew I could theoretically hit both Brenda and Caroline but I didn't want to. I didn't actually want to hurt them and I didn't want to be like Wenzel. I realised in that moment I was turning into him with my actions. I was angry with Brenda yeah, real angry and I knew I'd make her pay for that one sooner or later. I'd not forget easily but in another way I was relieved. Women made us, I'd learnt that somewhere. Without women we wouldn't be alive. Brenda had made me realise I shouldn't ever hit a woman and I stuck to it.

Brenda and Jim were forever going on that I should call them mum and dad. It was done politely "Tracie you can call me mum if you want to" I'd started by saying no to which she'd reply "But if you want you can you know?" I suppose she was trying to be nice but it was just pissing me right off. Nobody would replace mum. In the end I'd just say "I know" and she'd leave it until the next day. Jim only did it a couple of times and I just looked at him like he was an idiot. That's how I eventually got her back and made myself feel bad in the process. I'd presumed she was just being a cow all this time to get a rise out of me or exert her control like Wenzel had. I'd concluded that there was no way she could actually care. She got paid to look after us and had three kids of her own she must just want to feel like she's doing a good job and being nice in the process. Well nice comes from wanting to. Not from being paid to. That's how I justified it. She tried to hug me a few times. I didn't like it or understand it.

It was Mothers Day. Brenda was in bed and all her kids and Caroline had gone and given her a card or a gift. I knocked on the door and was told to come in. We were never allowed in. Little Jim, Caroline and Bob were already in there. She waved them out when she saw it was me. She had a nightgown on. I'd never seen her in a nightgown before. Somehow it made her look more human. She came around the bed and saw the card. "For me?" She asked delicately I threw my arms around her. She held me for too many seconds and I stepped back "Happy mother's day" I said and held the card out to her. She looked truly delighted. She opened it and her face fell rapidly and a part inside of me died too. Inside I'd written. "You're not my mum and you never will be". I put my best stern face on and smiled looking through her eyes. I held it for two seconds turned and walked out. I was unhappy with myself for upsetting her. Maybe she was genuine, But I was defending mum, my mum. Who nobody would replace. Brenda never asked again and seemed to accept I'd be my own person. I ate with the family, Abided mostly by their rules but I was out whenever I could be, reading or on the games console. I didn't like people. I liked being alone. I was safe alone and so were other people. Safe from me and safe from dying. I hurt everything I touched and I'd proved it by how I'd treated Brenda.

I'd been sent to a scout group once a week and a swimming club too! I figured they wanted me out of the way which worked for me because that's exactly where I wanted to be. At first I hated swimming, I couldn't do it and after being thrown in by Wenzel large amounts of water scared me. Inside a year I was going for my lifesaving certificate and I enjoyed it.

Scouts was ten times better. Our leader Larry was a five foot nothing, balding, quietly spoken man who ran the hall like a military camp. We had first aid training, bivouacking, knot making, camping, canoeing, orienteering, survival hikes, volleyball and raft making amongst a million other things. I was at home here. I learnt how to build a shelter from scratch. How to make traps, first aid and generally how to survive with nothing. Larry wouldn't always announce first aid training. He'd teach us one week then the following week we'd be playing football and an event would occur, usually it would be something simple "a boy fell from a tree outside" he'd point at who was to handle it and off we'd go. The injured lad would have a fake cut and pretend to have a broken arm and he'd tell us if it was supposed to be jutting out or anything. However on one occasion and not knowing my past. Larry took it a little bit far.

We were building indoor tents from poles and canes when Larry ran in and looked genuinely panicked. "Matt, Matt's fallen down, Matt's down" he said waving his arms around. Matt was a friend of mine I'd camped with a few times. A good lad and a quiet lad. He had a good sense of humour and was harmless. If Larry was panicking then something was certainly wrong. "He's not breathing" he said as I reached him. I was on autopilot. I wasn't even asked to assist. I ran past Larry into where I saw Matt on the floor on his back. A stick was poking through his stomach unbeknown to me totally faked by a piece of foam underneath his shirt. There was no blood. "Matt can you hear me?" I said calmly "Matt?" I asked again. "He's not breathing!" Larry shouted stamping foot to foot. I grabbed baconegg who was two feet taller than me and a few years older "Get him out of here, now!" I said shoving Larry towards the door. Baconegg took him outside. No time to waste. I leaned down next to Matt and listened for air with my ear whilst looking at his chest. Nothing. "Sorry mate, this might hurt" I said opening his mouth "airway clear" I said out loud *breathing?* I asked myself. His chest wasn't moving. No breathing but we had a heart beat. I put my finger on his solar plexus and linked my fingers "one!", "two!". I counted and got to three as Matt started coughing and laughing. Larry dragged me away suddenly calm. "Ambulance? Where's the fucking ambulance?" I asked from on the floor being held by Larry. "It was a test Tracie" Larry said calmly. "No fuck the test he needs an ambulance" I said and then I heard Matt laughing and looked over to see him pull the stick out. "Sorry man, I was holding my breath" He said as I walked off. Images of Nan and Alan engraved themselves back into my brain stronger than before.

I was outside the patrol HQ fuming at my friend Baconegg I'd met him because he was extremely tall and had a wonky haircut. He had an infectious smile and everyone called him Baconegg. One day I asked him "why they call you Baconegg?" and he laughed it sounds very similar to my surname. "So?" I asked. "Well it sounds like it so they call me it." He replied. "hmmmm okay" I said un amused. "Which do you prefer?" I'd asked him. "I don't mind" he said but I could tell he was lying. "You're baconegg" I said "yeah" he replied. We'd been friends since. It must have looked comical though me storming up and down outside the hall going off on a lad four times my size. "Who the fuck does he think he is? Larry? A scout leader! Shit! I liked him, and Matt! For fucks sake. All fake?" Whenever I said "all fake?" Baconegg would calmly say "yes" otherwise he said nothing. It wasn't until I said "I'm going to go back now, get out of my way I'll show him a fucking accident he was a friend" that Baconegg ever so calmly said "he didn't know." Baconegg knew about my past. "Neither of them knew" he said. "That's not the fucking point!" I said covering my face to stop the tears from flowing. "I'm the only one who went to help and I couldn't save her and Matt I couldn't save Matt!" I stormed half tears half anger.

"It's okay, Matt's fine" Baconegg said softly. Somehow I'd convinced myself that Matt was dead. He came out of the HQ "You okay mate?" he asked me. I lifted his shirt up. He was fine. "You pull that shit again" I said choking down a cry and broke into a grin. Matt was okay, I liked Matt. He laughed.

I'd learnt to listen to my intuition even when it was totally wrong. I didn't know what intuition was but I knew the feelings that spoke to me. They had warned me of danger with Wenzel many times and were there when I had to get help for Nan and Alan and again when I went into care. So when I was stood at the top of a bloody big hill on a scout camp next in line to use the zip wire I could see going way, way down into the distance and I felt *no, don't go.* I listened. I stepped back despite being next in line. "You're up next mate." I said to my friend also called Tracie. He was well built with long light brown hair. The girls loved him because of his looks and the guys loved him because he was hilarious. He nodded and grabbed the handle, slipped his legs through the hoist and off he went. He was three quarters of the way down when the line broke and he went face first into a log at the bottom. I was shocked but not surprised. I'd seen Nan twice before. Maybe she was protecting me. It didn't make me feel better about poor Tracie though, Especially seeing him walk around for the next hour holding a tissue to his bloodied nose.

Chapter 24

At home I had a guardian ad litem visit numerous times. He was a good guy called Drake who looked like a puppet from thunderbirds. He actually moved his arms in an animated way when he spoke and tried to put all the legal terms into a child's perspective. I liked Drake but didn't speak to him much as Brenda was always present or right behind the living room door. She was always listening in even when people thought she wasn't. I got the jist though. Wenzel was going to prison and I'd not see him, Jonathan and Jodie were to see us four times a year instead of every four weeks because they were going to be adopted and it was thought better for the children. They were so young that they wouldn't be affected as much as the older children and the sooner they had a stable base the sooner they could get to a normal standard of living. I wanted that for them didn't I? A happy home where they could be cared for by people with only one desire, to look after children they could call their own? No, I objected strongly. They are my family and I want them left in care. They are too young to know what they want and when they are old enough then they can decide, apparently Wenzel objected too. They were put up for adoption anyway.

I was getting on well at High street primary. Most of the kids left me alone because I was eerie and the teachers left me alone because I pretended to get on with my work. I was a lighting technician in Joseph and his amazing technicolour dreamcoat and my mate George was Joseph. Which meant he was a starring role which suited his personality as everyone seemed to love his charisma and confidence and I turned a light on and off. George was very good at chess, we played often and we'd always play five games. One week it was three- two to me and the next three – two to him. Other than George I was unbeaten in the school. I had to turn my light on when George came on stage. Turn it off when he left and do the same at the end of the show, on for his big scene and off after it. The first day the play was about to start and all the lights were already on. I was not happy. Now my job was "turn a light off" I spoke to the headmaster and explained "Look, whoever has turned that light on at the start has really messed up the show! I turn the light on at this point" I said pointing at my sheet of paper "then off after this act" I said pointing again "then on for when George sings and off when he stops". Naturally it turned out the head teacher was the one who had turned the light on! As luck would have it he also saw George and me playing chess. "If I get some chess boards will you two run the chess club?" He asked me. "No, I'll do it and George can help" I replied. He laughed "okay!" So we did.

Once a week chess club where George and I showed people how to play. Then we were entered into a competition against other schools in Cheshire. I loved it! We played competition rules and it was another level to what we were used to. I'd been taught by Wenzel. "White moves first, I'm white because I'm better than you" I'd get a slap if I did a move wrong and insulted if I took too long to make a move. In no time at all I was good at chess. I soon learnt to let him win. I'd get a roasting or insulted but If I was winning he'd knock his king over to forfeit. There was no "well done" no "good game" just "little shit, think you're good? Set them up." Then he'd beat me. Mostly because he was good and sometimes because I'd let him. I remember coming back to Brenda's with certificates and medals where I put them in my clothes drawer. Dad would be proud of me. Wouldn't he?

I saw his case on T.V It lasted about twelve seconds "A man in Cheshire handed himself in to the police this morning after killing his wife" that was pretty much it. The papers ran similar "From loving father to wife killer" yeah that was my dad. I'd finally got settled at primary school. I had friends and regular activities I enjoyed. I kept my head out of trouble when I could and at least tried to pay attention at school when It was time to go to High School. I convinced myself it didn't matter to me. More people I don't care about so what? Lessons I'll sit in on and do what I can be bothered to do, Who cares?

Unfortunately something or an accumulation of things was having an impact on me. My nose blowing got worse and so had my behaviour. I was nicknamed Rudolph at high school because my nose was red most of the time and my top lip cracked and bled. It hurt but it took my mind off things. I knew it was wrong and not helping me and so I tried to stop. The more I concentrated on stopping the more I noticed it and the more I felt the need to blow my nose.

Wenzel had been placed in a mental prison hospital near St Helens Merseyside. He was charged with manslaughter and got four years. He served two and a half, less than six months of that was spent in Walton prison. The rest was the prison hospital where he played pool and scrabble with staff. He was allowed contact and I visited him twice. A lady who seemed familiar with short red hair led me through to see him. He didn't talk much and looked like shit. I was told he'd tried to kill himself. I knew he hadn't. He'd bragged as a kid he knew how to really slit his wrists. He hunted rabbits and read loads of murder magazines. If he wanted to kill himself he would have done it I have no doubts about that. Everything with Wenzel was show and everything had a reason. This was no different. He wanted to put a face on. Become a stereotype people that people would accept. He had faint marks along his wrist. "You okay dad?" I asked playing straight into his game and trying to defend him at the same time. Look I love my dad and he loves me my body language screamed. I knew they didn't realise how he thinks. I knew he was using them. I knew because I know exactly how he thinks. I had to if I wanted to survive. That's a big statement he would immediately play down and sounds exaggerative, unfortunately it's one hundred percent true. I knew in that one look mum had to become the bad person and he had to look like the good caring one if we all wanted to be back together. I knew that was wrong but I wanted my family back. As if reading my thoughts he said "when I get better and get out of here we can all live together. We'll find a new mummy if you want" placing his hand on the nurse's as if by accident. She didn't move it.

I didn't want a new mum. It was my job to take care of Nan and Alan and they died. My job to take care of mum and she died and my job to take care of Jonathon and Jodie and I had no clue where they were. "OK" I said. I wanted dad out. With him out I could get my family back together. I'd had numerous meetings with my guardian ad litem and mostly ignored him. I'd done the same with social workers, sitting in silence until they left, Fuck them. Now I had to be different. I had to prove Wenzel a good man.

Brenda had started asking questions, Apparently the courts wanted information about Wenzel and mum. I lied my ass off. "Mum used to sit and watch snooker then have a go at us because we wouldn't eat fast enough", "She rarely cooked and when she did she was a bad cook", I'd cry thinking of Wenzel putting me in the corner and his heavy keys hitting me in the back as he'd thrown them. "Mum threw keys at me and used to get drunk a lot, it was always Wenzel who took care of us", "Wenzel had to take mum to hospital a lot because she would hurt herself". The lies were easy. I'd learnt from the best. I hated myself.

I didn't dare tell the truth. He wouldn't kill me but he'd kill someone I love and besides he was my only chance at getting the family back together. If I'd told the truth I would have said "Wenzel took her to the hospital because he wanted to make out she was crazy, he wouldn't let her out of his sight at the hospital because those cuts and bruises, he'd caused them. Those broken ribs and burns on her arms and legs, he'd caused them. So he'd get her drunk on Q.C sherry and take her to the hospital to prove how crazy she was. How addicted to alcohol she was and if she refused he would beat the kids in front of her." No I couldn't say that because that would be the truth and to be honest. The truth hurt me. What's more mother did want the family back together so I convinced myself I was lying because she'd want me to. Brenda and I did these chats every night where she wrote everything down and every night I looked right into her eyes, made her feel sorry for me and lied.

My inner anger started to show in high school. Rudolph was called out so much I'd drowned it out. I didn't care. What they didn't know is I'd started taking a ruler and scratching my arms until it bled. The friction causing heat, heat and then pain. The pain would temporarily block out my hate of life and myself. Then the bullying started. A lad called Lloydy was first nicking my lunch on the way to school, pushing me, It wasn't primary school. Not talking was not going to be enough to scare him away. At least twice a week he'd be there. Same routine. "Hey Rudolph what you got?" I'd try walking past without looking up and be pinned to the hedge or wall. He'd nick whatever he wanted and sometimes I'd take a couple of slaps or punches. I'd grab my bag and put back in whatever was thrown around and head to school. When I got home I'd always be told I did well for eating all my dinner or how much I was disrespectful because my lunch box was broken or my bag was ripped, again. Her son knew. He'd seen it happen a few times and done nothing. I didn't expect him to nor did I care. Hurt me! I screamed inside. It stopped me feeling the real pain.

Then there was another lad called Derek Baker who'd throw his attitude around. He never stole from me but was short wide with fat and very loud mouthed. "Ugly fucker you are" He'd taunt. He seemed to have a problem with everyone.

A new lad started shortly after I did called Toby Haslehgeist "I'm sitting here" he said as I sat at my wooden desk in history class waiting for the teacher to arrive. My bag disappeared from beside me and was thrown across the room. I got up and retrieved it keeping my head down to find he'd taken my seat. I sat elsewhere.

I didn't do a lot or work in high school apart from English. I got by on a bare minimal or just got in trouble for doing nothing. Mrs Hawlen was brilliant and I had a lot of respect for her. She used to treat us all like adults and was both polite and yet quiet. She seemed caring and put on a strong front when the kids got a bit over the top. I could see past the facade when she was finding it hard but she carried on anyway to teach them.

I'd got a couple of friends on the estate and one of them was Nigel Willowood. He also liked martial arts and did Karate regularly. He wanted to join the Navy and I enjoyed training with him in the summer on Brenda's lawn. He was a few years older than me with pale features and hair that always seemed to be in style, brown and with a quiff. He kinda reminded me of my brother who also had a unique quiff. We were playing basketball when LLoydy went past. He saw me and ran into the garden totally ignoring Nigel. I stepped back as he approached in fear and let myself be pinned to the wall. "Drop him" Nigel said from behind him. "leave it Nige" I said. "What you got for me?" Lloydy sneered in my face. "I've had enough of this" Nigel said calmly, He grabbed Lloydy by the arm and twisted his wrist up his back and walked him off the property. "If you go near him again you'll have me come looking for you" Nige told him quietly and walked back to me. Lloydy legged it. "What the fuck Nige?" I asked. "He'll kill me at school!" I added. "No, he won't "Nige said slowly. He went on to explain "How was it you can beat me but couldn't stand up to Lloydy and yet I can?" He had a point. He'd also just unlocked my confidence.

Chapter 25

Overnight I changed. I'd been thinking alot about what Nigel had said. He was right too, it was time I stood up for myself. Lloydy was first. He walked across towards me on my way to school. The road was busy with other kids and a stream of traffic. Little blue blazers dotted with white shirts marched along both sides of the road as every nerve in my body yelled "run!" He reached halfway across the road and I slowed down and unhinged my bag from my shoulder. I didn't look up. I could see him with my head down. He was two feet away when I dropped the bag and stepped forwards and one foot away when I jabbed him in the mouth and followed with a hard right. His head flipped sideways so I kept on going left, right, left, right. I stepped back as he hit the floor his head half wedged in the hedge I'd been thrown into many times and then I bowed like I had in Aikido before a session. I picked my bag up and went to school. I didn't look back but I'd be lying if I said I wasn't scared he'd come at me from behind.

Toby was next. "Move" he said entering the history lesson and standing right next to me. Why was our teacher always late? "No" I said remaining sitting and staring straight ahead whilst he stood to my side. "Move dickhead" he said and reached to grab my bag. I let him grab it and stood up reaching for his head which I dragged down fast towards the desk. He hit it but not as hard as I'd wanted. His face was protected by his arm so I punched him instead, holding him with my left and hitting him with my right. They weren't very powerful hits but they made my point. The teacher arrived just as Toby crawled to his seat on the other side of the room. "I'll have you!" He said looking around for approval from everyone. Nobody said anything.

In my next lesson which was science my friend Lee approached me "ere mate. I heard about Toby, he recons he's going to do you at lunch lad, watch your back yeah?" he said. "Thanks mate, But don't worry yeah?" I replied. "Scared?" He asked genuinely full of concern. Lee was a big lad dark skinned and looked the part but was a pussy cat, very friendly and very, very funny. "No mate, got bored of scared" I said honestly. Lee and I were walking towards the dinner hall after lesson when I spotted Toby within a group of other lads by the home economic rooms in the courtyard. "Hold this" I said handing Lee my bag. "Trace! There's loads of them!" I heard him call then I heard "fuck" as he followed behind me. "Oi dickhead!" I shouted making myself look as tall as possible and moving my shoulders wide. "You!" I leaned into the quickly spreading group and grabbed his shirt. "Gonna fucking have me are ya!?" I screamed into his face. "No mate, no mate, no mate," he said arms up. "Come on then dickhead. Right now." I screamed and dragged out the word right letting him go and turning my back on him listening for his feet. "Hit me. I fucking dare you" I said loudly without shouting. He didn't. I turned to face him "keep your gob shut and we'll get on just fine." I told him. "Okay mate, we're cool man, cool" he stuttered. I held his brown eyes and drilled mine into his "oh fuck" expression for a couple of seconds in silence and then turned to Lee. "Okay we're done here mate lunch time." I grabbed my bag and Lee pissed himself laughing. I didn't.

I remember clearly when my reputation changed. I was in my form room with Mrs Yeals, A lad called Pete had put a drawing pin on Mrs Yeal's chair and I didn't approve. "Miss" I said putting my hand up "later Tracie" she replied. Fuck that. I got up and walked up to her "now, I need to talk to you" She took me in the room where they kept all the exercise books. "I won't say who so don't ask but a lad has put a safety pin on your chair. You can stay quiet and I'll be fine or ask who it is and I'm seen as a grass. It's up to you but I had to tell you" I told her. She thanked me and as I left the room I could feel the eyes boring into me. Two things happened at the same time. Pete gave me a dirty look and nudged Mark. The same Mark I'd gone to primary school with. Mark looked at me like he might have a go because Pete wanted him to. I walked to Mark who was on the opposite side of where my empty seat was waiting for me "Got a pen I can borrow?" I said loud enough for all to hear and whispered "Problem?" with my head next to his. "No mate, we're cool man" he replied not taking his pale blue eyes off mine. I took his pen and told him I'd return it after lesson and I did. I had Mark's respect and I liked that because he'd never actually had a go. Mark was okay but that's when my reputation changed. I might have been seen as a grass, but I was a grass they wouldn't fuck around with.

It was during one of the chats with Brenda that I fell apart whilst explaining how mum had beaten me black and blue one night. I kept the stories the same but changed the instigator. Mum never hit me. I was in tears and told Brenda that mum had slept with my uncle which was true. So now I had to have a blood test to see who my father really was. Great, because hey, my life wasn't complicated enough.

I was in Mr Trent's English class, A funny man, tall with dark hair who I liked. However I wasn't in the mood for at all. I was too busy trying to figure out what name to write under the title "name" on my new clean exercise book. Tracie Wayne Daily? My name? Was it? What about the foster carers surname? Could I accept them? It wasn't me though, was it? My uncles surname? My mum's maiden name? Someone else's? "Idiot! You don't even know your own name!" Wenzel's voice rang out in my head. I stood up and walked out. "Hey where are you going?" Mr Trent asked "fuck off!" I yelled back. I got detention for that one and went home to get grounded for getting detention.

Wenzel had been moved to a place in Chester by now known as a halfway house. He had passed his anger related issues tests and was seeking contact. I said yes straight away and was on my best behaviour for a week before I was to finally see him. Maybe now after two years it would all fall into place. I was stood outside Brenda's looking at the sky and visualising that day I was given over to foster care. I could see Wenzel stood beside mum. I could see the social worker and I pushed her out of the image that was by now so real it was taking up the space I was standing in. Wenzel's hand was clamped around mum's hand but mums face had been replaced by a woman with red hair. I'd worry about that when it happened. For all I know they might just be friends. Wenzel wouldn't do that to mum. Besides I'll bet Clive killed her and it wasn't him at all. "Earth to Tracie?" I heard turning to my friend Baconegg "what?" I asked him sharply. He looked down at me and smiled "sorry mate" I was miles away I added. "Going for a hike?" He asked as we stood in the sun. "Nah mate, me dad's supposed to be turning up isn't it. Got a contact" I said "oh, what you mean supposed to be?" He asked. "He's over an hour late" I answered. Baconegg's face told me everything I needed to know about his thoughts. "He's coming, He'll be here" I said looking through him. "Er, yeah, sure, but if he doesn't it's cool ya know. You can come for a hike ya know?" he said. "He will turn up. He's just late. That's all" I said turning away and looking into space. *Why would he see me? He's free now he has no reason to see me unless he wants us all together.* Brenda opened the front door "He's not coming, car trouble apparently" she'd obviously just got off the phone as the receiver was still in her hand. It was a show of control. She was telling me whilst he was on the phone and in a way that said "I told you so". I smiled "Okay, next time is fine. Tell him I said hi" I responded. I nodded to Baconegg and we set off towards Whitegate way.

My mind wasn't in the mood for hiking, although I loved it. I needed to feel the burn in my legs to get any satisfaction from it. I needed to sweat and have the rhythm of movement pulse through me. We however were trundling slowly towards unknown ground we'd said we'd investigate next time we were here. Baconegg was happy and enthusiastic, I was neither. *Doesn't want me, nobody wants me, Nan dead, Alan dead, Mum dead, Wenzel doesn't want us,* what the fuck now? *Fucking idiots,* fuck all of them. We were walking through a field with a barbed wire fence beside us. I'd found a small stone and was chucking it up and and down one handed catching it as I walked. "Dickhead" I'd repeat over and over as I walked. I'd started by referring to Brenda and then Wenzel and then finally myself, Dickhead. *He'll have a new life now and you're not in it.* Dickhead. *You have a new mummy and you'll never meet her. You're the family he doesn't want. You're useless.* Dickhead. I must have been like that a while as Baconegg slowed down and walked beside me. He had no idea the junk going on in my head. He grabbed a stone and started mimicking me in a funny voice. I asked him to stop. He didn't. I told him to stop. He didn't "Look man if you're not happy go home" he told me straight. I was boiling up inside and Baconegg stood there smiling at me tossing this stone up and down his feeble attempts at making me laugh reminded me he's not like me. He has sisters and a mum and a dad. How dare he mock me? "Don't!" I said trying to fight the shaking in my hands that had started as the adrenaline pulsed through my arms. "Dickhead" He said smiling flipping the stone up and catching it again. He was mimicking me to make me laugh. He wasn't calling me names. I knew it but I couldn't find a way to calm down. We were both stationary stood side by side his grin had got wider he was trying to make me laugh. "Don't!" I said feeling like I was on a roller coaster now and the only way that carriage was coming off was at speed. "Dic..." he began as I jumped into the air and grabbed his head bringing my knee up and his head down at the same time. I caught him four or five times in the face. Both tall and strong he protected his face with his arms. "Dickhead" he laughed at me still trying to get me to laugh. The more he laughed the more angry I became. How dare he want me to be happy? How dare he care about me? Nobody cares about me! *Everyone I care about dies or hurts me.* I dragged him to the barbed wire fence and walked along it holding his head down. He had no choice but to move his arm from his face and leave himself vulnerable. I didn't stop when he moved his arm I just kept walking and pulling his head into the barbed wire until he broke free and pushed me off him "what the fuck man!?" He said touching his face where he'd been scratched. He walked away from me. *Fuck them, fuck them all, fuck Wenzel, fuck care, fuck friends and fuck God.* I stormed home to Brenda's. I was sick of liars.

My self-harming had become known. I'd had two therapists I'd sat with for an hour in silence despite their endless questions "Do you not want to talk?", "Do you want to play a game?" "How about I talk instead?" *Nice try asshole, I'm giving you nothing. I'm not normal. Not right, I hurt people, My dad killed my mum what do you know about that?* I refused flat out to speak to the amusement and sometimes respect of those two therapists and several professionals.

I was not a fan of authority which the therapists decided to tell me at every given opportunity They said I was grieving and I had depression. I was in a constant power struggle with myself. My problem according to them was me. They got all of this from information from other people. Back history and paperwork that Brenda had provided. My problem, My biggest problem was very simple. I didn't want to be in care. I wanted to be with dad, my brother and sisters. It didn't help that whenever I played up I was told by Brenda "you'll turn out just like your dad!"

Louise had listened to everything about Brenda and Jim on more than one occasion. Today was no different. I'd just explained to her that my nan and granddad died near Christmas. I hated Christmas. Brenda and Jim had provided a huge bag of toys for each of us and I'd sat and watched whilst they opened their bag of brand new toys. I wanted no part of it. It was all to do with money, they weren't my family. When Brenda asked me a few weeks ago what I wanted I'd said a mountain bike. I knew what I had in mind and half said it because I knew I'd not get one. However there it was right outside and looked okay. Fifteen speed, standard saddle and undershift gears with silver frame. It would help loads with my paper round which Nigel was going to let me take over. Then little Jim pulled his bike from around the corner twenty one gripshift gears which were brand new then, sports stream saddle, alloy rim and oversize frame. One again it was cemented how I wasn't family and he was. That stung. I went outside to the garage to get my old heavy mountain bike my granddad Alan had built from scratch. I'd use that, at least I had that connection left. I opened the garage door and flipped the light on. There was an empty space where my granddads mountain bike used to be.

Chapter 26

"Where's my bike?" I asked Brenda as I pushed the living room door open. The entire family was in there doing whatever it is families do at Christmas. "It's outside are you going to test it out?" She answered innocently. "My granddad made that bike, Where is it?" I asked feeling everyone staring at me but not removing my gaze from Brenda. "Oh it was old so we got rid of it for you" she said dismissively. I ran upstairs and threw myself on the bed crying "bitch!" I shouted. I reached down for what little I had left of my past. A fox Wenzel had made from the hospital and Gofax which Nan had bought me, both had gone. I lay there around an hour until I'd forced all the pain deep down inside. *Ok, you win if you won't throw me out I'll leave* I thought. I'd had every part of my past removed intentionally. I think on some level they thought they were doing the right thing and for some kids it may have been helpful. For me it was the worst thing they could have done.

Louise had sat nodding her head in all the right areas as usual humming to herself when things got too painful as I explained my situation. "Anyway" I said sighing "I'm off, not now but it will happen, I'll miss ya" I said giving her a nudge. "You won't go, you love me too much" she jested. "Tell me about J?" I said changing the subject. Knowing that she was right I did think the world of her but I knew it wasn't mutual. I was leaving and I'd told her. That was the best I could offer. We linked arms and walked down the hill just as it started snowing. It was beautiful. We got to the bottom of the hill and jumped up into a tree as the snow was getting heavier. There wasn't much room but we were well covered and it was warm enough. Louise had no coat but a thick jumper on "want my coat?" I asked her "No, I'm fine" she said staring into the snow. I'd known her over two years and listened to her every complaint. She'd heard a lot of mine too. I didn't realise it until I'd decided to leave but she was the most important person to me at the time. She turned her light green eyes to mine and said "As long as you love me". "Sorry?"

I replied. I wasn't up on the latest music. "Although loneliness has always been a friend of mine, I'm leaving my life in your hands" she sang it all the way through. "It's J's" she told me. I laughed secretly wishing it was mine. "last week it was Toby's" I said teasingly. "Shut up" she told me with a nudge. I'd never seen Louise as more than a friend but in that moment under that tree with the stars and the snow, she was beautiful. I sat there with her and me singing for hours. Then we walked home "you'll get in trouble for being late you know!" She told me. I shrugged "I'm leaving, remember?" she smiled and closed her front door. *Now....where the fuck am I going to go?*

Nigel was at my house, it was still winter out so we were allowed to play Stratego quietly in the dining room. Stratego is a game where you find bombs and beat players by having a higher rank or finding the main piece. The pieces are invisible to the other player. I was depressed but didn't realise it at the time. I just knew I wanted to be as far away from Brenda and Jim as possible and I was forced to play inside. I'd much preferred to have been in the middle of a field camping. Nigel kept saying I'd hit his bombs so I was losing terribly until I realised he'd said "bomb" more times than there were bombs in the whole game. "You're lying" I told him flatly. He looked at me blankly "want me to show you my pieces?" He asked lying to my face. "Yeah" I said leaning over him and grabbing his wrist fast. He tried to counter as I attempted a wrist lock and palmed me in the chest, as I went backwards I flipped his wrist side stepped and grabbed his elbow I threw him towards the conservatory half serious half pissing about. I intended for him to land on the carpet in the conservatory. I didn't realise the clear glass door was closed. There was a thud followed by a vibration. He staggered and came at me fist up. This time I was angry, I sidestepped blocked and threw him again this time fully intending for him to go through the window. He hit it face first as Brenda appeared behind me "Tracie!!!" She screeched.

I stood still slumped. *Here we go again.* "Nigel what happened?" She asked him politely. "He threw me at the door" Nigel said pointing to and fro from his chin to the clear window, his hair still miraculously in place. "Tracie is that true?" She asked me. *She saw me, why fight it?* "Yes" I replied. "Nigel I'll have to take you home, Tracie it's bed time" she told me. Nigel lived six houses away. "Why don't you throw me out?" I asked her calmly "we have had many, many children here Tracie and never thrown anyone out. We help everyone" she responded. "Whatever" I replied walking up the stairs.

The summer time had come around again and Louise and her friends were playing football with us opposite the farm. The ball kept going in the nettles near some big concrete posts that used to hold a fence up. I used to get the ball mostly not because of any heroism but simply because I was looking for places to hide if I could ever find a way to escape Brenda's place. At night I'd think of a new way of getting down the stairs and out of the front door. Since I'd moved in they had put in a two bedroom extension and a garage extension. Maybe I could climb on to that? I was up to my ankles in nettles when Nigel pushed me in. It was a bit of a laugh although it hurt I let it go. The same thing happened again the next time the ball went in although this time Louise pushed Nigel in the nettles. Nigel chased Louise and we all laughed. Shortly afterwards Louise kicked the ball and was told to go get it when Nigel went to push her. I shouted Lou! At the right moment but she slipped and scratched her leg. "I was only joking man" he said to me genuinely. I helped Louise up then turned to Nigel and pushed him hard into one of the posts. "I was only joking man" I mimicked. He went home shouting "you've changed! You used to be alright!" He was right too. In my head what should have happened was Nigel pushes Louise and she slips then gobs off and we carry on playing. However what actually happened was that I saw Louise's leg. I saw the cut and felt numb. *Cut! Man hurt woman! Drop him!* So I did. I wasn't thinking these things through. I was seeing things other people weren't and it was messing me up both inside and out.

By now I was doing an after school paper round which used to be Nigel's but he no longer had the time for. So if I was lucky I didn't have to eat with everyone else if I was a little late. I didn't like eating with them however I'd become more used to it. I enjoyed listening to Bob's adventures. Nobody else concerned me. I was also doing scouts and swimming lessons as well as school. It wasn't enough for me. Although I'd done two Cheshire hikes both times doing really well I wanted more. I needed the burn of my legs aching, feet hurting from hauling a rucksack thirty plus kilometres in the blistering heat or the stab of pain as another graze opened up on my arm. Anything to take my mind off the darkness. The part of me that had no clue who I was or where I was going. It come about in an odd way.

I had taken the habit of going to the library after my paper round. Brenda thought I was reading about Egypt or whatever the latest school thing was at the time. I wasn't, I'd started reading war books and basic history books. They soon progressed to S.A.S novels and to date I've read everything by Andy Mcnab however back then I was working through the Soldier A to Z an S.A.S series.

I rarely saw Mel a girl from school who I'd said hi to and was very much a tom boy. I didn't realise I cared about her at all until I saw her on my way to the library with her wrists covered in bandages "Bloody hell Mel what happened to you?" I said without thinking. Naturally my mind jumped to the worst conclusion. "Eh?" She asked. "You're wrists shit, what did you do? You can always talk to me you know!" I asked again genuinely. "Boxing" she replied. It was my turn to be articulate "eh?" I asked. "Monday, Wednesday, Friday, up there" she said pointing at a hill behind the library. "See you at 6:45pm outside, bring bandages and joggers" I asked Brenda what she thought of me doing a sport and she was all for golf, football, cricket or swimming but not boxing *perfect.* I went a few times and absolutely loved it. However money was hard to find and excuses were harder. In the end whenever I got the chance I would sit up on the embankment and watch everyone training. I'd copy the moves at a distance and when they ran I'd run on the spot. When they were doing their exercises I'd do the same.

Wenzel hadn't turned up for another contact. I was trying not to think about it and at the same time I was starting to be interested in girls. Her name was Paula she was born small and loved football. I used to play with her whenever I got the chance. Green eyes, quite dark with long brown hair. One day still in school uniform she invited me into the house. Upon entering the hall she had a stand up piano "wow can you play?" I asked. She winked and pulled a folder out and another folder. One had sheet music on. The other had her awards in. She had been playing since she was six and was qualified to teach. "Want to see?" She said flipping her legs over the seat I caught a glimpse of her legs and knickers. "Erm, yeah, yeah, play, play!" I stuttered admiring her legs. She sounded awesome but I had no idea what she was playing. Her fingers moved magically and her leg was touching mine. I didn't care what she was playing. Later we went outside to play football as usual until it was time for her to go in.

I'd started thieving as another distraction, pencils, pens and other stationary. Anything I could nick and sell that they had a lot of. It funded my boxing and my smoking which started around the same time as the thieving. Brenda's packed lunches now got given away. At lunch it was up to the chip shop with my friends Kap and Keel for a chip bap! Keel was ginger, comical and friendly, he always tried keeping me out of trouble, his dad was rumoured to be an English angel biker although we all knew he was a carpenter . He smoked and I'd go in to the local shop at lunch to get served for him despite being under age. He was over age but could never get served. Kap looked a lot like me. Thin frame, same height but with more dark hair and a bigger nose. Lot's of people mistook us for one another.

Mainly the teachers. Most of the school kids couldn't get served so I'd spend lunch there charging twenty pence or a ciggy to go in for them. It all added up.

Graham was small and round without fat. He had short shaved hair and was the cock of the school. I'd seen him at boxing but never seen him in the ring. Apparently he was very good. We rarely spoke to one another simply because our circle of friends was not the same. However one day our circles mixed and I found myself on the field eating lunch whilst his circle of friends sat smoking. I was still debating the best ways to get away from Brenda's My problem was simple. I had nowhere to go and didn't know where Wenzel was when Kap piped up "hey, what about Stoppy?"

"Who's he?" I asked Kap

"I'll introduce you. Don't worry about a thing" he said patting my shoulder. It felt good and at the same time I was cautious. Kap was a good lad but he might think is best for me might not be best for me. His heart was in the right place but was his mind?

We were back on the school field a couple of days later, Keel, Kap and I all off to meet a guy called Stoppy. "Why's he called Stoppy?" I asked Kap who just looked at me then at Keel "You'll see mate" Keel said twiddling a match in his teeth. A huge round fella in a leather jacket came over to us from the other side of the field. He was walking an equally big pit bull dog on a big thick chain. He was completely bald and worked at the circus putting up rides and general labouring. He had his own place and was in his early thirties however he had a mental age six years less than his actual age. Otherwise he seemed sound. He was called Stoppy because nothing could stop him. He agreed to meet me alone the next day at lunch just me and him to discuss things "Cool" I said. I had a word with Keel later and gave him some money. He skipped a school period and came back with a G10 pellet firing hand gun for me. It was Jet black and metal. If I was leaving, I wanted protection. It wouldn't do much but it would scare the shit out of someone if I pulled it out.

Chapter 27

It was a hot day and half the school had decided to skive off which wasn't that unusual. I'd got a hundred percent attendance my first two years of high school. Then a hazy few months which was the stage I was in now. Our bags were behind the goal posts on the field mine was further back next to Grahams where I knew it wouldn't be touched. He was lay on it when whilst the other lads played football as he was smoking. "What's this?" he said reaching into my bag after realising something hard was in it. "It's a Tampax" I said trying to change the subject and make a joke out of it. "A what?" he said ignoring me and pulling the gun out admiringly. "Real?" he said his eyes meeting mine. "No mate, Watch" I pulled the top sliding catch back and removed the safety with my thumb, Flipped the plastic front up and placed a 1.77 pellet into it and moved the plastic back down level with the barrel. Then put the slide back into place with a click. "Also fire's BB's" I said. "BB?" he asked. "Ball bearings mate" I told him. "Ah okay, hey guys! Trace has got a gun look!" He shouted. "For fuck sake Gray shut up!" I said hurriedly. "You don't have the balls to use it" he said standing up beside me his eyes meeting mine. I picked up some kind of threat. This wasn't going to go in my favour. He could out fight me in seconds and I knew it if I backed down I'd lose the gun and keep getting ribbed that Gray beat me in a fight. "Who?" I asked reading him easily and walking straight into trouble myself. "You choose" he said waving his arm towards the lads playing football as though they were all disposible and all belonged to him. I shrugged "Stuart, Here a minute" I shouted.

I'd never had an issue with Stuart, a good looking lad with a semi blonde fanny parting. The girls loved him, maybe I was jealous "Yeah, what mate?" He said full of smiles and a body that belonged in the movies. I pointed the gun at his leg "nah mate, we're cool" he said leaning backwards as I pulled the trigger hitting him in the thigh. "Fuuuuuuck" Graham let out bouncing around foot to foot with excitement. "You shot him!" He said looking less confident now. "Be alright" I answered dismissively. Stuart was on the floor bleeding a little and trying not to cry. I realised the pellet was still in his leg as I knelt down beside him. "You lot, fuck off!" I shouted to the gathering crowd. Graham get me my bag" he did and I pulled out my pen knife I kept for scouts as a spare. A long folding fishing knife with a thin blade. "No, no, no" Stuart quivered. "Relax mate, I've got to get the pellet out or you'll get lead poisoning" I told him. What I actually meant was "or they will have proof I shot you". "No, no,no" he rattled off again getting rather animated waving his arms around. I held the blade up a few inches from his face so he could see it clearly "sit still" I said calmly, he did. "Graham hold his leg still" I asked. "Ah, erm, no man fuck no I ain't having no part of this" he told me backing off. I dug the pellet out and chucked it into a hedge a few meters away, cleaned my knife and put the gun and the knife in a carrier bag. I'd ditch it later and come back for it after school. Then I had to square things with Stuart so I didn't have problems later on. "Sorry mate, listen up though yeah. It was dumb to shoot you, you did nothing wrong" I said "I know man, fuck, why man...what did I do to you?" he was genuinely confused and I couldn't blame him. I would have been too. "Shut up, what I'm saying is I'm sorry and I hope we are cool, but if we are not and you're pissed at me. Don't come looking you know what I'm saying?" I told him directly. "Dude, you *shot* me" he said looking down at his leg now red with a tiny hole in it. "If you come looking I'll fuck you up it's that simple. Okay?" I said leaning into his face. "Ok" he said. I was convinced I was OK as far as Stuart was concerned but it wasn't him I was worried about. People tend to have friends and it was them I was concerned about.

I'd had a visit from two NSPCC workers who asked me a ton of stupid questions. I ignored them all. One male, balding mid thirties and a female who was younger and cute. It was the first time I'd made a mistake about talking. The guy was the boss and he'd tried everything from "do you like school?" To "how much do you like scouts?" Nice try. I wasn't playing. I sat looking through him in a little room at social services base rented especially for my little visit. They had a box to tick and I didn't want to be it. "On a ratio of one to ten how much do you miss your mum?" The male asked me. I hadn't expected the question and he caught me off guard. I'd opened my mouth to speak and stopped myself. I leaned forwards staring at him and made as if to speak again. "It's okay" he said "go on" he added. *Nice try*. I opened my mouth again and closed it leaning back placing my arms along the chair I flashed him my biggest grin and held it-*fuck you*."I've had enough of this" he said. I held the grin "It's a shame you refuse to talk" the lass said, Smart girl. She knew I was choosing not to and not because I couldn't. "Because I know what it's like in care, you're not the only one" she added. My intrigue was spiked I checked her eyes and she wasn't lying. "Well if you won't talk to us then we can't make you" the guy said picking up his pad. I pointed at the woman and kept my eyes on him. "I talk to her and her only" he almost jumped out of his skin as I'd made a full sentence. "That's not how it works" he said. "Cya" I replied leaning back and crossing my legs. "It's okay, go for a cigarette" the cute girl said cocking her head at him. He left in a huff. "Sorry" she said and it's the first time I'd heard an apology in a long time. "You wanted to talk to me?" She added straightening her black trousers and leaning forwards on her elbows. I wondered what the best way to take this was? I had no idea. I didn't like talking. "He's your boss?" I asked. "Yes he is" she said "Then I'm sorry if I got you in trouble" I told her. "It's OK" she shrugged fake smiling. She had nice eyes they were warm. "He's an ass-hole" I told her. "Sometimes" she laughed. I did too. "You said you grew up in care?" I asked her. "Yeah I did" she said. We chatted for a while during which time she told me she loved skiing and ended up getting along OK with the people she grew up with. She picked me up a few times and I'd chat but never give anything away. I told her I wanted to be with my family and that she was cute. She told me she had a boyfriend but still let me play Spider's "You and me against the world now" in the car on repeat. I never let her closer than that. I couldn't tell her about the abuse or about my plans to run away.

I'd met Stoppy and his dog Buster again at a lunch time and agreed that when I was ready I'd look him up. Keel knew where he lived so anytime I wanted to leave Brenda's his was ready to take me there. I asked the NSPCC worker again how she'd learnt to get along in care because Brenda and I are so different and that's when she told me "My mum was a foster mother like Brenda we had care kids around all the time so it wasn't that hard to fit in" that hurt. I'd trusted her and been stung again. "OK" I said and that was the last thing I ever said to her. She tried talking and I refused to talk on two other occasions and then they were cancelled. *I'm a job, Just someone's wage. That's all.*

I was in another therapy session with a guy called Alan who was a top notch specialist in child behaviour apparently. I had high hopes for him as he was based in Macclesfield and he had the same name as my grandfather . Grey suit, clip board, quite tall and thin. He kept checking the clipboard and would forcefully make eye contact when he wanted answers and randomly look away when he was trying not to pretend he was getting nowhere. I didn't have anything concrete to dislike, but I had no reason to trust him either. I did my usual routine of staying silent and then after fifteen minutes he informs me I'm going to see a new guy called Nigel today, but only if I want to. I ignored him. "Nigel's an art therapist he works differently to me, he makes things. Do you like to make things?" Baby talking me. When will these people learn? My father killed my mother mate. There is nothing your books can teach me.

A few weeks earlier I'd seen Doris Tones the leading psychologist on when father kills mother. To be fair she wasn't bad and did get me to talk. She was a damn sight better than half of these so called professionals. I have the notes to this day and part of the communication goes.

Tracie – "Do you believe in ghosts?"

Doris "Their could be, I don't know"

I didn't believe in what I knew as ghosts back then. I knew they existed. I'd seen my Nan. She was a ghost, alive but dead. A ghost. Mum I'd seen in visions all over the place covered in blood. Not a ghost. My mind, bad images. I knew the difference.

The result came back that I was preoccupied with the past and couldn't move on until I'd spoken about it. The self harm stemmed from blaming myself for my mother's death. No shit. That and growing up with a psychopath and killing my granddad. It told me nothing I didn't know.

The door opened and Nigel came in. A big man, white but looked grey due to the amount of clay and paint covering his arms and clothes. Some was in his hair. Brown shoes. One damaged and brown trousers, dirty and a dirty shirt. His hair was all over the place. "Hi Tracie, you coming?" he said and plodded slowly down the hall. He didn't wait for a reply. I liked him. I watched his trousers as he walked. A big powerful man. Slow by choice. He could move fast. "You smoke?" he asked totally throwing me off guard. "I'm thirteen" I replied.

"I asked if you smoke" he said. I laughed and shook my head. "Terrible habit" he said "mind if I do?" He asked opening the back door and went to walk outside where he immediately banged his foot. "Shit!" he said loudly. No threat in his voice. I laughed "fucking hate it when that happens" he added. My attraction grew. He was a Macc lad and my appointment was at Macclesfield general hospital where we were born. He worked here daily and understood Macc rules.

I'd have to test him. But I could see me talking to this guy.

"Ok Tracie, what do you like to be called?" He asked.

"Dunno" I replied shrugging my shoulders.

"OK Dunno, here's the rules" he said not skipping a beat.

"Swearing is allowed in my room only, not anywhere else unless it's just me and you. Don't be late without a good reason it upsets other people that see me and means I can't have a fag, and finally" he said exhaling smoke into the sky "do what you want but ask first, paint, draw, make clay objects or talk, or don't talk it's up to you, but if we don't do something for three sessions it's over and I have to see someone else instead. Okay?" He said.

"Sounds fair" I nodded.

"Cool, let's see the room then, in here you do what you want, It's your room, nothing is wrong, no opinion is wrong no matter how bad it is or how wrong it sounds, oh no feeling is wrong either" he said it with amazing conviction, he meant every word. He pushed the door open and before me was a desk with a notepad on it, pens and pencils. One chair. To my right was a huge long shelf at waist height to draw on, sit at, make things. It was dirty. Beside it were hundreds of pictures and to my left was a shelf full of clay items. The floor was bare apart from a chair in the middle of the room. A box of toys beneath the desk which I'd later discover held army men and cars and a big box of air drying clay.

"Where do you want to sit? Or do you want to sit?" He asked me. I hate choice! Must be a trick. Nobody gave me choice. My choices were get slapped or get insulted. Drop someone or get dropped. I didn't have choices. "No answer is wrong" he repeated.

I could see his chair from mine a mile away. His was at the desk and mine was in the middle of the room. I pointed to his chair. "Okay, can I sit here?" he said grabbing his pad and pen and moving to the chair in the middle of the room. I felt uncomfortable. "You're the boss. Do you like the room?" he asked.

I stood up and walked around. "It's dirty" I said looking at his cup covered in clay and half drank coffee, "aye but it's fun, want a brew?" He said. A brew in therapy? Amazing! I'd never been asked if I wanted a drink in any of the other sessions unless as a means to get me to talk.

We had two sessions that stayed along that level of chat. I liked Nigel a lot and in one session I made a clay skull. Nigel asked me why I'd made it and I couldn't tell him. I didn't know. He asked if I'd like to add anything to it? I was scared. What if Brenda knew I'd made a skull? She already didn't like me drawing scary pictures. I wanted to add a dagger to it, right through the head. Nigel agreed he'd keep it for me and I could do that next week.

Chapter 28

Maybe it was the way he gave me time to speak or the choice not to. Maybe it was because I was allowed to paint, drawer or do whatever clay items I wanted with no repercussions if they were ghastly or of a horror nature. Maybe it was just because he was a damn good therapist and I was lucky or maybe it was the picture... I'll never forget that day. I was sat outside the waiting room in the hall. There were toys around a semi circle area some below chairs some in a box in the corner and there was a rocking horse in front of me, a big wooden thing with reigns and everything. The waiting area was empty all apart from me and Nigel was a little late. I didn't mind because I'd been in that position myself where I'd talked so much I'd hit a point where I needed to and that moment was so important Nigel had given me the time needed to do so.

The door opened and a small girl with dark hair walked out in front of Nigel. She walked head up straight past the rocking horse and not making eye contact. She seemed like she'd just found the ultimate confidence. Nigel walked a few paces behind her. I saw him smile to himself as he lifted his head up. I could see he was proud of her. The girl was pretty and I wondered what horrors she had witnessed. I felt good because we had this place and we had Nigel and it reinforced to me that no matter how alone I actually feel. I'm never really alone. There are people like me everywhere. This made me feel sad even though I could feel the strength of this girls energy as she rounded the corner and walked out. I turned to Nigel with my jaw open and stood up. "Hello! Good to see you" He said turning away for me to follow. When I entered the room I noticed to my right an amazing scene. A huge painting of a waterfall, I was awestruck. It was beautiful, a cliff face with a waterfall that appeared to wash away every form of abuse imaginable. I remember thinking "what has she seen?" and I hoped her waterfall would stay with her forever. I don't recall our session although I do remember thinking about the girl a lot. How could I be like her? Had she seen what I had? Could I be that strong? She was amazing and I wanted to run up to her and hug her, tell her I was proud of her and hope that one day someone would feel that way about me but I knew that if they ever did there was no way I would accept their sympathy.

I soon learnt to trust Nigel. I don't know how that came about other than the freedom to decide if I trusted him or not. Perhaps it was also because Brenda knew nothing of my skull or because Nigel didn't ridicule me. But during one session when Nigel was sat by the desk and I was just standing in front of my chair. I sat down and placed a freshly stirred coffee (complete with clay ridden pencil) by my feet. "My dad killed my mum"I told him convincing myself I was testing him after all I didn't have to tell him anything else.

"Okay" he said continuing his drawing of men and women figures. He'd started last session when I'd given him the silent treatment. It's hard to recall exactly how he got me talking. Yet I know he intrigued me. He made me want to know about him and become friends, But he never said or used the word friends. He never treated me like a client, a number or a wage either. He genuinely seemed to care. He had solid boundaries and ethics. I remember choosing to draw one week but I couldn't think of anything. I didn't tell him. I just sat there with my pen (My choice) and paper. I used to draw in Biro with my granddad and loved having black, blue, green and red to draw with. I didn't use the green at all. My figures were men fighting in martial arts and usually involved a lot of blood or were stabbing each other. Sometimes I'd make them as graphic as I could. The tops of heads missing with the brain hanging out and the spine sticking through. Blood everywhere or grim reapers chopping off arms and legs. I knew it made me feel better and knew in some way I was drawing things that others weren't. I drew on school books, at Brenda's and every change I got. I wasn't very good and didn't care. When Brenda saw them she said they were horrible. "Why would you draw that?" So I did it all the more to piss her off.

The images became Brenda, Jim, Clive, bullies and even my grandparents. But on some level all of them were me and Wenzel. None had identifying marks. It was impossible to tell who was who. I didn't want Nigel thinking I was crazy, So I didn't draw. I sat staring at this blank piece of paper most of the session. Nigel got some clay and made a shape mounding it expertly. He seemed amused at his creations. "Want to try?" he said squishing his man of clay and handing it to me. "How?" I said handing it back.

"Thud!" the clay landed on my blank sheet of paper crushing all the things I remembered drawing but hadn't touched. "I don't know it's your creation" he said smiling and returned to his desk.

I had ten minutes left of session. I started to shape the clay, arm complete I set to work on another arm. I remember so clearly concentrating to make each piece the same size. Somewhere I zoned into my own world without realizing. Clive I'd make Clive. Clive beat my dad we got made homeless, we lived in a car, we went into care, father killed mother, I'd make Clive, nobody would know who it was. It's just a figure. Clive two long legs, thick and strong. A big body. I glanced up "Nigel, I'm over time" I said.

"Today you can carry on if you want to I have nobody waiting" I got back to work on the body and head. I placed the figure stood up in front of me. Double checking. Two arms, two legs, body and a head. "Clive" I saw him in my head stood at Nan's. "I want a word with you" I felt my fear, Caroline's fear. I saw his drunken eyes and felt his intent. The alcohol smell I'd blocked out the instant I realised I had to run. I stared through the clay Clive. Alan was fighting him again this time in my memories. I saw Alan hit the floor and bite Clive. Then Alan grab his head and shout "run!" his face scared, scared for me not for himself. Then I watched my friend trip over my foot, toppling and slam into the darkness as the radiator vibrated then his head hit the floor with a hollow thud. The sound unlike anything I'd heard before or since. I stared at "Clive".

"Trace?" Nigel asked as we'd agreed that's what he'd call me in "my room". I looked at him. I could feel the pain my eyes. I closed down immediately. "What?" I asked with a look. "Want to tell me who it is?" he asked me.

"No" I said.

"Okay. You've done a good job, will you tell me if I guess?" He said sitting forwards.

"Yeah" I laughed.

"Is it male?" Nigel asked.

"Yeah he's male" I said glancing from Nigel's elaborative friendly face to the evil anger inducing clay Clive figure who just stood looking out at us. I lay him down gently.

"Why did you lay him down?" Nigel asked me.

I shrugged.

"No answer is wrong" Nigel said.

"I forgot to do eyes. It's not very good" I lied.

"And the real reason?" Nigel asked.

I started at Nigel for a full minute with zero response. He didn't fold his arms or lean back. He didn't end the session or go back to drawing. He just sat smiling at me with all this care on his face like my answer meant the world to him.

"I don't want him to watch us. To hear us". I said.

"Thank you" Nigel said cracking me a huge smile. His beard rising with his white teeth.

"Eh?" I asked.

"For trusting me, whatever you say to me stays between you and me, There's no wrong answers" he said.

"Then why do you write it down?" I asked him.

"I have to take notes but never specifics. I write to show my boss but never what's said between us. Would you like to see?"

My turn to trust him. "No, it's okay" I answered.

"You can see my notes anytime you like" he said "it's your room" he added.

"I'm way over time, sorry" I said grabbing my coat from the back of my chair.

"Do you want to go?" he asked elaborating on the word "want".

"No" I said.

"Then let me have a smoke and we'll talk about this clay man of yours, come on" he said heading out the door. I followed with my coat on.

"You won't tell anyone?" I asked.

"Nope" he said exhaling into the sky. A car went past "then what do you tell the boss?" I asked him.

"I tell them what I need to. If you used clay I say you made progress with clay and started talking me today. If it's okay with you I'll say today you started to trust me?" he asked me.

"But I won't say what we said or who you made. No personal

details". I nodded. A car went past again. Which is your car? I asked pointing to the car park.

"I don't drive" he said. I was stunned and saw him again with new eyes and realised I knew nothing about this man. "Why?" I asked. "Never saw the point. Lots of buses so I never learnt" he replied.

"Everyone I know drives" I said.

"You don't have to do what everyone else does" he said a wicked grin spreading across his face. The sun was out.

We went back inside where Clive seemed to take up the whole room. "I have a question" Nigel said making a brew. I looked at him in reply expecting him to ask about my clay man. "Clive" I said out loud. "sorry?" Nigel said. "Him-Clive" I replied pointing "My uncle".

"You're angry with him" he said telling me, not asking.

"What makes you say that?" I asked levelly. "See anything different or unusual on him?" He asked me. "No" I said "two arms, two legs, a body and a head," I said not looking.

"look closely" Nigel said. I did. My clay Clive had a head, two legs, a body and one arm. I'd checked twice, I'd taken ages over it. Only Nigel and me had been in the room. The door was locked when we left. I must have missed an arm and not even realised. "Why does he make you angry?" He said passing me a hot coffee cup covered in fresh clay fingerprints.

"He, he, he, shit, fuck, sorry" I said sighing.

"It's okay" he said with a nod prompting me to continue. "He, He, I can, can't, can't T,T,T,T Shit!" I said placing the cup down. "It's hard to talk?" Nigel asked me. "Yes" I nodded.

"Be right back" Nigel left and I heard him tell Brenda we'd be a while longer. When he returned I said "She's here, I gotta go, she'll be mad." I said.

"Fuck her, she can wait" he said and I creased up laughing.

I must have looked totally shocked "It's okay you can blame me" he said. I smiled Nigel was okay. "You were telling about clay man Clive?" He said.

"He killed my mum I know it, I was there." I said.

"When Clive killed mum?" Nigel asked.

"N,N,No, No when he, B,b,beat dad up" I stuttered explaining.

"Ah okay, bit of a bastard is he?" Nigel asked.

I nodded relaxing a little "Yes I was in the living room when the door went, Clive and Phil came in...." I recited how my uncles had beat Wenzel up and how Clive had used the ironing board to break his back and how Wenzel had said when they left he'd of used the hammer behind the curtain if he'd known it was there."

"Thank you". Nigel said pulling his chair close to mine quickly, before he'd reached me I'd stood up sending my chair flying and moved against the wall arms up ready to fight or run. "Sorry" he said still seated. "It's okay, I was going towards Clive, I didn't mean to startle you, I'd not hurt you" he added. I dropped my arms feeling foolish and ashamed. "Sorry" I nodded. "let's give him some eyes." Nigel said taking a pencil and doing two dots"

"What would you like to do to him?" He said to Clive standing on the large shelf that came out at waist height.

"No" I said standing next to Nigel. Nigel took a piece of clay from the sack rolled it and snapped it. "We can break it up" he said re rolling the clay then he pulled it apart "tear it limb from limb" he said smiling. He rolled it and took a plastic knife and fork out. "Prod it" he said poking it with the fork" or cut it up into pieces" he said slicing an end off his sausage shaped clay. He put the knife, fork and pencil down together next to one another and besides clay Clive and said "I'm going to get up and walk to my desk now, okay?" I nodded staring at the stood up Clive. I took Nigel's sausage shaped clay and gave Clive another arm. I sat down in front of him and lay Clive face up. I sat calm, arms in my lap and saw Clive, I threw myself into the images of him stood over me, strangling me, hanging me over the balcony, stealing from my Nan, fighting with Alan, hitting his wife. I felt the pain. I watched it play out all around me. Only Clive and me existed now. Him and I, no rules apart from mine. It's okay to do anything. I took the pencil and marked a cross on Clive's chest like the one on my nan's coffin and placed the pencil down gently. I sat back.

"Do what you want to do" Nigel said quietly. I heard him but I couldn't see him. Clive had taken up every vision, all of my perception. My hands had moved without thought or intent at such speed. I'd grabbed the knife and plunged it into Clive's hest and face over and over. The knife broke clean in half. I threw the broken plastic blade and carried on frenzied with the handle. "You bastard!. You bastard!" The knife handle slipped and cut my little finger. I threw it punching Clive instead into a little mess of clay. Nigel was holding me and I was on fire. Adrenaline sweeping through my body in volcanic waves. I never took my eyes off Clive. I swung again and again brushing Nigel off I collapsed in a heap on the floor. "Why? Why?" I screamed to the ceiling. Nigel was on all fours facing me. "It's okay, let it out" He said "bastard!, Bastard," I said calming my voice but not my body as I continued to pound the empty floor. Tired I looked at Nigel. "let me guess, you don't want to see me any more".

"Wha.." he tried to speak "it's okay" I said "I wouldn't either. You want to know what I want to do? How I feel?" I pulled Clive back into a ball.

"It's okay to be angry in here" Nigel said.

"Angry," I said totally calm. I stepped back seeing Clive's face in the ball and took up an Aikido stance. "I'll fucking kill him" stepping forwards I chopped the ball sending it splattering in all directions and hurting my hand a lot. As quickly as I was angry is as quickly as I became calm I turned to Nigel "I am sorry, you don't need this, I have to go". I said. I was totally relaxed. "I'll see you next week." He said smiling. "Yeah, right" I replied.

"I will" he said opening the door for me. "Oh before you go, remember you don't have to talk to anyone about anything you don't want to." He put his hand on my shoulder and it felt good. We walked to Brenda. "How did it go?" she asked. I looked at Nigel. "He's doing great, He'll tell you if he wants to" he said and walked off. Just turned on his heel and walked away. Nobody treated Brenda like that. I was dead impressed.

In the car Brenda repeatedly asked how it went. I ignored her. In my head I was in my own room with Nigel when she pulled up she said "I'm not sure you should go to scouts if you won't talk to me Tracie". I smiled "I ain't telling you shit" I responded.

Chapter 29

Seeing Nigel became a nice break from the chores of home and school, boxing was on and off when I could get the chance and my paper round was going well. The lady at the shop usually bunged me a packet of crisps or a wispa bar when I dropped in to say I'd completed the round. She was friendly and I liked her. She also didn't bat an eyelid when I bought my smokes from them and said they were for a friend.

Louise had started helping me in maths and I helped her with English. Louise knew I was self harming but she didn't know to what extent. She'd seen me etch marks into my arm with a compass but not seen the cuts I'd made with the ruler.

She was prodding me beneath the table in maths lesson with a pen whenever the teacher turned around and we were generally having a laugh. She'd do the Math and I'd copy her work as she explained it to me. I didn't understand anything Miss Lourne was saying . I grabbed Louise's wrist as she came at me again with the pen she grabbed my forearm with her other hand and I flinched away as the pain shot up my arm. "What is it?" she asked genuinely concerned "nothing" I said pulling my seat in further and moving my arm away from her. "Not your fault, don't worry about it" I added trying to pay attention to Miss Lourne a mid forties lady with curly hair and big thick glasses. "Well Tracie you seem talkative today, What's the answer?" She said turning to face me. I was relieved Louise wouldn't know about my arm because she'd give me a right roasting but I was horrified to be the centre of attention. My mind jumped to being against the wall at Wenzels and then being stood in front of the table at Brenda's reciting sums and I turned red with embarrassment. "Dunno?" I said quietly. "What do you think it could be?" She asked not letting up. "I don't know" I said louder "but what do you *think* it is?" She tried again. "I think you should fuck off! I don't know!" I shouted, "Outside!" She shouted back pointing a long ruler towards the door. She expected me to wait outside for a roasting. I was through giving people what they wanted. I walked down the hall, the stairs and right up to reception where I turned left and walked out the front entrance. I headed to the fields where I was both alone and free.

On another occasion it was a science teacher who caught the wrath of my tongue. I was chatting with my friend Lee when the teacher interrupted "Tracie I suggest you quieten down" He'd singled me out from others talking together and I wasn't backing down. I had it in my head that if I backed down to one person then everyone else would see it as a weakness and decide to have a go. If I was seen as a push over for just a second then I'd be hurt by others. I couldn't have that and to add to it I felt everyone was trying to parent me because I didn't have parents. I didn't make the connection that they were just doing the normal teacher thing. They were having a go at me because I didn't have parents to stand up for me or they were sympathising because I didn't have parents. Either way it amounted to the same thing *I was different than everyone else. I deserved to be treated like this.* I was sick of it. "I suggest you kiss my ass" I replied looking at my friend who promptly put his head in a book to cover the laughter. "What did you say?" Mr Jackclough said. A taller man with light brown hair and a small spot that was always white on his head. "I suggest you kiss my ass" I responded. "Get out!" He told me not taking his eyes from mine as I slowly walked out of the room. I returned the glare. He came out five minutes later.

"Right you!" He said stepping closer and pointing his finger in my face. "This is my lesson and if you think..." I didn't hear the rest I was watching his finger get closer and closer as his words sped up. He was getting angry and only just had control. I had to think fast. If I eyeballed him or ran I'd be hit I was certain. I didn't know what the answer was here so did what I felt was right as I concentrated on this finger getting closer and closer to my eyes. "Do it" I said as calmly and flatly as I could and looked up into his eyes flatly and as though I couldn't care less. I wasn't looking for confrontation. My body language said "I don't care"."If you're going to hit me, do it" I repeated. That's when the furnace started to build inside me. The familiar shake of adrenaline and fear. The flight or fight kicking in. "I'm a teacher at this school...." he began still with a raised and fast voice. He stepped back slightly I ignored him and walked off. He didn't follow me. My tempter was getting worse. I felt if I got hit then at least it took my mind off what was happening in my head. If someone simply asked if I wanted a coffee I took it as my duty to have already made them one or that I wouldn't be allowed so there was no point in asking and they were just taunting me as Wenzel had done. One of Wenzels games was to take a tune sweet from his pocket and ask if we wanted a tune. When we said yes he'd reply "tralala lala lala la" if I said no he'd reply "good, you weren't getting one anyway". I trusted nobody.

`I was in the playground on a concrete football pitch playing football with Kap, Keel, Graham and a couple of others lads when a tiny girl ran over to Kap holding her face and crying he eyes out. She was thin with long brown hair all messed up and she was red faced from crying. Keel held her closely "Keel's sister" Kap said reading my thoughts next to me. "Who did this?" Keel asked I could see his body tense where he tried to remain calm for his sister. She moved her hands to show us her nose was bleeding. I approached with Keel in tow as Keel's pale face turned red with anger making his ginger hair stand out even more. I'd never seen him angry. "Stuart kicked a ball in her face" he said looking out over her head as he stroked her hair. "Accident?" I asked her leaning down. "No" she said shaking her head and sobbing "I'll do him!" Kap shouted stepping forwards and moving the girl to one side "no" I said evenly placing my hand on his chest "what?" He said confused thinking I was protecting Stuart "I'll do him. You have family and you're on your last warning here" I said gesturing towards the school building. "Next time you get expelled. You're needed here." I added. I nodded to the girl. "No mate she's my sis..." he began "listen, you'll need a fucking job to take care of that sister and your family. I won't I don't have family. I'll do him. " I said strongly. "I don't have family" I said solemnly not looking at him. Keel looked at me like a brother for about three seconds. "Where?" I asked the girl before Keel could speak I'd later find out her name was Kristine. "Field behind economics class" she told me wiping her nose as Keel was holding her head back to stop the bleeding.

Louise's cousin was playing football with Stuart and Graham. I ignored Stuart watching us I was just here to play football. I approached James, Louise's cousin a medium build lad who I liked he was quiet and kept himself to himself. "Hey mate, what happened with Stuart?" He told me Kristine had asked if she could play and Stuart had told her "you want to play? Play with this!" Then kicked the ball into her face. James mimed the action to me, it was no accident. "Thanks mate. I know you're Stuarts friend and I like you but I'm dropping him don't get involved yeah?" I didn't wait for an answer. He'd try and talk me out of it and out of respect for Louise I'd not want to drop James to be fair I did hear a "no problem mate" as I walked away. "Graham!" I shouted up the other end of the pitch "here mate" he walked over all confidant I hoped he wasn't going to get in the way. He'd be a major problem if he decided I shouldn't do this but something about his over confidant walk told me he wasn't getting involved. He didn't want trouble but was preparing himself for it if it came. "I'm dropping Stuart let me play football for five minutes and make sure he gets the ball" I told him making it sound as much like a question as I could. "Okay" he said nodding to two guys and telling them I'm on their team. "What's he doing" I heard Keel say to Kap as I walked over "Sorting shit out, watch" Kap said. Kap knew me pretty well. If I said I was going to do something I did it whether it was smart or not.

The ball came to me and I sent it on to James who sent it on to Graham, He booted it up the pitch and nobody moved apart from

Stuart. I ran up behind him and punched him in the side of the head as he turned with the ball. He didn't see it coming but immediately tried curling into a ball, on the way down I jumped and brought my food down hard on the back of his calf. He fell covering his face and curling up into a tight ball but then sat up protecting his face. I Hooked him maybe four or five times trying to break his guard down before he just fell and brought his knee's up into a ball. I landed a boot to the curled up Stuart and bent down throwing punches. I hated ground fighting, I wasn't trained in it and hated more that he'd not fought back. Jab, jab, cross opening his guard and catching him on the chin. "What's your name!?" I shouted stepping back into the gathering crowd and looking at the young girl who's name I'd forgotten in the adrenaline fuelled moment. "Kristine" Keel answered for her. I took her arm and pulled her over with me then grabbed Stuart by the shirt "You so much as look at that girl and I'll kill you. Do you understand?" As I'd grabbed Kristines arm I'd seen teachers approaching. *Fuck it* "well?" I said throwing a jab then a cross into his arms to get the message across *I want an answer.* "Yeah, yeah, sorry" he said. I walked off giving Graham a thank you nod as I left. "That should have been me" Keel said beside me. "Don't be stupid. You get that carpenter job you want" I replied. "Why did you do that?" he asked me "because if shit was the other way around you'd do it for me" I told him, which was true. I knew he would and he knew about my father killing my mother however I couldn't tell him the truth it would be too weird. Kap and Keel were family they were people I could trust, people I could rely on and I'd never had that before. Besides I might have told them directly about my past but I felt everyone knew anyway, it's a small town and I doubt little Jim and Caroline keep their mouths closed for long so fuck it. Everyone must know I don't care if they didn't think I was crazy before they do now.

I'd finished my paper round and was on the rob at the local newsagents. I'd picked up a packet of Polo's and two packets of fruit pastels as I walked towards the till I shoved the fruit pastels up my wrist into the rubber band I had there. I placed the polo's on the counter "just these mate" I said. "And the fruit pastels" the big fella answered nodding to the C.C.T.V camera I'd not spotted. "What?" I asked "Empty your pockets" he said "Fuck you, keep the Polo's" I replied heading for the door. He stopped me just as I reached the pavement by grabbing my arm. "Get the fu...." I'd started as I noticed Paula watching me from outside the shop. She was stationary just twiddling something in her fingers. She shook her head slowly. I felt so ashamed of myself, I'd upset her and hoped I could make it up. I took the Pastels from my pocket "sorry, I stole them" I told the man. "Don't come back" he said leaving me facing Paula in the street her hair was down either side of her face like a waterfall circling the sun. She had tight jeans on and a football top. "If you needed money I'd of given it to you" she told me innocently searching my face for why I'd be thieving. I mean, it must be because I was hungry? Right? I could see myself through her eyes and I didn't look good to her. "I'm not hungry" I said, telling her the truth became so important in that moment. Maybe she'd understand, maybe she'd change me, accept me or still be a friend. I fumbled for words that should have said "hey, I was just stupid. I need a distraction from the shit I feel inside. I'm sorry! I didn't mean to hurt you!" But what I actually said was "I don't know why I....." I was cut off by the silence of her turning around and walking away. I felt awful why did I only realise how much people meant to me when I'd hurt them or they left? Why did I not see she cared before? *That's right, walk away, everyone else has.*

Chapter 30

I was grounded, I wasn't allowed out to play or to go to scouts and Brenda found issue with everything I did. I don't even know why I was grounded. Maybe it was when we went on holiday and I brought big Jim, who is welsh an ornamental sheep I'd told him "there's a hole in the back so you can you know.....hang it up?" With a smile, or the time I told him to fuck off. Perhaps it was because Nigel had promised to meet me for the blood test to decide who my dad was but when I got there Brenda wouldn't let me go and get Nigel. Instead she held me down whilst I had the needle and told me Nigel didn't care enough about me to turn up so I'd called her a bitch. Who knows? It could have been anything but I was grounded so I read a lot.

Brenda wanted me being a part of the family and I flat out refused so it was time to see Nigel again. He'd gained my trust by this time and knew my biggest problem was Brenda. I was angry with Nigel for not turning up for the blood test like he promised he would, so when Brenda got me in the car to visit I was not happy. I ignored him for twenty minutes then he went for his smoke."You weren't there" I said. "Where?" he asked me. I told him about the blood test "I didn't know" he said showing me his diary. He'd been told it was the week after. Brenda had lied to him and to me. Nigel apologised a lot and told me he'd be talking to Brenda about her behaviour. He did and Brenda never let up about what a bad therapist he was and how he is a bad influence on me. This just got me more angry with her. She was a constant irritation to the point that in the end I told her "He's better to me than you'll ever be" that didn't go down well either, seriously, honesty hurts.

During what was left of our session I told Nigel "my mum's grave is near here. I want to see it" He said that he'd try and get permission to take me off the premises and was there anything else he could do? "Yes, I want Brenda to stop asking about what I tell you. She's not my mum she has no right to know". "Okay, I'll deal with it" Nigel told me nodding and he did. Brenda ignored me all the way home. She must have had a right bollocking. The week went well. I was still grounded and it was the holidays. I was grounded until I apologised I remember that much but whatever it was I'd done I wasn't apologising for it.

Louise knocked on our front door "Sorry I can't come out" I told her.

"Why what's up?" She asked.

"Dunno but I can't come out until I apologise" I told her.

"Apologise then and come out sheesh!" she said rocking her head left and right. She had a ribbon in her hair, it was red.

"No chance" I said "but before you go, got a smoke?" I added. She handed me two in a pack and left. Brenda came to the door I explained it was Louise and I couldn't go out. I walked away leaving Brenda holding the door open "Tracie you can go out if you apologise?" She asked me calmly but loud enough for Louise to hear. "No" I said picking my book up and heading for the conservatory. She set the ironing board up in the adjoining dining room so I closed the door. I wanted to be on my own. She opened it "You've been in all day why don't you go out in the garden?" She asked. Ah I knew this game. Wenzel used to play it if I got up to go out I'd be told "if you apologise" If I didn't I was in trouble, either way I was screwed. I was dying to tell her I'd been in for two weeks straight but thought better of it and headed out the front door. Nigel Willowood was playing with a remote controlled car on the road. I stood talking to him from the drive for ten minutes checking the curtains every now and then to make sure I wasn't being watched. Nigel's parents were religious like Brenda and Jim but as far as I knew like me Nigel had little faith.

I lit my smoke and walked our of the drive behind Louise's hedge.

"Those will kill you if Brenda doesn't first" Nigel told me smiling. I laughed "fuck Brenda and fuck death I don't care mate" I meant it whole heartedly. I didn't care about me. We chatted for five minutes when Nigel said "big Jim". I crushed the ciggy into my hand and it stung like hell. "Tracie are you smoking?" Big Jim asked me leaning forwards and pushing his shoulders out. "What? Hell no" I replied facing him then turning back to Nigel. "I'm sure I saw smoke, Nigel?" Big Jim asked. Nigel said nothing. "OK well if you weren't smoking you won't mind swearing on the bible will you?" Big Jim said. I shot him a "what the hell?" look. This game was new. "You put your hand on the bible and repeat. I swear on the bible I've not been smoking" he continued "God will strike you down if you have" Nigel took two steps backwards and turned pale "don't do it man" he said. "okay" I replied slapping my hand on the bible my left still contained the brewing blister and remains of a crushed smoke. "I swear I have not been smoking" I said. "in the name of God" Big Jim added. "I swear in the name of God I've not been smoking" I repeated leaving my hand on the bible and meeting big Jim's eyes. He was trying to fuck with me, two can play that game. Big Jim moved the bible "okay then lads, carry on" he said walking home. "You crazy bastard!" Nigel said "what?" I asked peeling the paper and tobacco from the hand. "You swore on the bible!" He said. "Yeah, didn't even get to finish my smoke" I said pulling my last one from the pack and lighting up. Shortly after Nigel went home and I went back to Brendas.

I didn't think for a second at therapy I'd get to see to see mum's grave. I waited in the waiting room. It was summer. There was a rocking horse opposite me and Nigel was ten minutes late. A girl came out. She looked happy, healthy and normal with Nigel, She left. Nigel gave me a "hi!" Smiled and asked if I was ready to see my mum's grave. I said "yes, who's the girl?"

"She's one of my guests like you" he replied. I liked that but hoped she hadn't seen the things I had.

We went into his room on the wall was a huge painting of a freshly done waterfall. It was stunning. My jaw dropped. There was a huge cliff and trees and an enormous cascading waterfall. I was awestruck. That young innocent girl made this I thought. Beautiful. "What do you think?" Nigel asked me.

"I love it, It's great. But it's sad" I said.

"Why is it sad?" He asked.

"She just wants to be clean. To wash away the pain. To stand natural like a tree, Strong but clean. She can't though because the mountain is in the way. That doesn't make sense does it?" I asked.

"You'd make a good therapist one day" Nigel said.

"No, I'm joining the army" I replied as we headed out the door, we got to the cemetery and I tried to remember from mum's funeral where it was and was able to manage it. Nigel and I arrived to find the stone had other names on it. My granddads, my nans, my mums and one I didn't recognise. Which later would turn out to be my uncles' child. A baby cousin I never knew. Nigel asked me what I felt, but I couldn't say. He left me alone for five minutes. My mum's surname was wrong. She didn't have my surname. She had my granddads brothers' surname. (her maiden name) which must have meant my parents weren't married and my dad was actually my granddads brother. Looking back now this makes little sense but at the time. Not knowing who my dad was and seeing the wrong surname on mum's headstone I believed my granddads brother (who mum had slept with) was my father. I was in a state of complete shock. Nigel asked me questions on the way back to session. I ignored them until he asked if I was OK "Yes I'm not angry with you. I want to see your notes" I needed to know my name.

He showed me my notes. My name was Tracie Daily. My father's surname. I was totally confused. Was my mum even my mum? Who am I? Under today's notes Nigel had written "Tracie appeared Morose at mum's grave" I asked him what "morose" meant.

"Sad" he told me.

"I'm not sad. I don't need help. nobody's help. I'm not stupid" I replied.

I didn't even know who I was. I knew who would though – Wenzel.

Chapter 31

I was reading in the conservatory on account of my grounded status. "You can't read all day you know, play a game or put the computer on" Brenda told me poking her head through the double glazed doorway. "Okay" I replied totally intent on doing my own thing until and I don't know why that moment or where the idea came from, maybe I'd just had enough but the inspiration was instant. "Can I get a game from upstairs?" I asked her "of course you can" she replied knowing all the games were two player and I'd have to get someone to play with and make myself part of the family.

I had no interest in a game but off I went up the stairs into her room and routed through the drawer until I found a letter we'd received from Wenzel. I took one and left the rest as they were before I came downstairs. "Nothing you wanted?" Brenda asked me. "Erm, no It's okay, I'll put the computer on" I stuttered wondering how long before I was caught and kicked myself for forgetting the game. I turned the megadrive console on and waited until Brenda was taking the washing upstairs before I checked the letter. Finally! An address in Chester! I'd never known the address, we weren't allowed to know just as our letters all had to be checked by Brenda and Jim and redone if they said anything that could make them look bad. Twenty minutes must have passed and it was nearing 2:30pm my paper round didn't start until 3:30pm and although grounded that was considered my job so I had to do it. "You can't sit on the computer all day you know why don't you play in the garden?" She now insisted. I knew she would. She always did. When I'd asked for a game I'd done it in ear shot of the living room around her family where she would be as good as gold but as soon as their backs were turned she would make life as hard as she could for me and besides I was still grounded. "I'm grounded?" I asked her trying to figure out what was happening now. "No, you are ungrounded as of yesterday?" She told me. I snapped "I can't read, I can't play on the game I can't go out and I can't stay in. What can I do?" I replied looking at her questioningly. "He's off again" I heard little Jim pipe up from the kitchen. "Go outside and play" Brenda told me. I left the megadrive turned on grabbed my book and walked out.

I sat on the back door step reading. No more than five minutes had passed and she was out "what are you doing there?" She asked. I just looked at her. She should know by now if you ask me a stupid question you'll get a stupid answer. Several seconds passed before I informed her "reading" and sighed. I felt the letter move slightly in my pocket. "Go and play" she said taking my book. Fuming I stormed off "where are you going?" She shouted "paper round!" I yelled back carrying my bike and bag from the garage. "Oh no you're not it's too early!" She screeched walking purposefully towards me. "Yes, I am" I said throwing my leg over the bike and peddling away. *Bitch, bitch, bitch, bitch* I repeated over and over to myself as I threw my legs into a steady rhythm. Big Jim was home and he'd probably follow me in the car. I looked back to see no sign of him. Then he'd say something dumb then we'd argue then I'd go back...unless..I wasn't where he expected me to be?

What are your choices? I asked myself like my scout leader had taught me. Kap,Keel,Louise,Stoppy,Nigel,Paula? No, she knew all of them and I couldn't drag Paula into this. Where do you want to be? I asked myself skidding to a stop at the bottom of the hill. With my family. I remembered Nigel telling me to do what I want to do because it's my life and I should have the choice okay he wasn't referring to Wenzel but it was my life and it was my choice? I opened the letter and the address burnt into the back of my mind. How do I find Chester? How would you find it in scouts? I cycled towards the bigger roads until I saw a sign saying "Chester 24 miles". I had no idea how long that would take or how far a mile was as we always hiked in kilometres. I could do 4 kilometres an hour with a full rucksack on in hiking boots. How long would it take on a bike with no rucksack? You won't know until you start going. I was sweating a lot and had to regulate my breathing like on a hike. The Summer sun didn't help the sweating much either. What do I need? I asked myself I had nothing. Just my T-Shirt and trousers, my letter, my bag and my bike. I had no pen knife, map or first aid kit this was dumb. No! Don't think like that! Remember the pyramid in scouts. A fire needs fuel, air and a light source. A man needs his skills, food and water. With skills you can get food and water. What don't I need? I asked myself. Well you don't need that luminous orange fucking bag for a start! I chucked the bag in a forest and immediately felt bad. My scout leader would have a fit as I'd dirtied the forest even though it was a perfect observation sign and kept blowing out behind me. I had no choice. I couldn't do anything about the bike so I turned my T-Shirt inside out and put it back on then carried on to a big roundabout. I asked a dog walker for directions and was pointed towards Chester. How would I remember the way back? Are you going back? What happens if you can't find it? Shut up! Shut up! I insisted of myself and finally pulled in at Chester beside the zoo. I'd still not had a drink and was now searching for Hoole Thankfully the fourth person I stopped knew the location and it wasn't far. My attention must have lapsed as one minute I was riding on the pavement and the next a car was right next to me. I swerved and went into a wall. I was fine however my front wheel was buckled. I couldn't even push it without it grating. I spent ages trying to figure out where Hoole started and where it finished by now I was cooling down and so was the evening air. I asked more and more people for this address until one guy said "you having a laugh mate?" and stormed off. I looked at the building he'd come out of to find not only was I stood on the right road but I was outside the right address.

Chapter 32

It looked like a large house from the outside and had no features that suggested it was a half way house for criminals. I don't know what I expected. Maybe something that looked like a prison perhaps. Whatever I expected, this wasn't it. I looked at the door at the end of the path. It was blue then I looked at the series of windows on the left. Would he be in? Would he be happy? Sad? Would he be the same dad I knew before? I was certain he'd have changed for the better. In my head he'd hug me and tell me he missed me. "Everything would be alright. I'm sorry. Let me explain everything." That's what he'd say and it would be alright. I'd understand whatever it was he told me and we'd get the family back. I was certain that he'd changed into a version of Alan.

After prison he'd of had to see the light. Change his ways. It would be perfect. Did I really want to do this knowing what he was like before? I could go back to Brenda's and accept the roasting. I could tell her I went camping and grow up in care and work at the packaging company with big Jim. We'd play golf at the weekends and they would buy me a car. Perhaps they would even adopt me and when I'd made enough money I'd leave them forever and get married and my son would work at a packaging company and we'd all be a fake kind of happy for ever. No, fuck that, I may not have much but he's my dad. My way might be harder but.. I mentally slapped myself around a bit and just knocked on the fucking door. I didn't even know if he still lived there. I only had a letter. No answer. I knocked again harder and an older man in his late forties opened the door. He had greying hair and jeans which were too tight and a brown shirt that was too big. "hello, can I help you?" He said chirpily. "Erm, yeah. I have a letter. I'm looking for Wenzel Daily?" I informed him. "Nobody by that name here son....Daily...hold on a minute" he said chewing his finger nail. "It's okay Frills" Wenzel said from behind him. "He's here to see me" he added as the door opened some more and my father stood there.

"Ah Stella , there you are. Stella isn't your name then? We thought you were fishing" Frills told him. "Frills, that's my son" Wenzel said not moving at all and eyeing me like he half expected me to be there all along but he had other plans. He was intrigued and careful, not scared at all but there was something there which worried him. He wore a suede jacket open with a white shirt beneath and clean blue jeans with his trademark white trainers. He definitely wasn't going fishing. He appeared to be faking shock. "No visitors in your room Stella you know the rules but as it's your son come on in lad" Frills said waving me in. I pointed at my bike which I'd laid against the wall in case I had to make a quick getaway despite the fact that it wouldn't be that quick and I'd be unlikely to get away. "Oh it will be fine there" Frills said pointing to the inner hall way. I didn't move. I hadn't taken my eyes from dads nor him mine. I didn't know what to feel or do. Wenzel seemed to be trying to figure me out. "Put it in the hall it's safe there" he said and I did for once knowing which name to write.

I had to sign in to see dad. Where the halls were big the rooms were bigger. On the right was the office with a large kitchen at the back with no food just tea, coffee, sugar, milk and biscuits. The seating area could hold twenty comfortably. I'd later find out it was on a rota system where each client made meals for the rest of the group. All apart from Wenzel who had already got on the right side of the staff and ate out a lot. Most clients had limits on the distance they were allowed to travel. Wenzel wasn't one of them. "lucky you caught me in. If you'd turned up tomorrow I'd of been at work" he told me casually, something didn't sound right. I nodded and flicked my head to one side questioningly. "Fruit and veg I work the warehouse. It's okay" He was lying I'd caught it when he spoke to Frills earlier. "Come on up" he said turning his back and walking up the stairs. His room was immaculately clean. Kitchen was on the left the bathroom on the right, the toilet sparkled. It had three little ducks in height order along the back of it. I was shown the living room. A black portable television with a blue carpet and a large black chair with a matching two seater sofa. All very clean, the room had a large bay window with a black ash coffee table in the centre of it. On top there was pictures of Jodie, Jonathon, Caroline and me all lined up. I'd fallen into old habits as soon as I'd been alone in the room with him. I just stood there waiting to be told what to do next. "Well, what do you think?" he asked from the doorway and stood directly behind me. I was already in his head without trying. It was a perfect show home for social services, friends and anyone else really. It screamed look at me I'm a nice guy, I can look after myself. This is the home I always wanted but was denied because of circumstance. Did I tell you the story of how much you should feel sorry for me? Trust me? Then my own thoughts kicked in. It's not him. He's changed, maybe, he's changed. Something's wrong. This doesn't feel like it should. No hug, no good to see you, no I love you and no I'm sorry. My response was small. "You have pictures?" Which was exactly what people were supposed to notice and their fore exactly what I was supposed to comment on. "Yeah, I think about you all the time ask anyone. I never shut up about you! Want a brew?" He asked heading to the kitchen. "No thank you, do you have something cold?" I asked his back.

The kitchen was smaller with a tiny drop leaf table and two metal seats either end. A kettle, tea, coffee and sugar pots and an empty draining rack. Something was wrong but I couldn't put my finger on it. There were no pictures in the kitchen. He opened the fridge to get the milk for the coffee. Milk was the only thing in there *something's wrong!* My mind screamed. "I knew you'd come back" he said talking to the cup. "You always took care of people. You'd want to see me well. I'm alright" he said moving his shirt sleeve down. I'd only seen his gold watch, no marks. "I'll be right back I left the biscuits downstairs earlier" he said walking out of the flat. He left the door open and was back almost immediately. He was red faced and had obviously ran. What wasn't I supposed to see here? I checked the corners of the kitchen and hall *no camera's.* "Well you've met Frills, he plays pool he's very good. I got my own flat but

I'm usually working or fishing. I like to keep busy so, you cycled here?" He asked me. "Yeah, I cycled here" I replied. He handed me a coffee ignoring my request for a cold drink.

"From Brenda's?" He asked dunking a biscuit and eyeing me across the table. You killed mum! I thought. I could see it inside him. He wasn't scared of Clive any more or anyone else either. "What happened? You did well to get this far" he asked again. I explained how she'd upset me when I was reading so I left and that she kept trying to get me to call her mum. "I knew you know, I knew when you wrote what a great time you were having that you'd come, I knew when the writing stopped it would be soon" he said obviously in his own world. He didn't reach across and tap my hand. He didn't say I'm sorry. He just sat there with his head over his cup smiling like he knew everything. I knew he wasn't smiling because I was there, he was smiling because he'd been right and in his head he'd got one up on Brenda. "Yeah, she made us write stuff. I said mum was bad because I knew that would help. In the end I refused to write at all if I couldn't write what I wanted to" I told him.

"Bitch!" He said venomously without being loud.

"She says I'll be like you if I do something wrong" I told him. "What do you mean?" He asked me his eyes turning threatening. "She says you're a murderer" I told him looking at the table and waiting for him to explode.

"Oh she did, did she. That's deformation I'll have her for that." he said leaning back and shaking his head the old anger had never left. I didn't know what deformation was but I knew in all my time in care I'd not seen anyone speak or have body language like Wenzel.

"What?" I asked him.

"I'm not a murderer. I was convicted of manslaughter and that means she is lying and by law she can't do that."

"Oh" I said feeling both that he didn't care what she'd done to me and that he definitely had killed mum.

"What happened?" I asked.

"I will tell you but now is not the time. We have to figure out how to get you home okay?" He said.

"Home?" I asked defensively.

"You can't stay here. They won't let you. I have things to sort out here" he said dismissively.

"Sorry I disturbed you" I said honestly and stood up. I wasn't going back.

"No I didn't mean it like that. I want you here If you want to be but it was to be done the right way. Stay here whilst I make a couple of calls okay?" He said I nodded visualising the route down the stairs left into the hall grabbing the bike and out the door into....then what? I need not have started planning my escape. He took the calls directly outside the door and he was pacing. I could barely hear him and then he walked downstairs. This flat had one exit if a social worker or the police came I couldn't run. I went out and heard him on the phone. "Yes but I can't come tonight, what am I supposed to do? Yeah, Yeah, I'll do that yeah." As I approached his tone changed. "Anyway I'll pick up mars bars, yeah that's right mars bars, I'll bring them soon I have to go now" he hung up. "Okay?" He said fake smiling me. The feelings of wanting to hug him and hold on until I'd cried out all my pain were gone. I'd been here maybe an hour and he was cold, distant and had lied to me twice. "All good?" I asked. "yeah I just told my friend can't make it tonight. They understood though I mean fishing can wait it's not every day your son shows up is it!" He answered. "I should go now" I told him. "You do want to live with me don't you?" He asked as though he was uncertain as though he needed me there. "Yes" I said looking at my feet

"Caroline, Jodie and Jonathon too" I added looking at his eyes. "One step at a time. It's not easy. If I keep you here I'll get in trouble and so will you. If I say you came here looking to live with me and I took you home because it's best for you at the moment then when I get my own proper flat then you can move in" he said opening the door to the pool room.

I didn't move "it didn't work before" I told him flatly. I was remembering the last time I was left somewhere and told it was only a matter of time until they had their own place. "This time is different" he said not turning back to face me. I followed him into the pool room and he set them up. "I'll make a call right here and we'll sort it out" he said pulling his Nokia out. I didn't play pool, I walked around the table looking through the windows for exits. Two by bike and three on foot but I'd loose the bike as I'd have to climb the fence beside the property but then that would be the least likely way they would expect me to go. I could climb the fence and just hedge hop until I found somewhere to hide out. Dad didn't feel like dad I realised. Not like the dad I had in my head anyway but he was dad and he was all I had. "Well? Wanna game?" he asked. I kicked myself for not hearing him come off the phone and kicked myself again for not listening in to the call. "Brenda?" I asked him. "Social services first, I had to tell them and I told them you don't want to live with Brenda and Jim any more so they will find you somewhere else"

"Really!? I asked" "With you and the kids?" I was dying to jump up and down I was so excited for my family!

"Not yet, but soon. For now you go back to Brenda's tonight and then you'll have weekly contact with me if you wish it and only as long as you behave at Brenda's. That's the deal" he told me. I was reminded of a deal I made before where my granddad ended up dead.

"Okay" I said nodding ferociously. In my head I'd got the ball rolling it was only a matter of time before we'd all be back together again. Now I could help Wenzel look after the kids then they couldn't adopt Jonathon and Jodie as they had real family to look after them and Caroline would see I'm fine with Wenzel so I'm sure she'd come back too!

"Great! Okay, I'll be good" I promised.

"I need you to" he replied. Throughout the entire conversation he'd remained standing and impassive. Stood perhaps five feet away and he didn't smile for himself once. He was just "doing what needed to be done." He wasn't sad or angry but he wasn't pleased either. This smile seemed to be for my benefit as though he was smiling to tell me what a great idea this was and convince me it made sense. I knew it made sense and then why was he trying to convince me. I know how he thinks and something wasn't connecting between him and I here. He was still seeing me as an object. No hugs, no pleasure in his body at seeing his son? Nothing? And who was this friend who was getting mars bars?

He showed me how to play pool. He was very good and explained him and Frills play a lot and are the best two players there. He used to play in snooker competitions in Macclesfield too so it's just practice. It was soon time to go. I was silent in the car all the way back whilst my bike was tied down into the boot. I remembered other times I'd been in the car with him. This was a different car but it felt exactly the same only this time I was sat where my mum would have sat and Jonathon, Jodie and Caroline weren't there either. "With my bad back and you now on my side we'll have a flat in no time!" I wasn't sure at first if that was said because I needed to hear it or because he wanted it but he seemed genuinely excited about the flat. "If you're good" he added sternly. "I hate it there" I told him about big Jim knocking my arm. I didn't tell him I got so angry I could have killed him. "Fat welsh bastard!" he shouted. I didn't like him talking like that because big Jim had never really hurt me and he'd never killed anyone but dad was dad and it was my only chance to get the family back together. We pulled up down the road from Brenda's house I thought he had lost the directions when he suddenly stopped. "OK off you go, good to see you. Remember what I said" he told me rapidly as though firing off a shopping list at speed. "My bike?" I asked feeling like I'd just been dismissed. "Untie it, take it out. I told Brenda I wouldn't go on her road or get out of the car that's the condition of me dropping you home" he told me. "What?" I asked. "Stupid cow I know but needs to be done just remember the big picture yeah?" He said eyeballing me as I looked in at him through the door window. I was struggling to undo the knots "fuck it" he said getting out and uncurling a small pen knife "shhhh" he said meaning he wasn't supposed to have it. "Why you got that?" I asked him. "Fishing and for knots like this" he laughed cutting the rope. He lifted my bike out with no problems "go" he said tapping my shoulder. I wondered why he had tapped my shoulder and then realised big Jim was watching us from down the road. "Where's Brenda?" I asked Wenzel "she's the boss she always comes out" I added. "too scared I guess and she fucking should be too" he replied. "Go, remember what I said" he waved to big Jim and got back in the car. I pushed my bike down the road to meet Big Jim. He only left the front door step when Wenzel had gone.

Chapter 33

The atmosphere inside was terrible. Brenda stared into the distance whenever I was around her and hardly spoke to me. Little Jim passed me in the hall "you shouldn't have done that" he said without malice. Was he scared too? Why was everyone scared? What didn't I know? I walked into the kitchen "Hi Brenda, what should I do now I'm late for tea?" I asked her honestly. "You can do whatever you choose Tracie" she said staring through the kitchen window. It kind of reminded me of my first memory of mum. I was shocked she sounded like she really didn't care. She wasn't even fake caring any more she just plain didn't give a shit. "Thanks" I said and walked towards the living room where Caroline and Rita were sat. Rita got up and walked past me to go to bed. "What's going on?" I said to Caroline. "We didn't know where you were" she said shaking her head at me. Did nobody get it? Was I fucking crazy? I ignored her and went to bed.

Suddenly all grounding had stopped. I had purpose and things were working okay. Caroline and Brenda's family still weren't talking to me but to be fair I'd hardly made the effort myself. The scout event I couldn't have previously I was now allowed to go to. I really enjoyed Jamboree there were hundreds of other scout groups and girls in scouting which we'd never had and seemed very strange. It didn't seem right somehow. I'd not read about female soldiers and didn't expect any in scouts. We were split into two dormitories six people in each room. I was with four lads I didn't know and one lad I'd got chatting to at my scout group but who wasn't in my patrol. I didn't know him well. One of the unknowns had a big mouth he had an even bigger friend was was actually quite smart. The first task was to decide what to call ourselves. Our group outside the dormitory consisted of Kate, a brown haired girl, the mouthy kid, a big lad and a quiet boy. I knew nobody until Kate introduced herself. They threw ideas around until the big lad came up with "The northern lights!" Kate's eyes glazed as she went into a dream world.

Mouthy kid said "Yeah, yeah man like being high man and all that wicked shit!" Normal lad nodded and big lad looked at me. I knew nothing about the Northern lights but the way gobby kid went on and Kate's eyes glazed in her lightly tanned face I guessed it was drugs. "Yeah man, fuck, do it, as long as they don't get it we are on!" I said trying to fit in and sticking my thumb in the direction of the scout leaders "yeah, whatever" big lad said. Kate gave me a smile which was quite nice but seemed more sympathetic than acknowledging. "So what are the Northern lights man? Really?" Gobby kid shot off eyeballing me. I leaned in "drugs man, drugs" I must have sounded like a right loon and probably looked it too. I was wearing green camouflage jacket just like Rodneys from the T.V show Only fools and horses which had staff sergeant Brown on the side and the front pocket. I loved it as dad had bought it for me and I wore it everywhere.

Another day on camp and they had stalls out. One was boxing with giant gloves way too big to box with but it caught my eye. Opposite it was a magician, He made things in a box vanish and did a few slight of hand tricks, then he hands a girl a wand and as he did so it immediately turned into flowers. Her face lit up and I was amazed. Her face fell when he took them back and gave her a balloon instead. I sat having a smoke out of sign but watched him all day. I'd figured out all his tricks apart from the box and the flowers. "Here lad" he said calling me over "you've watched me all day. You like magic?" He asked me. He was tall and thin and looked like a penguin. He was also polite and I liked that it all added up to part of the show. "You're the only one I've seen sir" I said being extra polite in case he told my scout leader he'd seen me smoking. "What do you like most?" he asked me. "Well I know how to do everything apart from " I said leaning on his counter and knocking the box forwards accidently revealing a secret compartment at the back. As penguin clutched at his stall and hid things rapidly again I stepped back apologetically. "Erm, that actually. Sorry and the wand thing, yeah the wand. It's so fast. It's brilliant!" I said getting excited. He started laughing "are you sure you want to know how it's done?" he asked me seriously. "Yeah, yes please sir" I said with a cough. He handed me the wand and I examined it. "Push the button" he told me. I did and it transformed into flowers "wow! Cool!" I said "how do I change it back?" He took the flowers and began turning the end of them slowly until they vanished back inside the wand. "Thanks" I said suddenly depressed. Magic wasn't real. Their happiness was fake. They were tricked. It hadn't really changed into flowers it was just a tool and I'd fallen for it. What an idiot. I thought about it all day what was real? How do I know I'm real? Maybe that tree isn't a tree, maybe it's a wolf like the wand and I just see a tree.

That night in dormitory Gobby was on the bottom bunk opposite me talking to his mate who was on the top bunk above him. "Guys come on, it's late" I said trying to sleep.

"Yeah so?" Gobby piped up.

"So go to sleep" I replied.

"No, what If I don't eh? Eh? I'm talking la,la,la,la,la" he started raising his head higher with each word to be louder closer to me.

I ignored it and they carried on talking and laughing "lads, shut the fuck up yeah?" I said still lay down.

"Trace, they won't be quiet don't get involved they are just silly" quiet lad said from below me.

"Silly! Silly!" Gobby started singing and big lad joined in. "He's not silly, you got a problem with him then you got a problem with me" I heard movement as big lad sat up on the top bunk. *fuck it* I sat up "listen gobby shut the fuck up. Last time I'm telling you and shut your boyfriend up too" I stared at gobby keeping big lad in my peripheral vision. Big lad was dangerous but gobby was really pissing me off. "Or what?" big lad said blocking out the white wall behind him simply by leaning forwards. "Yeah or what?" gobby mimicked somehow resembling a tiny vulture. I took the fishing knife out of my pocket and opened it slowly so they could both see. "Now shut up" I said lying down flat. "You wouldn't dare" gobby said half heartedly. Without looking I threw the knife at him over the side of my bunk and down towards where his head should have been. It hit the post near him as I sat up and flipped my legs over my bunk just as big lad jumped down so did I. Gobby was in shock but not hurt "You want a go dickhead?" I asked him calmly eye to eye. "Get back in bed or I'll cut your head off and then your friend's" I said closing the two inches between us and holding it there. It was important I remained calm and looked like I'd do what I said I would otherwise their would be violence and to be fair I'd probably get my ass kicked. It was simple though I really didn't give a fuck. "leave it, leave it" Gobby piped up. "knife" I said holding my hand out to Gobby as he passed it to me big lad jumped back onto his bunk as the dormitory door opened. "Bed time lads" one of the scout leaders said "sorry, I dropped my knife" I replied giving quiet lad a wink. I wasn't going to hurt anyone but big lad didn't know that. I was pretty much a loner from there on in but two things stick out vividly and are good if not foolish memories from camp.

We were all in the main hall we had several scout leaders behind a long table against the wall and all the scouts around various square tables dotted around. I was on a table in the corner whilst Kate was in the opposite corner. We kept making eye contact, long brown hair which curled as it fell, she was beautiful. I sat saying nothing just listening to a lad talk shit on my table. Big lad kept approaching Kate's table and talking to the girls there. I had no idea what was being said but Kate leaned forwards to talk to him and turned her head away from me. Then she leaned back pointed straight at me with a smile. She seemed happy but what happened next involved me and big lad had started walking towards me. This wasn't going to end well for one of us. He walked over with purpose trying to be intimidating. My table mates vanished as he put his hands down in front of me. The entire room was now looking at us two. Kate hadn't taken her eyes off me. "Yeah? Want something?" I asked him. "You, arm wrestle" he said placing his elbow down and sitting in front of me. *What the fuck?* "Chicken" he said. I looked at Kate and she nodded. I smiled and looked back at him. I'd never done this before but I got the idea. Whoever slams the other guy down wins. He was a big lad but I knew I had aikido and the years of controlling pain to rely on. The Aikido meant I'd breath properly and the pain control meant the only way he'd win is if he broke my arm. Which to be fair was quite likely. We clasped hands via thumbs and I planted my feet apart on the floor, visible to everyone from beneath the table apart from him. I showed no emotion like being hit by Wenzel. He was strong with blonde hair shortly cut, blue eyes and was trying to make himself look bigger. My hand hurt just with him holding it. I tried to adjust my grip but had no chance, he was like a vice. I stared observing his eyes and let my focus change. When I felt the subtle vibration that was the little shake of adrenaline I said "ready?" He did what I expected and tried to slam me straight away. He moved back a half inch giving me room to push forwards and get a better grip. I clamped down as hard as I could. He'd moved me a half inch down and then an inch. He smiled at me *enough!* I closed my eyes and visualised all the power in my legs rushing up into my chest and my arm then down into my wrist and fingers. I started to shake inside. "Father killed mother, father killed mother, Alan's dead, Alan's dead, You're useless, useless, useless" I repeated it over and over. "Waste of space!" and back to "useless" over in my head as I watched Alan's head hit the floor again and again. I opened my eyes and met his as mentally I stood next to Pat's coffin and I smiled at him across the table. His face changed to Wenzels, then Clive's and then Kate's as my legs shook violently. I took a deep breath in and then audibly started chanting "da,na,na,na, da,na,na,na" it was the ultimate warriors theme tune I'd trained to it with Alan and I'd seen it a thousand times. My legs took all the adrenaline and I could feel them dancing around stamping uncontrollably as my top half remained stationary and calm. Big lad was in pain and red faced trying to force all his will into me. I needed a focal point to distract from the pain and keep my adrenaline going instead of falling. I looked at Kate, her green eyes somehow knowing what I needed and continued pushing.

"You're quite strong really" I told him my voice even trying to show no effort and keeping my eyes on Kate.

"You can't win!" He growled through gritted teeth.

My arm was killing me but Kate was soothing me. "Okay, if you say so" I replied dismissively ignoring the pain through my arm.

"Ten!" shouted a scout leader I didn't know what was happening until the rest of the hall started. "Nine!" , "eight!" and so on with each number we both gave everything we had. "Seven!" I watched Kate whilst the lad watched me. She was almost jumping up and down. "Three!" I turned to face big lad. I didn't have much left in the tank. "two!" And "one!"

We both growled and relaxed. My legs continued their dance beneath the table. Although we'd relaxed our fingers still took a few seconds to come apart. He rubbed his hand and arm where I simply let mine fall down to my lap *show no pain* I'd fix it later. He stood up "you're okay" he said holding his hand out to shake mine I took it and found a new respect for him. "You too mate" I said nodding.

"Dance, dance!" Our scout leader shouted. I walked to Kate who was still watching me "okay, one question" I asked her. "Yeah?" she said coyly cocking her head. Damn she was cute. "What the hell was that all about?" I asked. She laughed "he wanted to go out with me and I said no. He started bragging so I told him if he beats you in an arm wrestle I'd go out with him" she said. "How did you know he wouldn't?" I asked her gob smacked. "I didn't" she replied smiling. I didn't get it but hey the girl was talking to me, we'd been arranging into a circle to dance and I was beside Kate, I was happy with that. We had to dance in a circle one way and then another and then make the circle larger or smaller all by holding hands or wrists with those next to us. Kate took my wrist and my watch was in the way, A cheap plastic thing Brenda has got me. I couldn't undo it and wasn't taking the chance of her finding someone else so I just ripped it off breaking the straps and chucked it on the floor. "You're weird" she told me. I took her wrist and started dancing. "Do you like weird?" I asked her concentrating on her thin little wrists and hair that routinely rose out in front of me. "It's okay…" she said. We danced and chatted for ages. Her fingers felt great in mine. She wore brown boots she kicked out in front of her whilst laughing. "The northern lights thing?" she asked breaking away from the group and dancing with me alone.

"Yeah" I responded.

"Do you use drugs?" she asked me.

"Can I be honest?" I said.

"Yeah, I hope so. Well to me at least" she smiled.

"I don't do drugs. I just didn't know what the hell the Northern lights were." We threw our heads back laughing.

"I don't like Jamie, he's rude" she said.

"Who's Jamie?" I asked her.

"The lippy lad in your dorm, you don't know him?" she asked me.

"Oh him. Don't worry he won't bother you any more" I said.

"And why is that?" she said smiling.

"He got lippy so I shut him up." I replied.

"Really? I might have to try it" she joked.

"Chucked a knife at him, told him to go to sleep" I replied. She looked shocked and took her hand from mine. "Don't worry it didn't hit him and the knife is fine" I said trying to re capture the moment. Luckily she laughed hard just as the music stopped.

"Coming to my dorm?" she asked me. My arm hurt and I was dying for a drink with all the excitement I really didn't get it. "Need a drink, let me get my cup" I told her.

"You can use mine" she said with a cute as hell grin, her eyes widening.

"Won't be a minute!" I said running to get my cup. As soon as I reached my dormitory I realised "she was going to kiss you, you dickhead!" I downed the drink and flew back to the hut where everyone was talking "enjoy your drink?" she said with no smile. "Erm yeah, I'd like to have erm you know but I erm" she laughed. "You'd like to have what?" She asked me. "Had a drink with you" I replied turning bright red. We danced and chatted and generally got to know one another over the last two days of camp. I'd lied quite a lot and even told her my mum ran off with the milkman. She thought I was hilarious I felt like a bastard. I got her number before we left camp and I promised to call her. She didn't look back when she was in the car with her parents. I knew we were from two different worlds. Hers posh, a strong family with rules but mostly very caring, mine were dead and a killer, the rest, well I had no idea where they were. I wanted both her and her type of life so badly. I put the number in my pocket and recalled her words "if mum or dad pick up just hang up" she'd told me. Why was she so concerned? I didn't want her around my family. I didn't want her to see the real me. It was better to fake it. I convinced myself I was protecting her.

I got in Brenda's car and made a real effort "Scouts was great! We did canoeing, rafting, dancing, built bivouacs and climbing I loved the dancing!" It was part the high from Kate and part making an impression of how happy I was now I was back in touch with dad. Brenda gave me a few comments of "that's good" and "oh great" but otherwise no conversation. I didn't care I had a Kate's number tucked in my sock. I was seeing Wenzel once a week now and going to all my lessons at school.

I saw Nigel once during this time to tell him he'd been a very big help but I could take it from here. I'd live with dad and get the family back then I'd join the army. I'd see him again in full kit when I got accepted his reply was to put his arm around me and say "I'm proud of you. Well done. Do what's right for you and if you ever need me again make an appointment."

"Thanks man" I said welling up "thanks" I added. By now he knew a lot about me but not everything. I couldn't tell him everything as it would hurt him. I looked at the room one last time breathing in the clay and paint smell. This was home and Nigel might not be normal but he was a special kind of perfect. "Cya" I waved and turned to walk out two feet taller and three years older than when I'd first entered his room. "Oi!" he shouted. I turned back "You still owe me a game of chess" he said cracking a smile. "Go have a smoke" I replied smiling and walked out feeling like that little girl who'd painted the waterfall.

Chapter 34

I took a very active role in social services dealings now. They came to see me and I took my own notes at review meetings. I questioned everything. I had to I remember numerous awkward conversations where I'd notice the line of questioning was designed to trip me up and keep me within the care system. Since I'd been in touch with dad my social worker had changed also. This one I didn't know very well and wasn't around for long "So I believe you want to live with another foster placement?" He asked me with his pen poised to write down my answer.

"No, I want to live with my dad and he wants the same. Brenda has been great but it's time for me to move on. When will this be possible?" I responded. For me this was huge as I'd taken such a routine of not speaking I was now enabling myself to use my mouth in a positive way. A lot of the time I felt vulnerable, it felt like if people knew my thoughts they would know what I wanted and be able to counter it. However I had two choices remain quiet and let other people make the choices for my life or get my act together. I chose the second one.

"Well it's not that easy, we need to make sure you'll be happy and safe and that it's done properly. So we will move you closer to Wenzel with open contact okay?" It was a good answer however it had totally ignored my question. "I didn't ask if it was easy I asked when you could make this possible? He wants to live with me and I with him do you know a time when it will be possible?" I replied not being rude just level in tone and copying his body language when I wasn't writing down what everyone had said. "Well the sooner we get you closer the sooner you'll be able to move back if he passes his anger management tests and if it's deemed suitable and now it is but then he still needs a home for you" he responded. "You're a social worker send a letter to the council as being in care has been damaging to my health when I could be with my father. The more

I'm here the worse my behaviour has got. The more contact with Wenzel I have had the more it's improved. I'd love to move in with him but will accept a closer placement as a means to moving in with dad" I was reeling off what Wenzel had told me automatically and I'll admit I enjoyed having that little bit of power. I didn't have to just listen and take it any more I could say what I wanted as long as I used the right words and said it the right way. "Can I have a copy of the minutes please?" I'd request at the end "Brenda will receive a copy, you can read those" the latest social worker told me. "No, I'm at the review I want a separate copy in my hand. No offence to Brenda but if she gets them I'll never get a copy" naturally Brenda was at the review and this wouldn't help me later on with her but both mine and her hands were tied. She had to be nice to me and I to her so screw it. It needed to be done.

On the rare occasions that I couldn't understand or get around a situation then I'd simply state what I want and say "no talking until it's done". That worked okay for a couple of reviews until a social worker put on a review paper that "Tracie when asked about contact with his father told us he didn't want to take part in the review meeting any longer" which made it now look like I was scared of declining contact with my father. I wasn't it was just another one of their stupid games designed to do what they wanted to do regardless of the child's needs.

I'd handed in a twenty four page story to Mrs Howlen in English. It was the longest in the class and got a few comments from the kids in the room. I was behaving so I kept stum although I noticed when one lad said "you'll be having his kid next miss!" Her face flashed with pain and was gone again. Nobody seemed to notice it apart from me. Later in the lesson she was talking away and writing on the board when a lad called Rick started again "Hey Trace, bet you'd tap that ass right?" I knew she could hear him but also knew she'd say nothing. She was a good teacher but unless it was obviously irritating she'd let it go. I'd watched her arm lower with the chalk as he'd spoke. She was upset and hiding it again "Rick, don't" I told him flatly a little louder than his comment. I had a desk in front of me and he was in front of that one. We were all stood up as it was nearing end of lesson. "Trace loves Howlen" he started a little louder so half the class heard. "Rick, I'm telling ya, reel it in" I told him. Rick was a tall lad with one leg longer than the other. He was usually a decent lad I'd seen him go from shy to quite confidant he was just pissing about but it was upsetting miss Howlen and their fore me. He turned around to face me but I didn't give him chance to speak I stepped back and kicked the edge of my desk hard sending it into his stomach. He keeled over my desk as I stepped forwards he arched around to lean on his own. "What happened Ricky?" Mrs Howlen asked him. I swear I could see a slight smirk brewing. "Your stomach playing up again Rick?" I asked him. "Nothing miss, I'm fine" he mumbled.

After class I waited until everyone had left and just stood there. "Tracie?" Miss Howlen asked. "Are you okay miss? You seemed upset" I asked her.

"I'm fine Tracie, personal stuff, all good, honest. You did well with your story."

"Okay, if you're sure" I said waiting several seconds knowing I'm fifteen and she was a bit older and a teacher. Knowing there was no way in hell she'd speak with me but wanting her to know someone gave a damn. Whatever it was.

"I'm sure" she said smiling I left to catch up with Rick "Oi Rick! Put the word round" he turned to face me. "What word?" he said leaning back as I cracked him in the side of the head with my palm. He hit the wall so I grabbed his shirt and pulled him forwards "If anyone upsets her they will have me to fucking answer to, Got it?" I told him. "Shit man, yeah. Got it." He replied. I had a little respect for him and realised in that moment he was used to dealing with pain. He'd not tried to fight me but was capable of holding his own.

It was Physical education time and I didn't like gym but as I was behaving myself I'd got changed into the compulsory white shorts and T-shirt. Derek Baker who was always mouthy but generally as harmless as he was brainless was mucking around because he didn't want to do Gym. He didn't want to do Gym because he weighed three times as much as anyone else in the locker room and our teacher always made fun of him. He was hurling insults at the other lads but none were directed at me. He was however annoying Mr Klich our teacher and rugby coach. "Hey Kleechy! Is it rugby that makes your face flat?" Derek asked him. Mr Klich was a short wide fella with a big smile and he never missed a beat. "What's up Porky couldn't manage the Gym? Tell you what tomorrow we'll play football which do you want to be? The pitch or the ball?" I creased up laughing as Mr Klich obviously thought Derek was joking and replied in kind.

The session went well apart from Derek every so often complaining and we just laughed it off until it was time to get changed again. Derek stormed in after being told off by Mr Klich and started grabbing peoples bags and throwing them around. "Fucking dickhead, who does he think he is?" I noticed Derek was attention seeking. He'd not thrown Mark's bag or Grahams as they were his friends and Graham would spark him out but he picked on everyone else either throwing bags, pushing them or both. I retrieved Peters bag who was the oldest in our year but also the smallest and thinnest, A ginger haired lad who's family was made of money. He was amazing at art and very clever but rarely spoke. Derek grabbed it again and chucked it "Derek!" I shouted above the level of his screaming insults at Mr Klich who wasn't even in the room. I picked up Peters bag again and returned to find Derek had thrown mine into the shower room he was laughing and pointing at it. *Fuck it* I popped him with my right just enough to get the message across and all hell broke loose. He started swinging like a windmill both arms going in circles rapidly. No control, no technique just a big fat windmill coming straight at me. I jab crossed as he came closer and sidestepped but ended up in a crowd of coats as everyone closed in to see what would happen next "fight! Fight! Fight!" they chanted in the small changing room. I had to make space. I couldn't fight like this it and few too many pies was heading straight at me again. I grabbed him and started nutting him then turned his arm at the elbow and spun him until we'd gone one eighty degree's. I let go sending him into the crowd and me towards the door which led into a hall. The hall was thin but at least it was just him and me now. Ideally we'd be outside but the hall door opened inwards and there was no way I was turning my back on chunky. I tried a few punches but most got knocked out of the way by this arm circling, he kept it up pretty much constantly. It looked stupid but it was working. He punched me in the gut and I dropped my guard ever so slightly. I also had my mouth slightly open, as his left hook caught my cheek It opened up on the inside and my mouth was suddenly warmer than it should have been. I shook my head brushing the impact off and blood fell out of my mouth. I stepped back and he stopped circling. I touched my tongue and ran my fingers along my cheek not taking my eyes from Derek. My tongue and teeth were fine however the cheek was sliced all the way from the back teeth to the front. I put my hands up palm out "fuck it, you win. Okay?" I ignored the boo's and got cleaned up and shoved a gym sock in my gob and bit down on it. On the way out Derek shoulder barged me. *So that's how it's going to be is it?* I wasn't scared and knew I should have been which made me concerned about my mentality.

Why wasn't I scared? I was totally logical now with fighting. It was something that had to be done. If he'd let it go so would I as it stood he wanted to be an ass. That needed to be taken care of or it would continue. I gave myself a telling off *get better then drop him. If you do it now you end up worse off!* It went around the school for a few days how Derek had beaten me. It was as unexpected to them as it was to me. I tried to ignore them *get better, sort it, until then fuck em.*

I came home from school as normal expecting to get changed and head out to my paper round when I saw my new social workers car outside. I could spot it a mile away it was private reg and was the biggest red thing on the estate. Okay, change of plan I pictured the sheet of paper in my head as I walked down the hill towards Brenda's. Number one live with dad. Two move to care placement. Three lots of paperwork. It must be paperwork there is no way they are taking me to move with dad and there is no way they are going to move me this short notice. I'd of been told. Has to be more paperwork unless someone else is dead. Which is possible but that would mean Jonathon or Jodie and they are safe, Caroline is with Brenda so that could be Wenzel. I surprised myself by not being worried and immediately knowing it was paperwork. It had to be as I didn't feel that change that I get when someone dies. There was a change feeling but no loss feelings. *Fuck it I'll see when I get there.*

The social worker was in the hall a ginger guy slim just over five foot five he looked smart and had a briefcase and glasses. His face was covered in freckles. I'd seen him before he was in a meeting with a team leader one day training to be a social worker. His name was Patrick Benson. Brenda was also in the hall "I'll just get changed" I said knowing something was up but what? "Wait, you don't need to. Come sit down" Brenda said walking to the living room. I walked in and stayed standing. The last time I'd been asked to sit in front of a social worker I was told my mother had been killed. I wasn't going through that again "what is it?" I asked Brenda trying to read her eye contact. She looked like she was determined but hiding sadness, I wasn't buying it. "Patrick is here to take you to your new home" she told me. I glanced at Patrick stood in the doorway "what? Now?" I asked him. "Yes now, you got your wish. We enjoyed having you and hope you are happy wherever you go" she said without emotion. What a crock of shit I thought. I knew it would happen but now? "You don't need to pack anything it's all done" Brenda added Patrick stood there like a lemon. I looked at him "well?" I asked sitting down. "They are nice people with no children, just you. They are a bit older than Brenda and Jim and you'll have your own room" I'd heard enough. I was going whether I liked it or not. "What about Louise?" I asked "I'll tell her" Brenda said.

"Right, Lets go" I told Patrick. *Fuck it I'm not showing Brenda she's getting to me.* "Want to say anything to Caroline before you leave?" Brenda asked me.

I thought about it for a split second and it hurt. Caroline is my sister, she should know why I'm going, why I can't stay but then she did make her own choice to stay. "No, nothing" I replied. It's better she doesn't know I'm gone. She won't be asked a thousand questions later. I convinced myself I'd saved her trouble when in fact I couldn't face her. I headed to the door and put my hand on it for the last time and turned back "there is one thing" I said "Yeah what is it Tracie?" Brenda said with a mountain of hope in her tone. "My paper round, Graham can have it back but I get paid today?" I questioned. Brenda dug out my seven pound and fifty pence from her purse and handed it to me. "Thanks" I said and left.

Chapter 35

Patrick filled me in on the new place in the car. So far he seemed okay but I didn't trust him. His daughter played guitar, he left college to become a social worker. He liked money, he had a CD player in the car when most cars had cassette's and his shades were worth two hundred pounds. He bought me a ruler on a later visit from a shop and asked for the receipt. The ruler had cost him ten pence. I asked him what the receipt was for and he told me. "The company would pay me back for the petrol, the ruler and our lunch. It's like that for all the kids" I trusted him a lot less after that. Kids were a meal ticket a means of getting free money I got that now. My being in care kept him in two hundred pound sunglasses, lucky me.

Their names were Tony and Pip, their house was a two bedroom semi and the town was beautiful. Tarvin had one aquarium that sold reptiles on the only road with shops that was the main high street. One post office, one chemist, one youth club, a church, a pub and a couple of newsagents, best of all it was all surrounded by countryside. I decided then and there if I ever came into money I'd buy a house there and get a dog. I imagined Jonathon, Jodie and Caroline playing in the fields. I walked in front of Patrick to the new house where I'd been told to use the back door beyond a little wooden gate. As I reached the gate a border collie barked at me and Pip and Tony appeared in the doorway. At least mid fifties, no teeth that I could see and made no effort to appear smart for the social worker. I shook Tony's hand and he called the dog over. I bent down to play with him, he was brilliant! I grabbed my things from the car and was shown to my room. Walking through the kitchen I noted a pair of shoes on the floor but not tidy like Brenda's. It had a funny humid smell too. There was washing on the floor in some places and my eye glanced towards the sideboards to find the cooker, washing machine, deep fat fryer and fridge freezer were all caked in either dust or dirt. The sink had things in and an open butter tub was on the side with a knife left in it. "Sorry to disturb dinner" I said as I spotted the butter "Don't be silly, that's from hours ago" Pip said. I didn't like her, she had dark curly hair and her face was always contorting into strange shapes. Most things she said came out as though I should already have known. We weren't going to get along but I could try "Oh, okay, sorry" I said cheerfully. "What's he apologising for?" she asked Tony. Oh yeah we were not going to get along at all. "This is your room everything in it is for you to use" she told me as I walked into a small bedroom with a single bed, a single wardrobe and a window with no nets. It also had a radio cassette player. "Everything?" I asked both sarcastically and because I was genuinely grateful to be able to have my own room. "Radio is for use only not to keep" Pip told me. "No worries, thanks Pip!" I said cheerily trying to keep up the up beat nature. *Be liked. It won't be for long and for fucks sake don't let the social worker know you hate it already.* "Put your stuff away and we will talk later" Pip said leaving me and Patrick in the centre of my new bedroom.

"What do you think?" he said. "I think it's a shithole" I replied running my finger down the window frame and proving my point. The white paint had turned yellow but that was nothing compared to the dust and grime left on my finger. "Don't want it?" he asked me. I wasn't playing that game. "I'll make it work. It's not for long" I said thinking of ways to do up my new room. I chucked my bags in the wardrobe and realised I could hear the T.V downstairs even with the bedroom door closed. At Brenda's house there was no way they would have gone to watch T.V whilst they had visitors. As much as it was nice I was allowed my space it was also awfully rude to watch T.V when they had professional company. I laughed at myself *you're turning into a snob.*

"Well whatcha think?" Pip said and I noticed her eyes never left the T.V.

"Yeah it's nice, thanks!" I replied with as much enthusiasm as I could muster. "Okay luv" pip replied.

I think Patrick felt as awkward as I did as we both stood in the hall as they watched T.V and ignored us. "Do you have any rules Tracie needs to know about?" Patrick asked whoever cared to answer.

Pip appeared to inch her head closer to mine, even though she was a good two feet away ,with every word she spoke. "Behave yourself" Tony answered flatly. I was starting to like him purely because he just didn't give a shit. "No" Pip answered then stood up "no smoking, we smoke you don't. Don't steal and we'll get on fine. Eat what you want when you want. Don't ask us just go and make it. Tell us when you use something up and sometimes we sit at the table and eat with family over but not often. You should be here for that. Any questions?"

"A couple" I offered "what time's bed?"

"Anytime as long as you are in bed before us and you get yourself up for school in the morning. If you have dirty clothes put them in the basket in your room" Pip answered. I was starting to like this place.

"Okay great, great can I play with Geordie?" I'd clocked the name on the collar when I came in. I'd also memorised the phone number.

"Yeah, he's due a walk. Take this" she said reaching into a cabinet of mess and pulling a lead out. Geordie was beside me the second the lead was in my hand. "There's a field up there" she said not pointing in any specific direction just kind of holding her arm in the air and circling it everywhere. She turned and was back in T.V land immediately.

"Looks like I'm walking the dog" I said to Patrick outside. "You'll get on great here" he said "you've got my number" he added when I didn't reply. Then he was gone in a line of petrol smoke. The field wasn't hard to find it was three houses from where I was living and it was huge.

The bedroom was cleanable so I set to work with a sponge and water, then some old clothes for good measure as I couldn't find scourers anywhere. It was late by the time I was done and I still had no curtain for the window. "Tony could I have some sheets or something for the bed please?" I asked him. "Airing cupboard, here what do I call you?" "Tracie, Trace, Tee, lad...whatever" I replied. "Tracie it is then" he said and I went on the hunt for the airing cupboard. I didn't have a clue what I was looking for as Brenda always provided us with the duvet we simply put it on the bed. I grabbed two sheet's *it'll do.* Pip provided more sheets in the morning and a pillowcase. No duvet like at Brenda's.

I had no school for the time being and I'd packed away everything I came with even folded my clothes neatly in the wardrobe. What now? I sat there like a lemon for five minutes and then got the cassette player working with an old tape I'd found whilst tidying "Hello el le lola" rang out from it. I liked it, it was catchy even though I had no idea what the song was about. The only things I'd not thrown out were cassettes and a black bandanna with a rock band on it. I'd put holes in it and hung it over the window frame by the nails already there, it was no net but it was my kind of perfect.

I went downstairs in the morning "Pip want to see what I've done with the room?" I was kinda excited that they would approve. I was cleaning and helping which felt really good. "Okay" she said and followed me up the stairs. Her face dropped as she looked at the bandanna "where did you get that?" she asked with venom in her voice. "It was on the side" I replied pointing to where I'd found it. "That's not yours to move" she said "why, why did you do that?" she added sounding like I'd slapped her. "Erm, sorry" I said innocently as Tony appeared beside her "he didn't know" Tony said and Pip walked out. Tony took the bandanna down and folded it up religiously placing it where it was before. "Sorry Tony, If I'd known not to touch it I wouldn't have" I told him. "It's okay lad, we'll get you some curtains today" he told me.

"Thanks, can I walk Geordie?" I asked. My stomach was rumbling but I wasn't eating anything in that kitchen whilst it looked like that and I wasn't going to clean it after this morning's episode. What had I done? Silly fuckers shouldn't have said use what you want if they didn't want me to. Why leave it in here if I can't use it? And why leave it in the room after it's been taken down? Who's was it? I'll bet it belonged to the last kid that was here. *Fuck it* I spoke to Geordie about it all and it felt good to tell someone who couldn't answer back. When we got to the road between our street and the field Geordie automatically sat down, he was perfect on a lead and I wondered how he was off it. I'd ask Tony later how he was off it. In the mean time lets try "paw" and he responded immediately. "Roll over" just left him sat there looking at me inquisitively. I got down on my hands and knee's "lie down" I said and he did. "Good boy!" I sang making a big fuss of him. "Roll over" I asked pushing him back. I tried this ten times and no luck then I rolled over with him as I pushed him sideways "Roll over" and he copied me. Within five minutes he was going nuts at the new game rolling over then jumping up at me with his tail going ten to the dozen. I had to get him to lie down again to get him to roll over but it was a start. Throughout the day I'd routinely stop walking and order "roll over" to check he'd got it perfect. Geordie was a great dog and I remember showing Tony that he would sit and lie on command "he's done that for ages" Tony told me sat in the arm chair but ignoring the T.V "roll over" I said and Geordie rolled and bounced to his feet then sat down again. "That's new" Tony said "Can I train him?" I asked. "like what?" Tony requested half interested now. "I don't know, fetch shoes, jump fences and stuff" I replied. "No, but you can take him off the lead in fields and he'll come back" Tony told me.

Patrick turned up to tell me a cab would pick me up and take me to school. I was to be opposite the post office every morning at 7:45am, which wasn't a problem it was only five minutes walk from Pip's house and I was to stay at my usual school which is what I'd wanted. Patrick asked if I had any questions and I'd already made a list. "Contact with Caroline?" I asked. "It's to be arranged by Brenda and only if Caroline wants to, Wenzel is not to be present" he told me. "What do you mean if she wants to? She's my sister" I asked him. "Yeah, but you chose to move away with Wenzel she might not understand that choice Tracie" he told me. "Well, she chose Brenda and Jim's but I ain't making a scene about it. She doesn't have to see Wenzel that's her choice but why wouldn't she want to see me? That's stupid" I said stepping back from Patrick. "You can see her at school" Patrick told me. "Yeah, sure" I said thinking that if she didn't want to see me why should I bother? We didn't really talk in care anyway. "Jonathon and Jodie contact?" I asked him changing the subject. "Twice a year and to be arranged by and Lynne and Sampson" he said "ah, yeah...fine" I replied a number of emotions hitting me at once. The first being that I'd convinced myself that Jodie and Jonathon were still with their foster placement like I had been and they weren't as they had now been adopted. I'd been to a number of contacts and liked their foster placement but really didn't like their adoptive parents who I'd met perhaps four times in two years. I'd tried to convince myself Jonathon and Jodie were happy in a foster placement and that it wouldn't be for long, so every time I heard about them being adopted I felt a sting. Parental responsibility was now with the new parents so they weren't subject to even come to contact if they didn't want to. They made the rules, if they said I saw Jonathon and Jodie once in ten years then there was nothing I could do about it and I hated it.

"Can I still go to scouts?" I asked him my mind wanting to be in a field in the middle of nowhere at the thought of Jonathon and Jodie adopted. "If Pip and Tony want to take you, yes" he said. "What and miss Countdown? I don't see that happening. Thanks though" I told him. "Okay last question, what's with the bandana?" I asked Patrick and explained what happened. I wasn't upset with Pip and Tony it just didn't make sense and I wanted to understand it. "Ah, sorry I should have warned you. Pip and Tony lost a child in a car accident right outside the house, I didn't think it would crop up. Is that okay with you? I can talk to them if you want me to?" he asked me. "Nah, it's cool. I didn't know that and I get it. That shit's hard" I replied looking away as Patrick gazed at me wanting me to open up to him and give him a feather in his little ginger cap, he had no chance. "What?" I asked turning my head back rapidly and holding his gaze. He said nothing just waited. "People die shit happens, you can't replace real kids with care kids and they haven't they have let me do my own thing and that's cool I like them. Accidents happen it's fine" I said. "When do I see dad?" I asked him. "Whenever you arrange it, ask Pip" he replied.

Each morning I'd be up and ready before everyone else I'd cleaned the toaster and sideboards days before so I was now happy eating in there although I did keep a knife and fork to one side just for me to use. Then I'd wait outside the aquarium until my cab arrived. Generally the cabbie's were OK and didn't ask any questions and I even had one guy who was a right laugh for a few weeks however one day they didn't turn up. I waited ten minutes and then called dad. "What now?" I asked him "I'll call them" he said and called me back ten minutes later. "They said it was sent and you weren't there" he wasn't angry. I could feel his brain turning over how should he play this one? "I was here, they didn't turn up, what now? Pip and Tony aren't in" I asked him. "Fancy a days work?" He asked me. "Sure" I replied without even thinking.

That's how I started work at a fruit and veg shop. I worked the day cleaning the warehouse and learning to swap old stock with new. Wenzel being the type of person he was there was no inclination to start me off on the small stuff. My first job was to remove all the sacks of potato's then put the oldest at the bottom and the newer ones on top. Once I'd done the Maris pipers, I was to do the King Edwards, Nadines, Jerseys and so on. Each pile was a minimum of four sacks and a maximum of eight and regular sellers had two piles. Then I'd clean and brush out the warehouse and pile all the junk into a big biffa bin outside. I'd break up all the cardboard and pack it and use one of them flattened to place over the biffa bin and jump up and down on it to reduce the garbage costs. Then I'd be checked by Bob a huge man and quite easily the strongest I'd met, I'd watched four men drag a huge Hessian sack of nuts from the van and carry it between them to the shop where I watched Bob throw it over his shoulder like it was nothing and take it to the warehouse, once Bob was happy my tasks were complete he'd teach me something else in the warehouse.

Chapter 36

I loved Tarvin and Tony and Pip were acceptable. They hadn't tried to step on my toes and I'd made sure I was polite and decent with them too. Geordie was great and I'd revelled in what I'm not shy of calling a friendship, I thoroughly enjoyed discovering the little Roman walls behind the egg factory and running through the fields and woodland together every other day where we would train a new skill. He'd taken to lying beside my bed to sleep until Pip and Tony had gone to bed then I'd open the door and tap my bed and up he'd hop. He was a great dog but I soon wanted interaction of a human nature. I missed Louise, Kep, Keel, Nigel and Baconegg terribly, I also missed scouts and wrote to my old scout leader thanking him for the two Cheshire hikes I'd done. He wrote back telling me he'd read it out to the troop.

I called Brenda a few times to arrange contact and was told Caroline wasn't ready whilst I was seeing Wenzel. I understood that and asked to just meet up with me then perhaps we could go to the cinema? I was told "You should have thought about that before you left Tracie!", work kept me busy and at school I avoided Caroline as she didn't want to see me. So I took to lying. I'd got good at it as a kid and better at it in care. I started by realising Wenzel was just another person. I hadn't felt the strong bond I expected to when I got back in touch with him so it wasn't too difficult. Then I put it into action. My drivers were mostly different so didn't know what I looked like anyway, just that I'd be outside the post office in school uniform. I waited outside the newsagents and when he pulled up I'd head to the chemist and pull my phone out as though listening to a call. I'd turn around walking up and down a few times and keeping an eye out. If they were still there after a couple of minutes I'd head to the shop until they left. Then I'd call Wenzel who'd tell me to call Pip and Tony. I'd call them and let it ring once then hang up and call him back to tell him they didn't answer. He'd pick me up and I'd do a full days work. *Nice and easy.*

Stock rotation became second nature and I was set to replenishing stock with the same principles, old at the back. Before long I was cutting swedes, bagging potatoes, taking responsibility for the warehouse, and helping with deliveries in my spare time or helping Bob with the stock take. They had a fast turn over with a new delivery every day and sometimes of an afternoon too. I wasn't there long before Bob opened another shop down the road within a month I was carrying two sacks of spuds a time on my shoulder with double my previous speed. "Slow down, they don't care about you. You're just a number" Wenzel would tell me often. I was certain he didn't like the fact that I was now doing the same if not more than he was capable of doing. I didn't rub it in I just loved the job and got on with it. I've always been skinny and I admit I got a kick out of the some of the comments and looks I received as I shouldn't have physically been able to do the things I was capable of doing. I had the martial arts to thank for that as most of the lifting was in the technique. I'd gone from getting fifteen pounds here and there to getting the same as the adults at thirty pounds a day cash in hand. I was missing a lot of school though and my friends even more. Wenzel had spoken to social services about the cabs not turning up and then he spoke to Pip and Tony who insisted they hadn't had the calls from me most of the time. On the rare occasion they did answer I went home to them and the cab company would complain about having to send another cab which took an hour each way so there was no point in me going anyway. Either way the result was the same. I got a full day at work. I tried to avoid him at work "bet you think you're strong now don't you?" He'd ask me I ignored him. "Don't worry little dick, one day you'll be as strong as me" it started to grate on me and I realised I didn't actually want to be like Wenzel at all. I wanted to be like Bob, I wanted my own business and to muck in with the lads. I wanted to be an inspiration and to be friendly. I wanted to be me but had no idea who I was. I also realised I was getting to Wenzel albeit unintentionally, he took me to one side one day "slow down!" He told me grabbing my arm "I'm fine" I replied trying to walk ahead "You're not fine! You're doing twice the work as anyone else out there! And you think they give a shit about you? They don't! You're nothing. They will just get some other mug to shift shit for them!" I knew in a way he was right but my work speed was my choice and I wasn't doing anything that wasn't sensible or anything I couldn't physically manage. I hadn't tried to put his ego down it just kind of happened.

I told Geordie that I shouldn't have been able to distance myself from Wenzel so easily. I shouldn't be able to do that if he was my real dad and besides I still didn't know if he was my real dad. The long walks helped but it wasn't long before I was sat there with Tony and Pip telling Wenzel I was a liar and the cabs had turned up and then Wenzel fighting my case for me. He was getting more and more agitated, I just vanished inside myself. Into the car at Brenda's and then camping with scouts. It was then I decided I needed to feel the freedom of camping again and what an idiot I was to have left scouts, my friends and Louise. Perhaps I'd even get back in touch with Kate... "Listen you old bastard he's not fucking lying!" Wenzel snapped bringing me back to reality. This wasn't good, Wenzel was pointing at me and staring at Tony and Pip who were staring right back. "You should leave now" Pip said quietly. "Yeah now you can't handle the truth you old bitch! You think I don't know my own fucking son?" He said scrunching his face up. He was trying not to get violent and it was hurting him. He hated not being in control. He walked out and I followed because I knew Pip and Tony wouldn't see it as betrayal but he would if I didn't and I'd not hear the end of it. Outside he said "I'll ask you once and only once. Did you say the cab hadn't turned up when it had?" I could see his chess playing mind trying to read my moves, I could see his body calm as he was outside and that meant he had to make a positive impression and he was conflicted because he had this need to seem like a perfect father and that meant protecting me and I could see he just wanted to run away and say goodbye to all of us. He had "I don't need this shit" written all over his face but only if you knew him. If you didn't he was just another father talking to his son and I knew two things for certain in that moment. He didn't care about me I was part of some bigger plan he had. A bigger plan I'd not yet put my finger on but he needed me for whatever it was and secondly I could lie to him as easily as I could lie to Brenda and Big Jim. I threw my arms out well prepared "They weren't there! I have friends at school, I see Caroline at school, do you want to check my phone?" I held my orange bar phone out at arms length knowing that he'd have no idea how to use it and even if he did check I had an out going call log. He wouldn't though he'd need me to trust him and to do that he'd have to trust me. I didn't break eye contact until he spoke and then I was concentrating on looking hurt because he didn't believe me. "No it's okay, I'll call social services and we'll get you out of there" he said pointing at Tony who was now stood in the driveway waiting for me. "Look at me again and I'll knock your fucking head off!" Wenzel started. I went in figuring if I went in there was no reason for Tony to be waiting or Wenzel to stay. "You scared him" Tony said to Wenzel as I walked past "scared! Scared! He's not fucking scared, he's clever! He knows if I whack you he won't get to live with me! Ask him! Ask him!" They continued for about five minutes. I'd got bored after two and stuck my headphones in "Lola, I'm not the worlds most physical man but I know what I am and I guess I'm a man el le Lola".

Wenzel wasn't allowed near the property after that but he still picked me up right outside out of spite. I'd stopped calling Pip and Tony at all and he just picked me up for work. I called the social services and told them the cabs were unreliable and I'd go back to school when they got me moved in with Wenzel. I still didn't see what he needed me for but I knew there was something going on. Naturally Pip and Tony had ways of their own of getting back at Wenzel and they took me away to a caravan site they owned at Geenacres. I didn't know if it was to get back at Wenzel or to assist me for a couple of weeks but it felt at the time like a dig at Wenzel. The truth is I absolutely loved it there, it was beautiful and I spent most of my time on the beach. I had my own money and of a night they had stage shows. One night a magician was on and at the end he grabbed three bowling balls and juggled with them throwing them high into the air and then one crashed down onto his head. All my first aid training flashed by me instantly followed by Alan's head hitting the floor simultaneously I'd dropped my drink and was running down the seated crowd of people towards the stage. I'd got about three feet away when he sat up to a round of applause. I was the only one who moved. The crowd loved it however I was gutted. It wasn't funny. Pain wasn't funny. Accident's weren't funny and death was not fucking funny. I walked out and headed to the beach.

The air was cold and the sand was warm. I lay my back against a rock willing my entire body to sink inside it and become swallowed by the world. For a while I thought it had worked as the people going past didn't appear to see me at all. I must have fallen asleep because the next minute the sun is in my face and I have a bitch of a headache. I got up dusting myself off and swearing internally because Pip and Tony must be going nuts worrying about where I'd gone.

I headed in the direction of the caravan, mum was killed in a caravan so I didn't really like being inside one simply because I felt trapped but I didn't hate it. I was swaying from side to side with a combination of heat and my headache when three lads and two girls came into view up ahead. "That's him!" one lad said. "Yeah that's him, get the fucker!" Another shouted. I looked around to realise there was only me and them in sight. "It's not him!" A girl squealed. I was in trouble and I knew it. There was no way I could fight three of them especially in this state and I couldn't run I had no energy so there was only one option left. I had to scare the living shit out of them. I reached down for my fishing knife to find it wasn't there. I checked all my pockets as fast as I could and it wasn't there. *Fuck!* One of the lads was now leaning over me as I frantically searched again he was saying something about hitting on his girl but

I couldn't make it out. Then I heard "leave him!" from the third lad who was a fair bit smaller. I recognised it from somewhere. I was halfway through replying "what the fuck mate?" When I heard "Hey Trace! What you doing here?" As my mate Lee came into view from school. *That was lucky!* My first thought was why is Lee here? My second was relief I'd not got my ass kicked and then it hit me. *I'd reached for the knife.* Would I have used it? I'd in that moment definitely have pulled it out to scare them. *Well done dickhead you'd have stabbed your mate's friends and maybe your mate too!* Or you could have got stabbed yourself? I made a mental note to never, ever pull a knife on anyone unless they had a weapon themselves.

Chapter 37

After the argument Wenzel had caused with Pip and Tony the social workers were on my case about school absence. I told them I'd start going again if they helped Wenzel get a place to live. It's important at this stage to understand Wenzel didn't train me to behave this way. He wasn't bribing me or forcing me to try and get the place faster. He didn't have to, all he had to do was allow me the freedom to make that choice myself and I ran with it, not because I wanted to be with him as much at this stage. I didn't trust him, but simply because I wanted the whole family back together and I'd of done anything within my power to make that happen. The social services agreed they would write a letter that stated Wenzel needed accommodation due to my current circumstances effecting my mental health and education. As soon as I was back at school I was in trouble again, although I was trying really hard not to be.

I was walking down the coridoor to my English lesson when I saw a lad called Tod walking towards us in a line whilst our line of people were on the other side. He was tall and strong but thin. I'd seen him before out of school and I generally avoided him. Every few steps he was punching someone on my side or pushing them, not very hard but enough to cause a laugh from his mates. I put my head down and carried on walking, perhaps I wouldn't be hit? Just as he was walking past he caught me straight in the solar plexus and I fell back *let it go, you'll be with dad soon and get the family back together.* I told myself and I let it go. I got up and went to class. I couldn't concentrate but answered all the questions on Romeo and Juliet. *I could be earning now, Where's Caroline? What would I say if I did see her?* I just couldn't concentrate and could hardly tell Caroline "Hey Brenda was right Wenzel's a dickhead but let's live with him anyway?" It didn't seem right and I knew she'd tell Brenda everything I'd said and then I'd be out of Wenzels and there was no way Brenda would have me back. *Best to keep quiet.*

It was lunch time and Kap and I were watching the lads play football as we ate our lunch in the concrete pitch. He wanted to skive off but I'd told him I couldn't so he'd stayed in school with me. Derek Baker was playing and kept shoulder barging a smaller lad who almost fell over a few times until in the end he said "fat bastard" quietly to himself. "What did you say?" Derek snarled turning on him *perhaps he thought he was a snack?* Derek was walking forwards with his head touching this small lad's as the smaller boy tried turning away but couldn't from the momentum and then he fell over. "What did you say?" Derek spat landing a kick to the skinny boy "nothing, Shit" he said as the kicks landed. "I can't watch this" I told Kap as I stood up. "Trace!" Kap called but it was too late I'd made my mind up. I walked over calmly "Hey Derek, What's up?" I asked him looking down at the skinny lad as I stood next to Derek. "He called me a fat bastard! That's what's up!" He shouted pulling his leg back again to kick the curled up figure on the floor. "Well, he's right. You are a fat bastard" I said as calmly as I could manage. "What?" he laughed nervously then anger hit "I'll kill you! I beat you before you shit!" He stormed as he swung at me. I needed him angry as he faught a lot better when he was calm. He was big and I needed him to make mistakes. "Pick on someone your own size!" I said shuffling backwards. "Oh yeah, there is nobody your size" I said sidestepping and making him chase me the other way. I caught sight of Kap behind me with my bag and coat. I hoped if Derek landed one of those big whirling fists Kap would cover me up with my coat.

Derek ran at me I sidestepped and kicked at him catching him just enough to send him over landing palms first. He got back up quickly. "What you going to do? Eat me?" I asked him as I saw skinny lad laughing in the opposite corner. Derek placed his head down and like a rhino ran at me again with his arms flailing. I wasn't fast enough to move and took a couple of hard punches to the face whilst I tried to grab his arm, his momentum pushed me over and I had a few tons of fat on top of me. I don't like ground fighting but I learnt this day I could if I had to and I had to. I tried flicking a hip but it was like trying to move a bus with a toothpick. He was leaning back straddling me to take big heavy punches at my head. I kept my guard up until he leaned back to swing then threw a jab cross to his chin and covered up again. It wasn't hard but it was fast enough to let him know I was there and take a little power out of his punches. I needed him to make a mistake "Come on chunky! Hit me!" We continued the same cycle him throwing huge hooks and leaning back and me jab, crossing until he was bright red in the face and I could feel the power of his punches weaken as they hit my guard and rattled my head and then it happened, he made a mistake as he placed his left arm down to support himself and punch my face with a big straight. I wasn't waiting for that to make contact. I rolled up and to the right grabbing his head with my left arm and his right with my right arm and pinning it. Now he could hit nothing but my side or the floor. I pulled him to the left and starting swinging with my right catching him in the side of the head two, three, four times. I rolled off *get him on his feet. Tire him out!* He got up slowly as a couple of teachers turned up. There was some chanting from the crowd but I couldn't hear it my ear had been crushed for too long and amidst the adrenaline I'd not even noticed until now. "We done lardass? Or do I need to slap you around some more?" I asked him. It wasn't my day, he ran at me again this time punching correctly and a straight caught my chin and rocked me big time. I tried not to let it show and unloaded with lefts and rights over and over stepping forwards fuck technique! *I'm going through this fucker.* His head flipped backwards with each punch but his body remained upright. Two teachers grabbed him and one grabbed me as I instantly relaxed. "I'm calm, you can let go I won't hit him. I won't run" I said palms out defensively as the marbles continued to rattle around in my head. The teacher was Mr Fourth who I'd later find out was a diamond. "Okay, fine with me" he said from two feet above me. He had long features and was at least six foot tall. He was also very polite and skinny as a rake. He reminded me of a tall Charlie Chaplin. "Okay come with me" he said. I followed as Derek was trying to fight the teachers "I'll kill you! You prick! You're dead!" He shouted towards me. *Good luck with that mate.*

I was getting worse I'd had numerous detentions for stealing and quite a few for fighting. I was outside the classroom most of the time for answering back and even Mr Kilch had given me a roasting and told me next time I'd be expelled "fine with me" I told him. I was missing my mates more and more so when a lad called Jason said he was going to run away from home I saw an opportunity to go camping. "Meet you after school tomorrow?" He asked me as he stood there half my height with a ciggy hanging out of his mouth, his off brown hair dangling in front of his eyes. He looked like a little hippy. "Fuck that, meet me in the morning and we'll go from there" I told him. "Bring a knife and some tins of food" I added looking around to see if Wenzel had arrived to pick me up. In the morning Jason was waiting in school uniform with a change of clothes in his bag. I'd packed food, clothes, first aid kit, matches, a lighter, bin bags, my survival bag, a large Bowie knife and my 1.77 gat pellet gun. We hiked from the high school down Whitegate way into New pool and then through the village behind the fishing area into Petty pool. Jason wasn't used to hiking like I was and kept stopping for a rest. Apparently his mum had caught him smoking pot which is why he'd decided to run away instead of apologising and facing the grounding. He told me how his brother does LSD regularly and she doesn't want him turning out like his brother.

"Up there!" I said pointing to off the public footpath and away from the beautiful blue lake "Fuck man, why there man? Why. It's miles away" he asked catching his breath "The water falls down the slope leaving us dry and it's low enough we won't be seen from the other side of the hill. Plus if we don't disturb too much bracken nobody will see us from this side either" I answered. "How do you know all this shit?" he asked "scouts" I replied grabbing his bag and starting the climb up the hill. We got to the camp spot near the top. I'd been here many times before and would return many more. It's a beautiful large forest which we could see sailing down in front of us as the wind hit my neck. Below the forest was a huge pool of water that people weren't allowed to fish on and another forest behind it. One public footpath circling the lake ran in front of us which was only used by dog walkers and the odd farmer. There was a farm directly behind us but I'd met him before he was sound and we'd shared a brew on my camp stove. As long as I didn't leave a mess and didn't go into his field he didn't care. This was my home. No care placements, no social workers, no rules, no family, no bullshit, it truly was heaven. I showed Jason how to build a bivouac against the same tree I'd used last time I was there. Criss crossing the branches and covering the lot with bracken taken from further away. "Why not use that?" he said pointing to the bracken beside us. "it gives cover and stops some of the wind. It makes us harder to find" I said planting a sharpened stick into the ground as a support for the wind break. "Oh O.K know it all, what's next?" He asked "shit hole" I replied marking a square out with my stick. We were too tired to do anything larger and thankfully Jason had brought loo roll! "We sleep in there?" Jason asked waiting for me to magic two sleeping bags, a T.V and a games console out of nowhere. "Yup, fill these with leaves" I said handing him two bin bags as I got to work filling mine, tied them and chucked them in the bivvy. "keeps us warm and off the floor, like a mattress" I told him before he asked. We sat down and brewed up a hot chocolate from my camp pack. "Mate, mind if I say something about what you said earlier?" I asked him as I sat on the floor cross legged nursing my hot choc. "It's OK man she's a bitch that's all" he said looking at the floor and rolling a smoke. "Sounds to me like she cares about you man" I said.

"What? Well maybe, but brother smokes why can't I? It's dumb, she's dumb!" He said biting his lip.

"Maybe he's beyond help. Maybe she doesn't want you doing the shit he does and ending up like him? Sounds like she's worried" I said putting my half drank hot chocolate down and grabbing my ciggies.

"You sound like her" Jason said honestly.

"OK, listen up. I'm only going to say this once then forget it, just forget I said it. – Right?" I said lighting my cig and not waiting for a reply "I lived in Macclesfield... " I told him everything from moving from Macc to going into care. He looked very pale. "So, seems to me you need to sort some shit out. How important is pot to you? How much pot can you do your mum doesn't need to know about?, Buy deodorant and cover that shit up for fucks sake or steal your brothers. How important is your mum to you? Now I'll tell you this" I added lighting my third ciggy "I love baconegg like a brother, I'd never tell him that obviously but I do and I'd kill him in an eye blink if it would bring my mother back" I said looking out over the field and not being able to look at Jason.

"I'm sorry man" he said holding the tears back.

"Nothing to be sorry about. You didn't kill her" I replied. "Here, check this out" I added pulling the 1.77 Gat from my belt at the back and handing it to him. It was getting dark so we got some beans on the go and settled closer to the fire. Jason was shooting the odd tree with the Gat. "Oi get the bread out man" I asked him. We'd picked it up from a newsagents come post office on the way down. I stood a stick in it and toasted it. "Butter?" I said the heat from the fire blurring my vision slightly. "No mate, no butter," Jason answered from somewhere beyond the fire. I could hear small animals settling into the forest. Some seeking the warmth most running from it. I should have said "OK mate no problem we'll stick it in the beans it'll be fine" what I actually said was "what time's the newsagents open?" To which he replied "about 6am I recon".

"That early?" I asked.

"Yeah man" he said.

"Okay if we walk down now we'll be there by time it opens, grab a load of grub and stuff our faces. Deal?" I said.

"It's dark" Jason said listening for invisible monsters.

"Yeah, so? Come on bring the gat if you're worried". I said leaving all the gear at camp apart from my Bowie knife, pen knife, money and the gat gun which Jason had. *No weight makes us faster.* We hit the road after taking some pot shots at random tree's. I ditched the Bowie knife out of habit and said I'd pick it up later. I still had the pen knife and wasn't willing to lose it versus the risk of getting caught with it. The post office was closed and we had around twenty minutes to wait. "Ditch the gat mate. We'll get it later" I said just as a silver BMW pulled up beside us. "Alright lads?" A male voice said. Looking closer I saw black and white uniforms. "Yeah, just waiting for the shop to open mate" I replied as out got two coppers. *Great, just great.* "Mind emptying your pockets boys?" one asked.

"Why?" I asked him honestly. "In case you have anything on you that you shouldn't have" he said flatly. "Ah okay" I replied handing him my knife and money. "What's this?" he asked. "It's a penknife, we've been camping" it's under three and a half inches long" I replied feeling smart. "I'll decide if it's legal or not for now I'm taking this" he told me. "What? That's mine!" I said as Jason was going through similar with the other copper. "Hey! This ones got a gun!" One of the coppers said standing beside the other cop and holding the Gat like he's 007 where he spread his legs and moved the gat from hand to hand. "This loaded?" he asked us. "Yeah, 1.77 gat gun snap catch not a push in" I explained. "Why do you have a loaded gun outside a post office at six fifteen in a morning I wonder?" He asked. I hadn't thought of that "need butter" I replied honestly. 007 was pointing the gat at a mound of earth a few feet away and pulling the trigger looking more and more puzzled every time nothing happened. I swear he did everything apart from look down the barrel. "The safety is on" I said trying not to sound like I was talking to a complete moron and stepped forwards to show him the lever above the thumb grip where I was stopped by the other cop and slung in the car with Jason beside me. I heard a ptooey as my mate Gat finally spat out a pellet. The cop got in the car with a smile and placed it on the floor "figure it out okay?" I asked him as Jason pissed himself laughing. I wasn't trying to be funny. I needed these guys on side.

"Names?" The more abrupt non gun toting cop asked. "My name's" I started. "Not you, him" he said pointing to Jason as I raised an eyebrow. "Jason, Jason Smith" he told him "address?" He asked and Jason told him. "You!" He pointed at me. "We needed butter, what's the problem here?" I asked him not moving and not raising my voice. "You have a gun outside a post office?" He fired back. "Yeah? And? We were camping..." I went on and was cut off again "you'll be picked up by your parents later where if you insist you needed butter you'll be released and your items returned to you – name?" He insisted. I wasn't happy he'd said parents. I was less happy he had my fishing knife. "Jason" I replied. "Two Jasons seriously? Surname?" "Argonaughts, can you guess my middle name?" I replied as Jason cracked up with nerves, fear, tiredness and laughter. "Have it your way". After twenty questions Tony was called to pick me up and I'd got to keep the Gat and my knife. I was released with a telling off and no fucking butter.

Jason had been driven home and was in a world more shit than I was. "Come on, home now" Tony said. "No Tony, I'm sorry I really am sorry, I mean it but I'm not going home without my stuff" I knew if I needed to run away my bag, hiking gear and penknife were essential. I could get food anywhere but my bag and shit were my lifeline. "Where?" He asked and drove me towards the fishing site. I walked the poor bugger through all of Pettypool and he was really decent about it. We had a chat about his camping days and he was real impressed that I knew so much and I had even managed to calm him down enough to convince him we had a small fire that was perfectly controlled. As a plus I'd even pretended to take a pee and retrieved my Bowie knife on the way. So when we hit Pettypool and a big ball of fire could be seen at the top of the hill he wasn't best impressed. "A small camp he says", "well controlled fire he says" he kept muttering to himself. "Not far now he says" dragging his feet behind him. He sounded more like Jason with every step. "Picking up fucking butter he says". I half expected him to tell me about a brother he once had but he didn't "grab your stuff and lets go, and do not tell Pip about this". That threw me "what?" I asked "she thinks they found you walking the streets lost and I'm not putting that thing out." He said spreading his arms and gesturing towards the fire. Tony was okay. I bent to pick my stuff up and my Bowie knife fell out of my belt "erm, hold this" I said making it seem as natural as I could "what the hell! Oh forget it, I don't want to know, just hurry up" he told me. So Tony and I shared a secret which was kind of nice. On the way home he told me they had lost a child. I told him he'd hinted at it with the bandanna thing and Patrick had filled in the gaps. "She misses him terribly, that's why we fostered" he said sadly. "I know. I'm sorry I'm not him but I can't be someone I'm not" I said. "I know lad, It's okay" he told me.

I was in work the next day and got the roasing I expected off Wenzel. "What do you think you're fucking playing at?" He hissed in my face "making me look bad and just how is that going to help me get a flat? We need to show you are happy with me not pissing about playing soldiers. You are happy aren't you?" It wasn't a question it was an order. I was going to be happy because he said so whether I wanted to be or not. I turned out after that and just said "yeah" and "sorry" in the right placed. He'd continue that shit all day until I just made him background noise mentally. It was lunch time and I was sat upstairs in the staff room with Wenzel on a two seater green sofa. "Well, you going to behave or what?" He asked me holding his baguette near his mouth and eyeballing me waiting for an answer. I said nothing as I had my mouth full and then out of nowhere he knocked my arm so hard my bacon roll hit the floor. I looked at him "look just don't make me mad. I'm not a foster carer or a fucking social worker" the threat was there, he wanted to hurt me. I stood up standing on the remainder of my bacon roll intentionally "I have things to do" I said. I'd made it to the stairs when he grabbed my arm "I'm sorry, I want you to live with me and emotions aren't easy for me. I do though. You know? Which just makes me mad" I presume he meant "love you" but he'd never said it. He was faking a fear of losing me. His anger was underneath. I could feel it travelling down his arm and into mine. I could see it in his eyes. "I know I have things to do" I said breaking free and wondering if he'd shove me down the stairs. He didn't and my thoughts turned more and more to running away.

Wenzel wasn't good for Jonathon, Jodie or Caroline and he certainly wasn't good for me and he constantly made vulgar jokes. Maybe I'd run to kate's? We didn't talk and I was sure she thought about me as much as I did her. I had to call her but what to say? Wenzel was great with women they seemed to love his humour. "Tell her she's gorgeous and you can't stop thinking about her" he told me. "No that's corny" I replied. "Tell her to suck your dick then" he said. "No, that's too much" I replied. "You want her to though don't you eh?" He replied. That was enough talking to him. From there on in Kate was my secret.

Chapter 38

It was lunch time at school and I didn't want to find Keel or Kap and I didn't really want to be in school either. Kate had been in my head for weeks playing the same scenes over and over again. Dancing, talking, walking hand in hand and I'd made myself a promise that the next time she asked if I wanted a drink I'd be there. I was nervous as hell pacing back and forwards in school uniform outside the call box at Over square in Winsford, what if she forgot me? What if she had a boyfriend? What if she didn't answer? What if it was the wrong number? Until finally I talked myself into making the call. "Fancy meeting up?" I asked. "I've missed you!" she told me and I used all the money I had left on that call but I was on top of the world. I told her I'd moved back with my dad and that I'd go to the zoo with her and it would be great! She sounded so excited I could hear the shrill in her voice and imagined her bouncing up and down! I was skint but it didn't matter. Kate had spoken to me and I was overjoyed. We'd talked about scouts and holding hands. Her parents now agreed that she's that little bit older she can do what she wants so we made a date for two weeks down the line. I told Wenzel about it and he agreed he would take us and drop her off again at home afterwards. For those two weeks I was as good as gold everywhere apart from school.

Wenzel had allowed me to go to a kickboxing class and they were pretty hardcore. I loved it but the conditioning was hard and it was a lot more physical than boxing. We would have to stand against a wall for one minute being hit in the kidneys and stomach whilst we controlled our breathing and took the punches and then we would swap around. We'd repeat this for a long time. I still had shoulder problems and again press ups were almost impossible so In boxing I'd done sit ups instead. Where my arms never built up my stomach was perfect from boxing but this wasn't boxing and the rules were a little different. It was a case of "do it or get out". It helped a lot with my anger and I usually felt better when I left. I was there around six months but insisted on going alone as one day Wenzel turned up early to collect me. He was watching me and it was press ups time. I was slow and in pain Wenzel got a kick out of that. "Come on! Keep up!" He shouted numerous times. He laughed when I collapsed and when we finished I headed towards the car. He slung his arm around me on the way pulling me close "no son of mine would be that weak" he said letting go. *Thanks dad.* I was used to it, he had to be better, always.

I'd written to Baconegg and he'd cycled to visit me whilst I was out I was so pleased! He was great! I called him and he cycled up again the next day. We went to play pool at the local pub, a nice quiet place and everyone was polite and friendly. We took a walk around the countryside and he cycled home again. When I got back to Pip and Tony's I got a roasting for being in the pub. "But I didn't drink?" I queried. "Doesn't matter, makes us look bad. My lad would never have done that" Pip replied. "I'm not your son!" I yelled feeling bad as soon as I'd said it and stormed up the stairs. I called Wenzel "I want out, I can't take this bullshit any more" he spoke to social services and told me to tell my social worker how I felt. I did and we all sat down and had a bit of a chat about it apart from Wenzel who wasn't allowed in the house. I was upset I didn't have a normal family and Wenzel's put downs were starting to affect me. Why would anyone want me? There's no reason for them to do so? *Behave at school and you'll get the family back.* I told myself over and over. Even saying the word *family* hurt. I hadn't seen Caroline, Jodie or Jonathon since I left care. I'd not seen Louise either *fucking concentrate!* I told myself as I found I was drifting into my own world again.

I was in motor vehicle a class I was way behind so had decided to catch up because I thought one day perhaps I'd impress Kate, however I was totally unknowledgeable when it comes to vehicles. It was a big woodworking room which we used to work on car parts. I needed to know something for my paperwork whilst everyone else was mucking around or doing a practical I'd caught up on weeks worth of work. I approached the teacher a thin quiet man called Mr Stockwell, Whilst talking to him a ball of sawdust hit me right in the neck. I was immediately pissed off and ready to fight *I'm trying to fucking work here!?* I turned around and my good friend Keel was stood right behind me smiling at me. I presumed he was smiling because he'd thrown the sawdust and found it funny that I wasn't impressed so I nutted him, I don't even know why. I just moved my head back an inch then shoved it forwards rapidly. When he stood up his front tooth had gone and the one beside it was wobbling. I turned back to Mr Stockwell. "Sir can you help me with....." pointing to my pad I said as he cut me off "Tracie don't you think we should clean Keel up first?" "Erm, okay, yeah. Sure" I replied wondering why Keel had turned on me? Why was I in trouble for trying to work? I approached Keel and walked him to the nurses office where he explained Derek had thrown the ball of wood and Keel had ducked at which point it had hit me and I'd then.... he let it hang there like a guillotine as he pointed to his tooth. I felt like a bastard but what could I do? I'd promised to behave so I couldn't slap Derek but I'd snapped at Keel and I should have known Keel wouldn't let me down.

Wenzel had got the flat and told me there would be a two week probation period until I could officially move in and then it would be six months of social services checks before we would be left alone but then it would be fine. I promised to behave and it really was a great time because Kate was going to be involved and eventually the family would be back together and Kate would be a big part of it! I was thinking about Kate day and night. What would we talk about when she was here? Would we get along like we did at scouts? Would she still like me? I knew she wouldn't like dad and also felt I wasn't good enough for her. I'd have to lie to her about mum too and I wasn't looking forwards to that. How could I expect her to love me when my dad didn't? Why would I want her to experience my life? The violence and the danger? She has a perfect family and she deserved better. I'll never forget the day I called her.

I'd paced for twenty minutes by the same phone box I'd used previously and then dialled. It was hot and I was sweating from heat and nerves "Hi Kate!" I said. "Hiya! How are you! It's nearly time I get to see you!" she said as we only had three days to go. I was about to make us both feel bad. "Yeah, I'm real looking forwards to it and all but the thing is...."I said, "my mum can take us if your dad can't she said she'd love to meet you!" She told me as a part of me died inside. "I hurt my shoulder playing rugby and I need to rest" I lied. She was silent so I added "I went in for a tackle and hit a post. I've broken my collar bone" I added. Kate was silent for two whole seconds and then said "oh you poor thing I wish I was there with you. Here was me only thinking about seeing you. Get well and then call me okay?" She said. I was holding tears back "Yeah, yeah I will" I lied and hung up. How low can you get? I thought slumping my shoulders. I lied to someone I love to protect her from your life my inner voice replied. No to protect myself from being hurt I told it. Push her away before she hurts me I added they all hurt me and she doesn't deserve my life. I hurt everyone even Keel. I never spoke to her again. She always remained in my thoughts along with Nigel.

Chapter 39

I was sat at Tony and Pip's bored stupid and waiting for the days to vanish when Pip said "why don't you go to the youth club?" I didn't even know their was one. Come to think of it I'd seen no kids the entire time I was there. Perhaps once a week a couple of cute girls would walk past but not like Macc or Winsford where they played in the streets. "Where is it?" I asked.

The youth club had two pool tables and was hidden away by the side of the only church in the village. It was run by a huge fella with a leather waistcoat and big silver rings. I knew the moment I saw him that I wanted rings like that. I had a small skull one but I'd lost it at work and his were huge. He was playing chess with another lad and was winning big time. "Come in, come in" he motioned to me with a big smile and slid a tin towards me "how much?" I asked. "No charge first time" he said and winked at me. I liked him straight away. I looked beyond to the pool room where five or six lads were playing pool and maybe another twelve around the other table whilst a tall thin guy with a leather jacket and jet black hair stood alone by the wall drinking from a plastic cup. He'd seen me the second I came in but turned away. He was doing a good job of pretending he didn't take everything in. He was at least six foot tall and very pale.

"Want a drink?" The big guy playing chess asked me as he took another of the skinny lads pieces. "lemonade please" I replied noting the pop bottles on the wall behind him "I'm Phil, everyone calls me Dude" he said showing me a huge paw covered in silver. I shook it and he was gentle. "Got a name?" He asked me "yeah, I got a name" I replied smiling. He laughed a huge belly laugh then as suddenly as it started he stopped and took another piece "checkmate" he said. "Shit" the skinny lad replied. "Set them up" dude answered him and then looked at me again "you play?" He asked nodding towards the board. "I'm good. You carry on" I nodded sipping my lemonade. The tall lad hadn't moved nor taken a sip from his drink. A couple of girls clocked me. The lads were too engrossed in their game. Tall boy had black jeans on, black shoes and a dark shirt. "You can call me dude too" Dude said watching me watch everyone else. I paid attention to the chess game and Dude won again at which point skinny lad turned to me "welcome to youth club." he said half genuinely, half as though saying nobody could beat dude. I laughed because in Winsford youth club we got "pay here and go over there" it was a lot nicer here. The lads were soon done with pool and piled out together one pushed into the tall lad by the door intentionally and knocked his drink over him. He didn't even react he just picked his beaker up with well practiced actions and approached Dude. The lads laughed at him "watch where you're going" a lad taller than me in a red football top shouted then, he stopped and walked back towards the pop bar and stood behind the tall guy. "Oi, I said watch where you're going". Dude spoke up "that's enough lads, you've had your fun."

 "No, not until he apologises" red shirt said. "I'm sorry" the taller lad who had done nothing wrong and was now leaning on the bar said. A baseball bat appeared on the bar in front of me clutched in a silver paw "out, now" dude said calmly. They left leaving me, Dude and the tall lad. The girls giggled from the pool room. I guess it wasn't so unlike Macc after all. Dude poured tall lad a fresh drink on the house. "That happen a lot?" I asked whoever cared to answer. "Meh, just kids" Dude replied "ever had to use it?" I asked him nodding behind the bar where the bat had vanished too. "Not yet" he said smiling. I looked at the tall guy "I'm sorry, I'm Mark" he said holding a hand out like he was expecting me to cut it off. "Tracie" I said shaking it gently. "That happen a lot?" I asked again. "All the time" he said not smiling. "It's because I'm tall and Welsh they don't like me.""they think picking on the tall guy makes them look strong" Dude explained. "Makes sense" I said. "Pool?" I asked Mark. "I'm not very good" he said. "Neither am I, lets go" I replied. About five minutes later a girl grabbed my ass. I've never liked that and it irritated me but I ignored her. She came around a second time and I said "stop it" and continued my game. I guess I'd embarrassed her in front of her friends because she started gobbing off at them and then came around behind me again I turned when she was less then a foot away. "I'll tell you once. Fuck off!" I said as her face turned ashen. "Uh oh, you shouldn't have done that" Mark said. "My brother will kill you! Who do you think you are?" She said running off. "That's why" Mark added. "Who's her brother?" I asked him "know that tall lad earlier with the red top?" He told me. "Great" I sighed.

"What are you going to do? You should go" he warned.

"Fuck that, I'm playing pool" I answered.

"What if he comes back?" Mark asked.

"Well firstly he has to get past Dude and then you can beat him up for me" I said calmly.

Mark stepped back and I smiled. He cracked up laughing. "Listen mate, I don't want any trouble but if he does get past Dude and if he does find me then if he does have a go at a new guy, which I doubt he will because he's a bully and no offence mate but bullies only pick on people who let them. Then and only then will I sort it out" I told him bending down to take my shot.

"How?" He asked.

"With this" I said holding up the snooker cue. Mark started laughing and then stopped when he realised I was serious.

"Oh, erm okay" he said.

I walked back with Mark that night to find he lived just a couple of roads down from me. He was a good guy and we became friends to the point he'd knock on Pip's for me and we'd go hiking together.

He was bullied a lot but this lad who owned a farm close by. Mark never fought back. Sometimes we'd go to his house and that's where I first encountered a normal family and It was amazing.

His house was quite a big semi detached. His dad was rarely home but wasn't working as he'd broken both his wrists in an accident at work which both laid him off and ruined his hobby of Aikido. He was a friendly guy who told so many far fetched stories his wife had to tell him to shut up when the T.V was on. They welcomed me with open arms. Marks mother had previous jobs but at the moment looked after the kids. I felt comfortable telling her I was moving into my fathers in a couple of weeks and she smiled warmly. They were all Welsh and I felt their accent warm and caring unlike my previous foster fathers who was also Welsh. "Not yet dear, it's not time yet" she said about moving in to my fathers. Mark nudged me "mum used to do Tarot readings, She's never wrong". I laughed at Mark but my eyes stayed on his mother and I believed her. Mark and I listened to Placebo and Texas in his bedroom. He fancied the lass from Texas something rotten. I didn't care much for the music but it left a calm atmosphere as did the household. We were playing Killer instinct on the games console when a beautiful five foot nothing blonde appeared in the hall. "Mum wants to know what you want for tea?" She said just as her eyes briefly met mine and she immediately went shy and quiet. "Hi" I said into her light blue eyes. She ran off. "I didn't know you had a sister?" I asked Mark. "That's Anne, she's aight" he said. "Staying for tea?" He asked me. As much as I'd of loved to play happy families I was scared. It felt too nice and I knew I didn't belong. I said my thank you's and made a sharp exit. This was their family, not mine.

School arrived again and I was in the third year by now. Not much had changed, I'd stopped kickboxing when the coach asked me to spar with a girl and I'd refused. He said "Spar with her or you spar with me" in a threatening manner. So I let her hit me a few times but wouldn't retaliate. "Hit her" the coach said so I walked out. A week later he was in the paper, Some guy had a go at him in a pub and the coach had bottled him and got sent down.

I'd been back at school maybe three days and was playing football with the lads when Derek Baker shoulder barged me. After two other fights I'd thought this shit was dealt with. I ignored it and carried on playing when he did it again "drop it" I told him as I turned out of the shoulder barge and regained my balance. "Or what?" he said squaring up to me. It was automatic, I didn't even think, the jab was thrown as he'd stepped into my personal space and my right foot had gone behind me. I jabbed twice more catching his face and followed with a right just as he threw a right hook. I'd blocked before it was anywhere near me. Everything was happening in slow motion unlike our two previous fights. I hit him with two straights and clinched his neck giving him a one, two with my knee's as I brought his head downwards just like in kickboxing. Where as before everything was a struggle to keep calm, get the hits in or out think my attacker. This time everything just happened effortlessly, it was surreal. I caught him twice in the chest hard before I dropped an elbow into his rib cage. He was smaller than me in height but awful round and my elbow did nothing. He pushed me back towards the floor trying to bring me down with his body weight, I pivoted and slipped out of the way sending him another knee to the chest on his way past. He stood up straight and took three steps backwards before coming at me fast throwing punches. None of them hit me. Block, counter, block, counter, move, block, counter. I wasn't being big headed I was simply better trained by then. He stepped back after a few hits to the face with no real damage done and threw a kick. I shocked myself when my shin came up to block it without me telling it to. I was even more surprised when I regained my balance and kicked him in the chest hard with the same leg. I heard the air go out of him and he bent double. "Now leave it, It's done" I told him and walked away.

I'd got perhaps two steps before I heard a growling sound

"Arrrrgh!!" He screamed as he hurtled himself at me. His arm caught my face slightly as I turned on one leg to face him and grabbed the flailing arm. Fuck it, I unloaded elbows and punches to his head and he hit the floor with me falling on top of him the momentum rolled me over and he had me pinned to the ground. He was bleeding but I couldn't see from where. I crawled downwards giving him less room to hit my head and more room for my legs. What I had in mind was risky but if it worked I'd win. If it didn't I'd end up with lardass sat on my head and I didn't fancy that. By now I knew he'd go for big hits. He always did standing and here he'd feel totally in control. Sure enough he threw his whole body back and came down with wide arching hooks to my head either side. I blocked maybe six and they hurt but not as bad as they would had my arms not protected my head, by six he was tiring and I seized the opportunity I pushed myself down a little further as he leaned back to take another big swing and flipped my legs up and around his neck from behind. Then I rolled forwards pushing down with my legs. I spun over and crawled on top of him throwing him a hook here and there, enough to keep him guessing not enough to do any damage. The next time he tried to hit me I grabbed his arm with both of mine and pulled him forwards and flung my feet underneath his back and linked my legs. Now one arm was trapped beneath my leg, His head was stuck between my legs and at an angle and I had hold of his other arm. He was pretty much fucked. He did the only thing he could do and tried to bite me at which point I simply tensed my legs together tightly cutting off his airway. A few seconds on and off of this every time he tried anything and he very quickly mellowed out. I released most of the pressure from his neck and jabbed him in the face. "It's over" then followed up with a cross which would have made his head moved had it not been wedged against my leg. "Okay?" I asked him. He grunted as one of the lads shouted "Hit him!" I ignored him as everyone else was shouting "fight!, Fight!, Fight!" How had I not heard them before? They weren't important. Removing the danger was important I gave

Derek a final squeeze with my legs and got off him and walked away. A lad called Jon approached me from behind. "What if he wants another go?" He asked me looking to cause trouble. "Fuck off or I'll drop you" I said turning to look back to see if Derek had got up. "Ok mate, cool, cool" Jon said.

I was finding myself at Mark's house more than I was at Pip and Tony's. Patrick Benson had just been to visit to tell me it would be another two weeks before I moved in with my father I didn't mind. I liked being at Mark and Anne's house. I'd been playing on the games console with Mark when we were called down for tea. I made my usual excuses and left for an hour. I didn't go back to Ben and Rona's instead I'd walked the fields. I wasn't hungry and I couldn't get Anne out of my head. I replayed the conversation in my head. Anne had said "Mum said you can stay for tea anytime" to which I'd replied. "I'd love to really, but I should go". I'd followed Anne down the stairs watching her golden hair fall over her shoulders. Mark followed us taking the stairs two at a time. "When you're ready to join us it's okay you know" Marks mum said not waiting for an answer and stood watching me from the kitchen. I smiled a genuine big smile as I looked at Anne in her usual place at the head of the table. I'd love to be a part of that family.

"Thanks" I said heading for the front door. "See you in an hour then" Mark's mum said from the kitchen. I felt warm inside.

I kicked a stone "What did she know about me that I didn't?" I wondered. I trusted them all totally and had told them nothing. When I returned everyone was in the front room. Dad on the chair watching T.V. Mum in the chair knitting. "Move up Anne let him sit" the dad said. "It's okay. I'll sit here" I said even though Anne had made space I knew I'd go red sitting so close. I sat on the floor in between Mark and Anne, Leaning more towards Anne who had blue jeans on. "What are you making?" I asked Anne's mum as the conversation soon turned to their previous jobs. Then to music and

Anne's schooling. She was quiet the kids in Wales had bullied both Mark and Anne for it but mainly Anne so they had moved to Tarvin where the bullying had continued by other children. Anne wasn't good at Maths or English explained Anne's mum. Anne had turned red with embarrassment I smiled at her apologetically. "I have homework" she said going to the kitchen and sticking her head in a book. I remained seated on the floor "I grew up in care. I am in care, we were homeless, I'm trying to move back in with dad, two weeks they told me but who knows?" I said.

"Would you like to know?" Marks mum asked placing her knitting down.

"Yes, Yes I would" I said thinking the genuine question over in my mind.

"He doesn't want a reading mum" Mark said. I didn't know what a reading was but Anne's mum had taken a box from beside her chair and sat in front of me on the floor. "I can use the cards to tell you but only if it's something you really want to know. I know you're hearts been broken and I know you'll always follow your own path no matter what I tell you. Do you want me to read?" She asked me with her big wise eyes on mine.

"Yeah, yes please" I replied.

"What's your question?" She asked me.

"When will I move in with dad?" I replied.

"Can we say, what will it be like when I move in with dad instead?" She asked.

"Yes, yeah that's fine" I replied.

She went on to pull some cards which I took no notice of. "You will move from here soon. You will find everything you asked for and there is a lot more than just dad. You'll find it all because it drives you. You want answers but I must tell you it will not be what you expect it to be. It won't be what you want. You will return to Tarvin. You'll look for us and we'll be gone. You'll try to find us....that is all I can tell you" she said looking a little sad but smiling.

"Thank you, I won't lose you. I like all of you even Mark" I joked punching his leg. He smiled but I could feel his mum's words had hit him harder than any of my punches could have. I looked back to his mum "Thank you, can I have a drink?" I asked her and headed to the kitchen where Anne was sat. She looked up and pretended she hadn't. "What you up to?" I asked.

"Homework" she mumbled. "Okay" I said going back to the living room.

I was sat there maybe five minutes watching T.V then thought fuck it what's worst that can happen? "Can I go and talk to Anne?" I asked looking at her mum. "Of course you can" she smiled and I had that feeling again that she knew me better than I did. As I walked past her chair she touched my arm gently and her energy shot up it. I felt it like a little electrical current she was humming with it. "You know" she said slowly. I nodded, I knew what she meant. One day I'd do for others what she'd just done for me. I felt it when she read. She wasn't really here and the atmosphere changed. Nobody else caught it but that energy was thick in this family and particularly the females. I had no idea what it was but it was the same thing that let me feel Nan in the chapel of rest. "HI, You okay?" I asked Anne. She didn't look up or reply.

"What you working on?" I asked.

"Maths" she said tapping the book with her pen and keeping her eyes on it but not reading anything in particular She was just waiting.

"May I sit down?" I asked pointing to the other chair beside her.

"If you want" she said with a little smile curling her head away from me slightly.

"I do, but only if you want me to" I said gently remaining standing.

"You can sit" she said waving a pen in the chairs general direction.

"Thank you" I said

She looked at me but without making eye contact. It was a question.

"For letting me sit" I added.

I waited perhaps forty seconds whilst she pretended to study another page lay on the table in front of her. "Looks hard" I said.

"Yeah" she gave.

"Having trouble?" I asked.

"I don't understand it" she admitted.

"That sucks, mind if I take a look?" I asked her feeling as though I was turning into Nigel.

She turned the book a fraction "Mind if I come closer?" I asked. She smiled so I pulled my chair towards her. Now we were both leaning over the book. "Ah okay, It's a pain and they have worded it really stupid but what they mean is..." I explained the sum making a point of giving really colourful explanations. "Imagine four bags of marbles each bag holds ten marbles and you give me a bag because I've lost my marbles. How many are left?" I wasn't sure if she got the joke but she didn't laugh. She did answer the question correctly though. "Well done!" I said"so now you give Mark a bag and how many marbles are left?" I added.

"Twenty Marbles, two bags" she smiled.

"I'm real impressed! Let's write down twenty!" I said.

We went on for about half an hour before Anne went really quiet. Quieter than her usual quiet self. I let her stay in that phase for a while. It seemed important to her. "Why are you helping me?" she asked her eyes meeting mine fleetingly, She smelt great.

"Because I choose to" I replied.

"You don't have to, you're here to see Mark" she said putting her head back down.

"I don't just come to see Mark. Would you like me to leave you to it?" I asked genuinely. She shook her head but made no comment.

"Cool because I like talking to you" I said as her head flew up off the table in a look of complete shock that did make eye contact. "And these sums won't do themselves" I added turning the book back to her and tapping it with my pen. We chatted for about two hours with me only moving to get another drink or help with the homework. Every night after that I'd spend an hour with Mark on the games console then say hi to his parents before going on the hunt for Anne, I'd spend the remainder of the night with her.

Chapter 40

Anne never went out. The girls who bullied her from school lived close by. I was outside and she was stood in the doorway. I told her about giving my word to Alan and that my grandparents were dead. I didn't tell her how but I did tell her that I've made myself a promise never to break my word again, ever. "You have some strong morals, that's a good thing" she told me as I moved into the hallway. I didn't know what morals were, she had to explain. I told her I've done some bad things too, things that I blame myself for and couldn't tell her about, but that I'd never hurt her. "Okay" she said innocently.

I desperately wanted to hold her and tell her that she's amazing but I didn't. I couldn't...one day I'd have to tell her everything and that would hurt her. I couldn't have that but then I was leaving and had no reason to drag her into my world...

Mark and I had taken Geordie for a walk over the fields for a few hours where I spoke for hours about Anne. "Goodnight guys" I shouted to her parents as I stood leaning in through the front door. "later mate" I said to Mark as he turned into the kitchen and I noticed Anne stood in her pyjamas on the bottom step of the stairs looking straight at me. She was stunning. I used her full name "Goodnight Anne Marie Owen" I said and walked out.

I didn't see Anne for a few days but I never stopped thinking about her. Why would people bully them? They were perfect as people and as a family. I was tired from working and Ben and Rona were getting the ass because I used the place as a bed and breakfast. Wenzel said I should spend some time with them whilst he picks up some things for the flat and moves them in. I was less excited than I thought I'd be but at least I'd be back with family. Wenzel needed a hand a few times so I'd help with lifting furniture, His bad back didn't play up at all unless I asked him how his back was in which case he'd tell me "I'm always in pain but I'm not a pussy" or similar.

On a comical note we had to wait to park up his battered old Rover because a van was unloading sand. This lad flipped a bag of it over his shoulder like I did daily with the potato sacks at work however he'd put too much power into the throw and chucked it straight over his shoulder where the bag exploded on the road in front of him. We sat there straight faced whilst this poor fella cleaned up all that sand and then bust into fits of laughter the second he'd drove away.

Wenzel wanted a black ash theme for his oriental figures, little men with fishing rods etc, odd really as he had no interest in China or Japan nor any connection with them. He was also quite racist if we went into a shop and the cashier wasn't English he'd walk back out again. He'd decorated the living room with stripes on the bottom and fleur de lis patterns on the top with a dado rail to separate the to. I got no say in anything naturally apart from my room. I did try to tell him the fleur de lis pattern hadn't been done correctly at which point he told me "I've matched them up fine they are done!" in a tone which said "don't mention it again!" So I didn't and his fleur de lis as far as I know are still on the wall upside down to this day.

I wanted to know about mum before I moved in "Can I ask you something?" I said as he stood leaning next to the kettle in the flat kitchen.

"Yeah, Anything" he replied.

"It's about mum" I said stood against the wall beside him I was aware to get out I'd have to walk around him and his hot kettle to reach the door.

"What happened? That night" I asked.

"We were arguing about the kids, she wanted to pick Jonathon up, just Jonathon and move back to Macc" he said like he was reading from a script. There was no emotion in his voice.

"Yeah?" I asked.

"Well I said no because Clive was there. Then she said she was going anyway, she'd had enough of life and being homeless. We'd get all the kids and move back to Macc" he added.

"I said we couldn't because of Caroline and with Leslie living near there but she said we could live with Betty until we got our own place" he recounted.

"We argued around and around then I saw red, picked up a knife and" he made a single stabbing gesture.

"Just once?" I asked.

"Yeah" he said "then I realised what I'd done and handed myself in to the police. They said I'd walked around a while but I don't remember. I was out of it" he told me looking up from his cup and making eye contact. He was pretending, something wasn't adding up. He was trying to read me.

"OK" I said.

"Here's your brew it's just like you" he said passing me the cup.

"Eh?" I asked.

"Weak" he said laughing at his own joke.

"So, you want to live with me or what, now you know everything?" He asked.

He was lying. I could feel it. The story was too easy to tell like he'd had it written out a hundred times and when he'd said "everything" his voice faltered slightly. I didn't know everything that much was clear. My mind swam with options, Kate? No, Anne? No...maybe....no it didn't leave room for Jonathon, Jodie and

Caroline. "Yeah of course" I said pushing the image of a big house with a white picket fence back into my mind where we were all playing in the garden.

"This is your room" he showed me before we left for Ben and Rona's. It was large and had a single bed, wardrobe, chest of drawers and huge bookcase in it. "I know you like to read. You can put all your wild life fact files in here" he said tapping the bookcase. "I won't go in your room and you don't come into mine. Okay?" he said jovially "Cool. Looks good" I said honestly, picturing Anne lay on my bed. Somehow the image didn't fit. I couldn't make her or me smile in the image whilst Wenzel was in the flat. "Can I put a dart board on the door?" I asked him. "Sure" he said "I used to play at Brenda and think of this day all the time but Jonathon, Jodie and Caroline were here too" I told him my turn for my voice to falter, this time with emotion.

"Soon, we'll get the bastards!" He snarled making me jump. He meant the social workers "They never understood me, what I went through with her, but you. you understand, don't you?" His eyes met mine again. They had turned colder, no emotions. He wasn't seeing a person any more I'd become an object again. By her he'd meant mum. "Yeah, urm sure" I said.

"Good, remember don't go in my room" he said with a cold serious breath.

"I don't want you routing in my stuff" he added half lifting his arm to point at me but not quite making a pointing gesture. I couldn't help but realise I'd heard that line somewhere before.

"Okay dad" I said smiling and instantly cooling him.

I was at Mark and Anne's with Geordie. "Came to show Anne my dog" I told her mum who knew I wanted Anne to come out. Mark and Anne appeared in the doorway and made a fuss of Geordie who lapped up the attention. "Coming out?, We're going for walkies?" I asked Anne who shook her head and stepped back "Go on you'll be fine" her mum said "Mark, hold this mate" I said passing him the lead. I stepped into the hall and nodded to Anne's mum who made herself busy in the kitchen. I stood right in front of Anne and took her hands "Do you trust me?" I asked her. She nodded looking downwards at the floor. "Remember what I said about my granddad?" I asked her. She nodded slightly "Yes" she said almost inaudibly. "What I'm going to say now isn't easy for me, but it is true. Okay?" I asked her and got another nod.

"I give you my word whilst you are with me I will not let anyone hurt you. I won't hurt you and neither will anyone else. I'd really like you to come out with me but if you don't want to that's okay. It's your choice. What do you say?" I released her hands and held mine by my sides. I heard her mum let out a sniffle from the kitchen. Anne looked me in the eyes and I'd seen all I needed "Come on" I said smiling and grabbing her coat from the bottom of the stairs "Have fun!" Her mum shouted as we left.

We walked the dog stood in a three. Mark, me and then Anne. When we reached the woods I let Geordie off the lead and Anne took my hand without a word and I felt happy. She'd made that move. I'd told them I was leaving soon "you'll never see us again" Anne stated reciting her mum's words. "I'll visit" I promised. The mum's always right echo went unsaid.

School was pretty much off this entire week. I was helping Wenzel decorate, at work or where I really wanted to be - with Mark and Anne. If I wasn't watching films with their family I was upstairs talking to Anne about everything from music to bullies whilst Mark played Killer instinct beside us.

On another walk out Anne had my hand and Mark was close by when Anne stopped dead in her tracks. A couple of girls and three lads had come around the corner ahead of us. "What's wrong?" I asked looking around. "Ah" I said noticing the problem "Ignore them they won't do anything. Come on" I said walking with her. I could feel the fear through her hand. She walked three steps and released my hand but carried on walking. "Aw Annie's got a boyfriend!" One of the girls shouted. "Idiots" Mark murmured. I smiled down at Anne warmly whilst my blood boiled. "What do you see in that!?" A lad shouted. Two things happened simultaneously in my head, the moment I heard "that!" One was "That!? You're dead".. and the second was remembering how I felt after Nigel stopped Llloydy from from bullying me. I knew what had to be done. I was already five strides towards the lad who I recognised as the fat girl's brother "Nooo!" I heard Anne yell and looked back briefly to see her curling into Mark's protective embrace. She was sobbing. "Ha! She's crying" fat girl said at the same time I'd reached her brother at speed "what you .." I presume he was going to say "gonna do?" But he didn't get the chance. I hit him square on the nose with a big hook. Fuck technique I was mad. He flew back against the hedge, before his hands had a chance to reach his face I'd grabbed his shirt and headbutted him. His sister screamed and their mate ran off as did one of his boys. "Trace, Leave it. It's okay" I heard Mark shout "listen you little shit" I said pushing his face into mine. I wanted him to know I was crazy, to dream about me. To feel as every bit as scared as little Anne had...as my mum had. "If you go anywhere near that girl" I jabbed him in the face then pushed him into the hedge hard without releasing him then brought him back towards me even faster his nose met my forehead and I held him there. "I will bite your fucking face off!" I sunk my teeth into his nose without drawing blood "And" I said now laughing like a maniac. "If you don't keep your bitch on a lead, guess what?" He was clearly crapping himself by now and not lifting his arms in case I hit him again "That's right - I'll bite your face off" I said laughing and rocking my head side to side half deciding whether to nut him again or not. "OK man, OK cool. It's okay he won't" his mate said gingerly tapping my shoulder. I wasn't done yet "You fucking want some?" I screamed into his face turning on him. He jumped at the reaction and fell over as I bumped into him. I walked back to Anne and Mark. "Anne, it's okay. It's done. They won't come near you again" I said calmly

"You're, you're just like them" she sobbed and to say that hurt would be an understatement. I felt like I'd just had a hook placed in my stomach and wrenched up into my throat forcing my organs out through my nose. I wasn't angry, I was just, empty.

"No, no Anne. I'd never hurt you" I said heartbroken. We walked off as three. Me ahead with Geordie. Mark beside Anne.

Twenty minutes of them talking and me not later and Anne approached me from behind and slipped her hand into mine. "I'm sorry" I said. "I promised I'd never hurt you" I added wiping a tear away and hoping she hadn't noticed. It was her turn to be strong. "They won't come back" she said pulling my hand to face her and taking my other hand. "I'm okay, It's alright" she said cracking me a smile. Fuck it. I hugged her and it felt good. "Sorry mate" I said to Mark.

"It's okay, Mum said this would happen" Mark said.

My best memory of this time wasn't going into the flat with dad, wasn't skipping school with my mates or even feeling part of a family with Mark's parents. My best memory from this time and for a long, long while later was lying on my bed at Pip and Tony's with Geordie behind me when Mark and Anne walked in. "It's not much but it'll do until I move" I said. Mark sat by my radio flipping through my cassettes. "Cool, cool, shit, shit. What's this?" He asked finding a blank tape I'd taped over.

Anne looked lost in the middle of the room. I smiled, she wore her hair down. White blouse and blue jeans. It was raining outside so we were staying in. She sat down on the edge of the bed beside me as I was lay down. Her golden hair shimmered in the light. "Geordie,

Down!" I said and he jumped off the bed nutting Anne's hand for a stroke. "If he's bugging you, You can always lie down here with me?" I smiled. "No, no he's fine" she said turning her head and catching my eye. Our eyes met and she caught herself "well, yeah, yeah okay" and she lay back against me. We spent the next two hours making small talk with Mark. Anne purred when I ran my fingers through her hair. "When do you go home?" Anne asked. "I am home" I said moving a strand of hair from her face and holding her a little tighter. Lola was playing on the radio.. when in the back of my mind I knew I would have to move soon.

Chapter 41

Wenzel had to prove to the social workers that he was okay looking after me. We had a three month trial where a social worker came around weekly to check on me. During those three months Wenzel took me to Wales to go hiking. I liked hiking but not with him. It wasn't the same. He was very controlling and passed comment almost constantly. I was walking up a hill a little in front of him "Oh don't worry about your old dad will you?" I ignored him "no, oh OK then I only feed you, give clothes to you, drive you to school, no don't worry about me. I even get a flat for you but will you wait? Noooo" I stopped and turned to him. I was calm I'd half tuned him out ages ago back at the car when he was complaining about never having a free ride when he was a kid so I was happy just looking at the scenery. It was beautiful. Grey but beautiful.

"You okay?" I asked him. "Yeah don't you know when I'm joking? Idiot" he said. "My back's playing up. That's all" he added. "Want to rest?" I asked him half heartedly - after all he'd only walked up a very small hill. "No, rest is for pussy's, you rest. I'll meet you at the top" So I let him go ahead "Come on slow coach, thought you were a big hard hiker?" He shouted from his four foot advance ahead of me. "I've seen social workers faster than you!" He laughed at his own joke. I didn't but he did get to tell the social workers that "we went hiking in Wales, we had a great time didn't we Tracie two?" Tracie Two was his new name for me. I was Tracie two, He was Tracie. If I wanted my family back I had to reply "Yes dad it was great" and that's exactly what I did.

Kathleen Goslin was a key worker who had helped Wenzel with paperwork whilst he was in the prison. Later they became friends and used to play squash together. That's the story he told me and it did explain how he'd managed to type up the life story work and how his spelling was suddenly spot on even if the information within it wasn't. He said squash was his way of getting the anger out of his system. I soon found out differently when I met her. She was blonde, tall, good looking and married. I could see his attraction but instantly took it as a betrayal to mum. If he loved mum he couldn't have had others people since....could he? He'd been out of prison over six months since I'd met up with him and now I was living with him. Work had to become Saturday only and I was in school Monday to Friday, so he had plenty of free time, although he always said he was working. I didn't trust him. I wasn't exactly being honest either though. I'd get dropped off at school walk into reception and sign in and then walk straight back out again. I'd find Kap, Keel or Stoppy and we'd head to their house or the fields it didn't matter...it was just away from everything.

I was in the living room with Wenzel watching rubbish on the T.V and waiting for this key worker to turn up so I could say hi then head to my room to play darts when the door went. Wenzel and I rarely spoke when alone and there was always an atmosphere. One I still cannot explain just like there was always an elephant in the room. I'd already told him I'd learnt to be a loner and was naturally quiet so apart from his "she's fit, I'd fuck her" comments to the T.V we had otherwise been in silence. All saints were playing their newest song Never ever and generally being depressed. Wenzel was really turned on by how upset the blonde girl looked in the music video. I exchanged hello's with Kathleen and told Wenzel I'd go to my room so he could have the living room to talk. "No, it's okay you stay here. You've never seen my room have you Kathleen?" He said taking her through to the bedroom and trying to hide a smile. "Erm, no not yet" she said her eyes twinkling "this will do just fine" she said as the door closed. Judging by the noises coming from that room they weren't doing paperwork. I went to bed and sat staring into space. This was not what I'd had in mind. Not at all. It was only then that I realised I'd seen that woman once before. I was with Brenda and we'd gone to a social worker's house for brunch. I remember it because I'd never heard of brunch before and was intrigued as to why anyone would have an extra meal. She was there then on account of it being her house we were at.

After Kathleen had left Wenzel came out of his room and knocked on my door "Yeah, I'm awake" I shouted "so, what do you think?" he said. I didn't reply "she's cute isn't she?" He asked. "Yeah, you two together then?" I asked him. "Nah, She's married. She's fun though" he said doing his belt up. "Brew?" he asked. "Nah I'm tired" I told him I replied "suit yourself. Bet you were listening by the door weren't you eh?" He quipped. I lay down as he closed the door laughing. I was playing streets of rage in my head. I was Max big and strong and I was walking through crowds of people, snapping necks and hitting people with a metal bar. I was snapped out of my daydream by my 6am alarm going off. It was time for work and I'd not slept all night.

Straight after work I noticed Wenzel was driving in the wrong direction. "This isn't right?" I asked him "We're going to see an old friend" he told me. "This might jog your memory and let you see what I've done for you" he added. "What?" I asked him. "You're too quiet. You need to talk more" he told me. "I talk" I answered purposefully pulling an invisible cloak around me and blotting the world out. "Where are we going?" I asked him about twenty minutes later "You'll see" he told me as we arrived in Wilmslow. We passed the park I went to with mum and Wenzel before I went into care. "Remember this?" He asked. "No" I lied. "You came here before as a family. I played Frisbee with you, Jonathon and Caroline, we had a nice picnic and a chippy meal" he lied. "I don't remember" I lied back. "Your mum sat there. She didn't want to play with us" he said pointing to a swing. "I remember that" I said looking him in the eye and hoping he knew I was lying and that I remembered every detail. Hoping he'd just die or kill me or do something other than keep showing me remnants of my family. We headed to the bed and breakfast we stayed in where I saw nan.

Barry was exactly the same as I remembered him. He held up a large cactus "remember this?" He asked me "no" I said genuinely. Barry and Wenzel were obviously friends and chatted happily. "You gave it to me as a gift. You stood right there and handed it to me" he said pointing to a spot on the kitchen floor. I'd had only one cactus and it was a gift from my Nan. As far as I was aware it had been left at our house in Moorhill road Macclesfield "No, sorry. Nothing" I lied to Barry shaking my head. "I remember bacon" I said suddenly angry that I couldn't sense Nan here any more "yeah your dad made lots of jokes about my bacon" Barry said laughing. I looked out of the window and could see Caroline and me swapping sweets. "If I'd known then what I know now I'd never have been so mean" I thought. I saw the younger me running through the end garden looking for my nan hopelessly. "Want to see your old room?" Barry asked me. "No, no point" I replied not turning around. I'd seen all I needed to. Nan wasn't here and mum was still dead. I interrupted their chat as they sat at the kitchen table. "I remember Sandy" I said as Barry gave Wenzel a look I couldn't grasp. It was a question - does he know? Is it okay to talk? I couldn't place it. "Go play upstairs" Wenzel said. "No" I replied. "What did you just say?" He asked laughing to conceal the threat behind his words for Barry's benefit. "OK outside?" I asked Barry. "Of course!" He smiled and opened the door for me. "Good to see you back where you belong, Thanks again for the cactus!" he said. I stood there like a lemon half an hour whilst they talked. I looked into the pond we'd previously tried to find frogs in with no success. Mum wasn't upstairs like before. Caroline, Jonathon and Jodie weren't here and nan wasn't either. Why wasn't nan? Where was she? Could she hear me? "Pat, what do I do?" I asked the pond. Nothing happened. The green shit just floated around like green shit does.

"Are you here, Nan?" I asked again and once again nothing happened. Wenzel drove me home all happy with himself "You've got something else to tell social workers now! We visited a park where we used to play as a family and visited our old friend Barry who has a bed and breakfast" When the social worker arrived a few days later Wenzel had placed a picture of Barry with the cactus on a page and had Kathleen type it up as he couldn't spell "an amazing day with Barry!" I had to agree to tell the story that everything was brilliant and I did. It was bullshit.

This pattern would continue. We visited Wales a few times to hike even though most times he just sat in the car once we got there. We didn't actually do anything and we rarely spoke. There was never any affection, ever and I didn't want him to touch me. By now I'd become more and more wary of him and more withdrawn. I'd taken to running the Roman walls in Chester of a night because then I could be out of the flat and have a smoke. I knew he'd been in my room every night because my fag packet had always moved when I opened the drawer. He never took any and only asked me the once "Stacy's" I told him "I don't smoke. You shouldn't either. They will kill you. I don't like Stacy smoking but if it stops her getting in trouble at home I'd rather I save them for her" I told him.

"Why don't you invite her over then?" He asked. *"I'll ask her"* I replied and I did.

Chapter 42

Louise said yes and we went to Chester Zoo together. We were quiet in the car from her place to the zoo and I knew she would know straight away something was wrong with me. Wenzel asked basic polite questions but I could tell he wanted to fish for information. I kept eyeballing him via his rear view mirror and he did the same back. It's then I realised I thought more of Louise than I did my own father. If push came to shove I'd protect Louise over him. I realised for the hundredth time I really didn't trust him and it wasn't because of mums death. There was something not right about him. People really were like a game to him. To be used, played around with and put down and if it breaks well he'd just get a new one. Louise was far too polite to say anything and I wasn't sure what she felt but I could tell how he looked at her and it wasn't right for someone of his age to look at her the way he did.

As soon as we were through the ticketed gates and it was just us Louise asked how I was? "It's alright". It wasn't alright but what good could come of upsetting her? We went on the monorail and both were disappointed it was so slow. Louise looked at every item of jewellery in the gift shop saying "that's nice" but refused flat out to let me buy her anything. I wasn't impressed but what could I say? We went back to Wenzel's and had bacon sandwiches before we headed off to my room. "Give her one from me" Wenzel said as I carried the bacon in for Louise. I made a mental note right there "she doesn't come here again". Louise talked for a fair while but I can't remember what she was saying I just recall thinking "I won't see you again, like mum, nan, Alan, Kate, Anne and it's because I love you. Everything I love turns to shit, everything I touch dies or leaves. You can't be here. It's not safe" "What's up with you?" she asked half turning to face me as I stood in the doorway and it had become obvious I wasn't paying attention. I was, just not to her. I'd put myself between her and the door in case he came in. I was listening for foot steps and trying to figure out how to save our friendship and keep her safe. "Nothing. Thanks for today" I said just to kill the silence.

Perfect day by various artists played twice on the radio in the car as we drove back to drop her off. I watched her lips move along to it both times as the sun hit her face through the window. Wenzel didn't speak all the way. Sure enough the next social worker visit it was right there in Wenzel's notes "Tracie enjoyed a day with Louise his friend from care. He got upset because Caroline wasn't there" I'd not even mentioned Caroline. I knew she couldn't come if Wenzel was taking us. Whilst Wenzel had been thinking of ways to have stabs at the social services I'd been doing some thinking of my own, It was kind of always there since he'd lied about going fishing and then it just grew, it formed in different ways like a jigsaw but I couldn't see the complete picture. I could only see parts of it falling into place and each part felt a different way until suddenly I had perhaps a quarter of an image and then I could make a decision. It hit me when he said I'd missed Caroline...perhaps I should have missed Caroline. Maybe a normal person would have but I hadn't said I'd missed her nor had we mentioned about her going with us at any point. This day was about me and Louise spending time together and then Wenzel mentions it..it hit me he was all about him there was a master plan that he had and I needed to find out what it was. I couldn't do that whilst I had some emotional connection to him and I needed to feel secure and right then I didn't.

I had a plan. I had to see Wenzel for what he was with no emotion. I had to see him not from his son's view or from his view. I knew both of those very well but from the view of someone he could attack, maybe even kill. How could I stop it? What would prevent it? Where would I go? It's the only way I could feel safe.

I walked through the school gates and approached cap, briefly looking over my shoulder to check nobody could overhear me. "I need a gun" I told him.

Chapter 43

"What for!?" He asked as we both bent to sit on the concrete. "I know your dad's in a bike gang. No questions. I need a gun can you get me one or not?" I asked him.

"I can try" what if I can't?" He replied.

"A knife, but better a gun. Nothing big, a handgun. Something I can hide like a Sig, G10 or magnum" I told him.

"What?" He said shaking his head obviously having no clue what I was talking about.

"Just a handgun or a really big knife mate" I said without thinking.

"I'll see what I can do" he replied with a concerned expression. I knew he was worried about me but also knew he'd trust my judgement. He'd know I was protecting him by not saying why but then I also knew he'd worry more because I couldn't say. It was a catch twenty two. He'd either have to trust me or I'd get my own knife and then he'd not be privvy to our chats and he'd worry more. He'd help me. He always had before.

"You okay?" He said standing up from where we were crouching on the concrete football pitch. "I will be, I will be" I said hanging my head and trying to convince myself as much as him.

"You're erm, not going to off yourself are you mate?" Kap asked looking pale I slung my arm around him "no you dickhead, thanks for caring though. I'm not done here yet mate. Not by a long shot" I told him.

"Promise me something" he said not making eye contact.

"No, no promises mate. What I might have to do leaves no room for promises" I told him genuinely.

"Just listen, I'm your mate. I've got your back if you need it. Now hear me out. Promise me if shit gets too much. I wasn't asking cos I know you, you won't tell me, you're a stubborn fucker but, if it does, you come find me before you do anything stupid?" I could feel his concern like a low humming in the air. "Depends what you mean by stupid?" I asked trying not to cry. Kap was still beneath my arm. "If you ever feel you want out. to end it. Shit you know what I'm saying" he said clasping my neck. "It's not me you should be worried about mate" I said my body suddenly turning cold "But I promise. you have my word" I added feeling like I was talking to Alan again.

"Hey, Stoppy still got that place if I need it?" I asked kap as I walked towards class.

"Yeah man. I'm sure he will" he shouted.

I ran back towards him "Tell him soon man. I don't know when but soon. Now - go get me that gun" I said turning on my heel and walking away.

I thought about Anne a lot as I ran the Roman walls, legs pumping up the steps and past the clock, down the other side and beyond into my favourite straight. It was night time, the odd homeless guy was sat in the shadows. I'd met a homeless girl who called herself ghost in the subway a few nights earlier. She seemed sound and introduced me to a few of the others. I felt totally safe in Chester at night, fourteen and running the walls. The best street earner was an old fella who drank too much but because he made people laugh he got a lot of tips. "Hey mate" he shouted as I'd ran past the first night. I ignored him but slowed down. "You've stood on something!" he shouted. I looked beneath my soles "The floor!" he said cracking up and rocking backwards and forwards. I felt like a right dickhead and then...I started laughing too. I had no money but I gave him a smoke. He was a diamond and never hurt anyone. He flashed through my mind as I ran my feet thudding against the pavement. There's always someone worse off I told myself. Stop being a pussy, pussy? like Anne's pussy? Or mums? I felt bad thinking of mum like that but that's how he thinks of them isn't it? Women are to cook and fuck! His words echoed as I pummelled the the path with my feet and swung my arms fast increasing the momentum until I couldn't hear him. Couldn't feel him and the image of Kathleen smiling as she entered his bedroom vanished. I looked up to see rows and rows of soldiers in the yard below to my left and ones with ten spaces in between them on the footpath, as I slowed down they vanished. I could feel them but I couldn't see them any more I stood at the corner overlooking the race track. Where did I go from here? Where do I belong? Who am I? Were the soldier's ghosts? Do I have to go home to Wenzel? I imagined Anne asleep curled into her arm with her hair all over the place. I sighed into the night sky and lit up another Lambert and Butler, the silver selophane flickered in the night air.

Wenzel was watching T.V when I came in. He got up and locked all three locks he'd had put on especially. He never slept unless those were securely locked. "Good run?" He asked not looking up from the chair he'd re seated himself in. The room was dark lit only by the T.V and his lamp. "Yeah" I said sitting in a chair a good distance away from from him. "Want a brew?" He asked. I didn't even answer I got up to make him and me one. "Want a biscuit?" He asked as soon as I'd sat down again. "What's your thoughts on ghosts?" I asked as I brought the biscuits in "load of shit" he said "they don't exist but the mind is a very powerful thing it can make you see very real things that aren't real. Why?"

"I know what a hallucination is" I told him

"Why you ask then? You don't believe that shit do ya?" He enquired.

"Well, I didn't but I thought I saw something earlier and.."

"yeah, go on?" He interjected.

"Well, I saw my nan - not a ghost." I said shaking my head "but Pat, really there. Solid. She moved a door. I wasn't dreaming" I told him. "Not you as well, your mother was into that shit and look how she turned out" he said looking back at the T.V.

I didn't know if he meant crazy or dead and I didn't ask. "When I was in hospital she came to me. It wasn't her but it drove me nuts. She kept asking why over and over like I had some kind of fucking answer. She was everywhere. It took lots of pills to sort that shit out" he said. "Trust me there are no ghosts it's just your brain fucking up" he told me.

"Why are their books about them then?" I asked him genuinely.

"There's books about God it don't make it real" he said.

"I got a book, it's about astral travel. Heard of it?" I asked knowing mum had told him that one day when he returned from what that she'd seen him on John's boat that day when she'd left her body and his face had dropped. Then he said Lizzy must have told her so mum described the boat to him and all the people on it. He called her all kinds of crazy that night. "No, your mother told me she had a dream about it once that's all I know, why?" he asked.

"Well I figure if I do this guys exercises for say a week every night and nothing happens there are no ghosts, if it does work and I do leave my body then they're wrong and their must be ghosts." I explained.

"Whatever, yeah you do that and if it works you come prove me wrong" he said.

Chapter 44

"You'll be alright on your own won't you?" Wenzel asked stood outside his flat in his leather jacket and white shirt. He was making an effort for someone.

"Sure" I said thinking he'd be gone perhaps a few hours. "Great I'll be back tomorrow night. No visitors and call me if you go out and when you get in" I didn't think I'd go out. I knew where he was going. Well, roughly. He'd told me earlier he was helping a friend with debt collecting. I went straight back to the flat and closed the door. I waited a whole hour after his car had left before I checked all the windows and then took my shoes off in my room and walked barefoot to his bedroom. I didn't want him knowing I'd been in there. I searched the bedside cabinets first whilst taking great care not to move anything. They were white with little brass handles on each drawer. I took a mental picture of the positions so I could put them back exactly as they were even though all of them simply hung straight down. I was concerned he had some sort of way to tell whether I'd been in there or not. The left one was filled with socks and underwear and the bottom drawer had the usual elastic bands and odd junk everyone has lying around. The right hand one had all his personal stuff in. Condom's, old receipts, spare wallets, etc. The bottom drawer had a brown box with an open top and lots of folded papers in. They were letters from someone called Cass. She'd signed off "Cass x" on each one. I was scared so didn't look further and came out checking three times that I'd not disturbed anything. There was a piece of paper from a fliar or leaflet of some kind because it had a plastic coating on it folded by the bedroom door that I'd not seen earlier. It took me a while to figure it out and then I Hooked it over the door and closed it gently letting only a tiny bit show. I sat thinking for a while. Was Cass the friend he's said about? How long had he known her? Since leaving hospital he'd said, That's a lot of letters since leaving hospital. Since before mum was killed? I couldn't think it. I wouldn't let myself.

I stared at the Chinese monk fighters he had decorating his window sills and wall units. Why did he collect them? Chinese figures and ducks in the bathroom? Why? Come on - think like him! I told myself. He had a carpet hung on the wall of Knicklesfield in Austria because it was his mothers, he loved his mother a lot and was heartbroken when she died. I only found out when I got back with him. A shame really I liked her but at the same time I didn't feel a huge loss. I hardly knew her, why did he keep the carpet from his mum but kill my mum? His mum had a brick thrown through her window after Wenzel killed my mum in a revenge attack, she had a heart attack and died. Macc rules.

You're thinking about it all wrong I told myself. Pretend you are new here. A social worker if you like what do you see when you come in? A secure door a clean hall and immaculate kitchen and then a living room that's quite dark but clean and tidy. The man likes tradition and history. He loves his mum, collects lighters, Chinese figures and has pictures of his kids on the window sill. I walked around to the bathroom, two toothbrushes, paste, three pot ducks, soap, hair gel, shampoo, towels and sparkling bath and toilet. I'd answered my question before I'd got to the bedrooms. Everything is perfect, A clean functional family man. What don't you see? I half heard half thought to myself. I don't see put downs, arrogance, violence, anger and his controlling nature. "What don't you see" I asked myself again out loud realising I was missing something. I could feel it like a strand of hair on my tongue but couldn't grab it. "What can't I see?" The unseen! The hidden! Something is hidden somewhere. If I was Wenzel where would I hide shit? Somewhere else I answered. "No, I don't trust anyone" I answered as Wenzel "They think they know me but they don't. I only ever would tell anyone too scared or too stupid to be able to do anything about whatever I chose to tell them" I scared myself with my accuracy. Everyone trusts someone. I told myself who doesn't he trust? I ran through twenty faces in my head and dismissed them all. What kind of person is he? A controller you're mine, that's mine. I'm the boss. you do what I say.

you think what I want you to think.

What else? I queried. Manipulative, he can make anyone do anything. He's charming and funny until you get to know him. - I know him.

I was walking from the front door to the living room over and over again slowly. Then what? Well he's a controller and a show off he was getting his kicks visiting his sister to demonstrate how he still had family when I hadn't, he got a kick putting me down about the hiking and kickboxing and a kick out of having my nan's key ring. He's not changed at all. What did he want with me? I wasn't waiting to find out. When mum was no use to him any more he controlled her. When she turned to leave he'd killed her. I headed for his cabinet with the black bowls with gold rims on them. They were too perfect and seemed to serve no purpose. That wasn't his style. Everything had a purpose What would be the ultimate kick for him? Why did he show everyone the cabinet and the T.V area with the pictures of kids on? Because it was right in front of them. "I could control them and they wouldn't even know it. They are stupid, all stupid" I answered again as Wenzel. I searched the bowls - nothing useful just paper clips and junk. Was I wrong? "No, you know him" I felt more than heard. "Keep looking, you're close" I felt again. My instincts wanted to tear the place apart. I didn't. I couldn't. I opened the cupboard door and saw three boxes. One was wooden like a fishing hook box. One cardboard and full of little notes and papers, a fishing license and a black plastic box that I couldn't reach without moving a table. I left it alone and closed the door then checked the windows again. No car, I'd left sweaty hand prints on the door. Fuck! No time! My brain screamed. I pulled the wooden box out, more letters were inside, mostly foster care stuff. I didn't read them I knew they'd be lies. My nan's keyring was in there and some odds and ends I didn't recognise and there was a yellow cassette tape which had Bernie written on it in pen. My heart stopped. Found it. Mum had taped her music on it I was certain. If there was a message it would be on this tape. Maybe even her voice. I couldn't hear her in my head. I could visualise her but not see her face properly apart from in my memories but I couldn't hear her at all. I felt a hand on my shoulder and "It's okay" sail into my chest. I knew it could have been anyone. I didn't care. "No, it's not" I replied. "This is mine, she'd have wanted Jonathon to have it. He should have told me he had it. He said Clive had everything" I thought and told whoever said it's okay, "It's not okay" I added. I stood up holding the only thing I had left of my mum and started to cry "No!" I screamed in my head as I put the tape back. "Later, I promise" I said out loud. I closed the cabinet and ran to the kitchen, I grabbed a duster and sorted out all the black ash cabinets then searched his VCR collection. One tape said "Mask" which was obviously a kids film. I opened it up and found a blank tape. I don't remember watching it but I know it was of him in an interview right in front of everyone. I was right. I did know him. I dusted it and put everything back and then went to my room to see if he'd moved anything in there. He hadn't. I opened each knife to see if it was still in good working order and then tried to relax. I needed to concentrate and my mind was doing somersaults.

I went into Aikido mode and bowed to the closed bedroom door. If he kicks the door open and runs at you? Everything was you, everything was said in the third person. If I said me I'd personalise it and get scared. I was turning into him and in doing so had to turn him into an object. If I didn't I couldn't defend myself. If it runs at me I said turning him into an item not a person. I visualised him in the doorway running towards me I pushed both hands forwards hard towards where his chin would be then stepped right and grabbed the fact file with my left throwing it at his invisible form grabbing the blade and unsheathing it in my right at the same time. Then what? Then you get him to shuffle out of the way do not go in grabbing distance. you leave and call the social worker. No! He won't help. you run, where? Pettypool. I decided I'd stop a night in Tarvin as he'd expect me to run to Winsford. Then on through new forest to Winsford until I decided where to go from there. What if you're by the window when he attacks? I two stepped to the top drawer of chest of drawers pulled the knife from the top and spun the blade out at head height. I was getting faster and feeling safer. I went through each motion numerous times. Each location. Every part of the room. What if you're in bed? "Thumbs in eyes, roll, grab the cutlery and chop at his ankles" I told myself - No! Too many what ifs and it takes too long. "Thumbs in eyes and lock knife from bedside cabinet" much faster. I practiced each for ages over and over until I was comfortable I could at least attempt to survive.

I left the bedroom to judge distances in the hall. I was less comfortable in the rest of the flat but knew if I could make it to my room I had a chance. Wenzel's spare coat was slung on the door to the living room. I searched the pockets and found an envelope full of twenty pound notes and another roll of notes in the other pocket. How did he get so much money? We earned thirty pounds a day at the fruit and veg shop and half of my days pay went straight to him for rent, electric and petrol even though I knew social services paid his petrol.

Chapter 45

Wenzel said he wanted to spend some time with me. He'd said it as though someone else had totally recommended it but he obviously wanted to talk. We never did anything together otherwise and so I'd suggested darts as it meant that it was in my bedroom and that at least fifty percent of the time I'd have something sharp in my hand. "Cass would really like to meet you" he said taking the darts out of the board. "Okay, your girl?" I cocked an eyebrow. "Yeah, you'd like that" he told me. "Sure, your shot" I replied finished on a double top. "Brew?" I asked after he'd thrown to start a new game. Despite thinking I'd feel safer in my room I didn't like him in there. I felt trapped with less space. "What the fuck is this?" He said calling from the hall. I looked out and he was stood there with my Gurkha blade fuck I thought. "Mate gave it to me" I told him trying to play it off as no big deal. "So why do you have it? Do you know what will happen to me if I get caught with this in the flat?" I didn't answer him. He had a fucking big blade and although seemed shocked and calm he could turn any minute. I kept my hand on the kettle. Boil! Boil! I panicked trying to speed it up. One step and it's going over him I said to myself. The front door was locked, it was always locked so either way he'd have time to grab me but I'd cross that bridge when I came to it. "I'll go back to fucking prison that's what!" he exploded "Is that what you want!?" He stormed. "Do you know what it's like in there? If it hadn't escaped your tiny little brain I killed someone with a knife and you bring this fucking thing home!"

The kettle had boiled and I slowly poured the water into two cups. I placed one to my left not taking my eyes from his feet now he'd moved a step into the kitchen blocking my only exit whilst I kept my right on the kettle. Then I moved the other cup to the left with my left hand too. It was hard trying to keep track of him and not make my actions look like I was obviously covering all the bases. Which ever side I was on if he moved something hot was going over him. "You idiot! Get rid of it!" he said stepping forwards, as he did I lifted the kettle and stepped back bringing my arm down fast. The room seemed to stand still for a few seconds and then he placed the Gurkha blade on the kitchen counter and said calmly "Get rid of it" then he walked off. "Fuck! Why me?" He shouted slamming his bedroom door. I don't know what changed in me but something did. Maybe it was those few seconds, maybe it was the build up of emotional shit I'd not dealt with, maybe I wanted to die or maybe it was the thought that maybe just maybe I'd cut his head off if he attacked me. All that and the fact that I was terrified and trying not to show it made me snap. "I didn't know did I!" I yelled "It's a Gurkha blade! It's beautiful! I liked it, It's mine!" I don't know why I suddenly expected him to crumble and be crying beneath the bed sheets but it didn't happen quite like that. The bedroom door flew open "You didn't know?" he took two steps forwards with his head down. My head went down not meeting his eyes out of instinct "You didn't fucking know?" he sneered two steps between us. "Do you know how stupid you are?" After all my practising I couldn't move. My arms were by my sides and I was back a little child unable to move and preparing to be hit. I watched his feet. He calmed instantly "I'm sorry, of course you didn't know. It's okay. I'll get rid of it for you. Let's just forget it yeah? We'll see Cass tomorrow and it will be great. It's only for a few months ....until we've settled in. Got to know each other. it's just teething problems that's all" his voice was sickly sweet throughout the whole speech. He was up to something and it wasn't good at all. He was being too nice and I'd caught it. He'd tried to hide it but I got it "only for a few months" He had plans that either didn't include me or worse were for me. "Sorry" I said. He lifted his hand fast to pat my head as I blocked and sidestepped automatically. He left his hand against my forearm. "I won't hurt you" he smiled seeing my fear through my response "Come here" he said gently. I knew he was turned on. "It's okay" I said "I get it you were mad at me. We're good. Sorry it was my fault" I replied taking a step back and with ice cold tone which seemed to vibrate through the air and through me he said calmly"no you don't get it. I've been through a lot more than you'll ever know. If I was mad at you you'd fucking know about it. Clear?"

"Clear" I said softly.

"Where's that brew?" He added.

I won't lie. I thought about it. Take his brew in with the Gurkha blade stuck down the belt of my trousers. Hand him his brew and take his head clean off whilst he's preoccupied. Had he just threated to kill me? I thought fantasizing about his head hitting the floor with a thud.. What if I couldn't do it? What if the head didn't come off? What if it shocked him and he bled but didn't stop coming at me? Then what would I do? I took the brew in.

We were in the car on the way to Cass's. A song by the Police was playing in the car. Apparently my music was shit so we were listening to Wenzel's Police album. We reached ST Helens and Wenzel said he just had to see a mate first. I could come in but not to touch anything and to do exactly as I was told. We went into a big house. The kitchen was massive and had what looked like marble sideboards. The guy we met was white, at least six foot tall with a bald head and was around thirty-five. He had arms the size of my waist a white T-Shirt and blue jeans on. "This your boy?" He said "Yeah" Wenzel replied. "He won't say anything" he added. I wasn't sure if he was talking to me or not "wait in the living room" the big guy said glancing at me. His eyes were grey like Wenzel's I looked at Wenzel who gave the slightest nod. A warning "don't touch anything". There was a girl sat in the living room doing absolutely nothing. His daughter? She sat bolt up right staring straight ahead. I nodded as I'd been told not to talk. She didn't reply. I tuned out the room and everything in it and tried listening to Wenzel "Sort it for me" big guy said "Yeah. I will" Wenzel said. He was scared of this man but trying not to show it. "Yeah, do it" I couldn't hear the rest just some kind of exchange by the sounds of it. When we got back in the car I asked "what was that all about?" , "Nothing, you never went there" Wenzel said. We never went back.

Cass opened the door, she was four foot eight at most. Smaller than me and I was fifteen years old. She had close cropped shaved red hair. Older than I expected and thin. She wore blue jeans with white trainers and a cream top. She seemed happy to see me. "You don't know what he's been through. He missed you so much! I'm just happy to see you again!" she said seemingly genuine. "Again?" I thought. "To see him" Wenzel said. "Yeah, well. I've seen pictures haven't I?" Cass said catching the lie. Something wasn't right. Cass was nice but she was hiding something. "Bet you're hungry aren't you?" She asked me. I looked at Wenzel who nodded "Yeah" I replied. She made the best burger and chips I've ever had and I ate the lot. The hall was tiny, as soon as you entered you were in the living room. Chaplain street wasn't exactly big though. The living room had a huge stone fire place and an alcove leading to a dining area we never used the entire time I was there. The display cabinet was brown and had porcelain dolls in it. At least I thought they were. It turned out that each was a lladro which is a special type of expensive doll. She had others in the corners of the room that wore dresses. As I was taking in the details of the house Wenzel was speaking "Here I am Tracie one. You are Tracie two. Whilst here you're not my son. You're a work friend. Don't call me dad. We don't want to upset the kids do we?" He asked me sat on the sofa in just his jeans with his damaged foot on show. He twitched it when he talked. "Okay" I said matching his flat tone with my own. This was no surprise. I'd felt for a while I didn't exist and when it came to him that's just how I liked it. "Brew Gilbs?" Cass asked "Gilbs?" I asked automatically surprised. "It's what people call me around here" he said flatly and then shot Cass a look. Larry and Jade were brought downstairs. Jade was small and round with jet black hair. A cute kid. Larry was skinny and taller with fair hair and he reminded me of Jonathon. He was younger than Jade. We all played football in the garden which was also tiny. I needed to be out though. There was a field about twenty feet from where Cass's house was. Not like

Tarvin but it was better than nothing. We could see it but weren't allowed to play on it.

I was to be seen with Wenzel as little as possible. "Why the big secret?" I asked Wenzel when we were alone. "If social services know I have a girlfriend she'd be investigated and she has two kids already" he said. "So?" I asked. "Well there is only two bedrooms for a start they wouldn't have you sleeping on the sofa would they?" He told me. "I don't mind" I replied knowing that something wasn't adding up and that I could actually get used to Larry and Jade, they were cool and Cass well she'd never take the place of mum but she was okay too. She was out on night duty a lot at the hospital. Larry and Jade went to bed and that left Wenzel and I watching T.V. It was more fun when Cass was there because she'd watch music channels and sing along. I often wondered if mum hadn't been killed or hit by Wenzel would she have sung along too? Wenzel would often wind Cass up the same way he had done mum but not as bad, usually taking the piss out of whatever was on T.V until I sided with her. I did it the right way. I'd explain why she was right about something as trivial as a guy on T.V wearing a pink top not meaning he's gay. I'd get the same answer most of the time "Don't you start too!" He'd say but then that was usually the end of it. However on this particular day he'd been jibing her for ages and slapping her ass when she walked past and then he'd indicated he wanted me to slap her ass and I hadn't. The next time he told me to shut up I replied "Okay dad!" It was funny because he was my dad and whether I liked it or not and because I wasn't supposed to call it him. He couldn't say anything back. I had him and he knew it. He was sat in blue jeans, white T-Shirt and suede jacket with a gold ring on that Cass had brought him for his birthday with an onyx in it. She'd cracked up laughing and I laughed harder because she laughed he slapped her leg but not hard enough to be meant. She moved back laughing. "Do you want a slap?" He said. I looked from the T.V straight at him. He looked at me. "What?" I didn't move my eyes from his. I could see the scene in my head. He was just another lad at school now and If I hit him I wouldn't stop. It wasn't vindictive, it wasn't ego nor revenge. I was just past caring it was clear, concise fact. I felt no anger just a logical sequence of events which would occur. He must have seen it too because after a good five seconds he turned to Cass "I'm only messing aren't I love? Come here" he said jokily. She curled up to him as he lifted his arm. I didn't take my eyes off his. I was miles away surveying a different scene. I was hitting him as he stood up. Hitting him as he retaliated as Cass was screaming in the corner behind me. The kids ran down the stairs as I kicked him over and landed a boot to his face. In reality we were still making eye contact. He pulled a funny face at me like we were best friends mucking around. It broke my fantasy and I turned back to the T.V without a smile nor a word. "Goodnight" he said later throwing me a sleeping bag.

"It's haunted though be warned" he said walking out.

Final Thought

I hope you enjoyed *Tracie's Story* as much as I enjoyed writing it. From my earliest memory until age fourteen my father was abusive. A story of this depth, this magnitude if you like has several emotional implications and it was as much a healing process as was a need to share my work. *Tracie's Story* allowed me to demonstrate how it is possible to survive many issues and come out the other side. I'd like to think if there's a child out there that's going through similar experiences, they would benefit from my story.

The rest of my story continues in *Checkmate* by Tracie Daily. This will detail how I finally broke free of Wenzel and how I've handled the consequences of my past and become the person I am proud to be today.

This quote was given to me on a tiny slip of paper by a neighbour when I was twenty one. It means so much to me and aided me through a large chunk of my journey. Find out why in *Checkmate.*

"If I have the belief that I can do it, I shall surely acquire the capacity to do it even if I may not have it at the beginning."

— Mahatma Gandhi

Printed in Poland
by Amazon Fulfillment
Poland Sp. z o.o., Wrocław

54618563R00164